STAR WARS
CLONE WARS
VOLUME 4

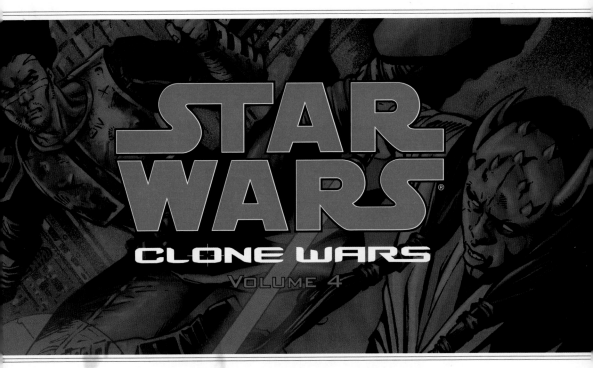

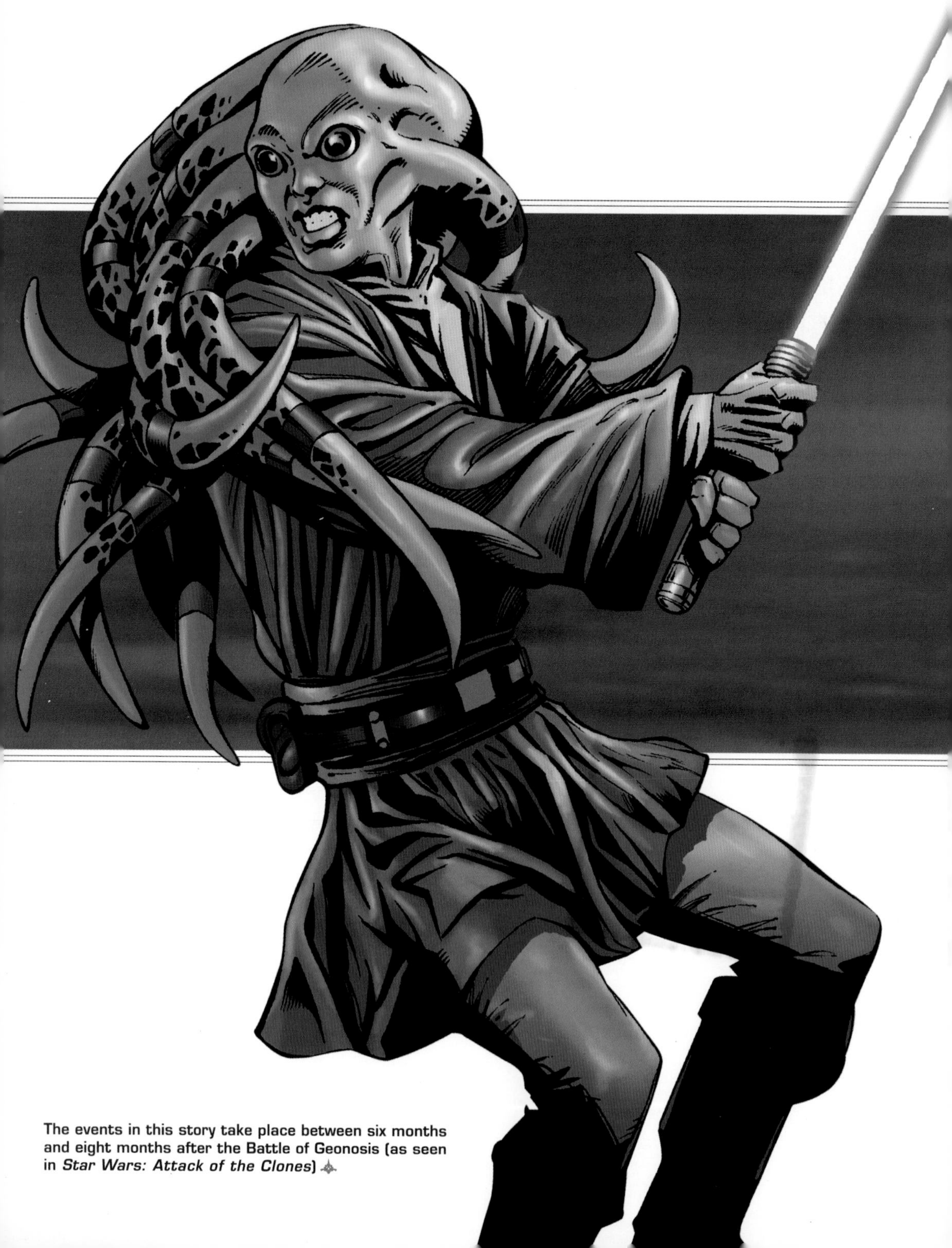

The events in this story take place between six months and eight months after the Battle of Geonosis (as seen in *Star Wars: Attack of the Clones*)

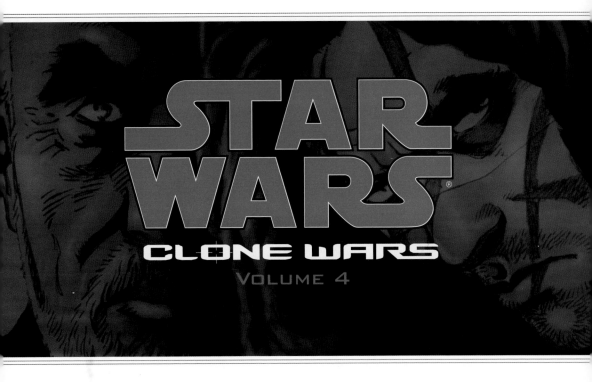

STAR WARS®

CLONE WARS
VOLUME 4

Light and Dark

writer **John Ostrander**

penciller **Jan Duursema**

inker **Dan Parsons**

Dark Horse Books™

colors by **Brad Anderson**

lettering by **Sno Cone Studios & Michael David Thomas**

cover illustration by **Tomás Giorello**

publisher **Mike Richardson**

collection designer **Darin Fabrick**

art director **Mark Cox**

assistant editor **Jeremy Barlow**

editor **Randy Stradley**

special thanks to **Sue Rostoni**
and **Amy Gary** at Lucas Licensing

STAR WARS®:CLONE WARS VOLUME 4

Star Wars © 2004 by Lucasfilm, Ltd. and TM. All rights reserved. Used under authorization. Text and Illustrations © 2003, 2004 by Lucasfilm, Ltd. All other material © 2004 by Dark Horse Comics, Inc. All rights reserved. No portion of this publication may be reproduced, in any form or by any means, without the express written permission of the copyright holders. Names, characters, places, and incidents featured in this publication are either the product of the author's imagination or are used fictitiously. Any resemblance to actual persons (living or dead), events, institutions, or locales, without satiric intent, is coincidental. Dark Horse Books™ is a trademark of Dark Horse Comics, Inc. All rights reserved.

THIS VOLUME COLLECTS ISSUES FIFTY-FOUR AND SIXTY-THREE OF THE DARK HORSE COMIC BOOK SERIES
STAR WARS: REPUBLIC AND THE DARK HORSE COMIC BOOKS *STAR WARS: JEDI – AAYLA SECURA* AND
STAR WARS: JEDI – DOOKU

PUBLISHED BY DARK HORSE BOOKS, A DIVISION OF DARK HORSE COMICS, INC.
10956 SE MAIN STREET · MILWAUKIE, OR 97222

WWW.DARKHORSE.COM   WWW.STARWARS.COM
To find a comics shop in your area, call the Comic Shop Locator Service
toll-free at 1-888-266-4226

FIRST EDITION: JUNE 2004 ISBN-10: 1-59307-195-7 ISBN-13: 978-1-59307-195-0
5 7 9 10 8 6 4
PRINTED IN CHINA

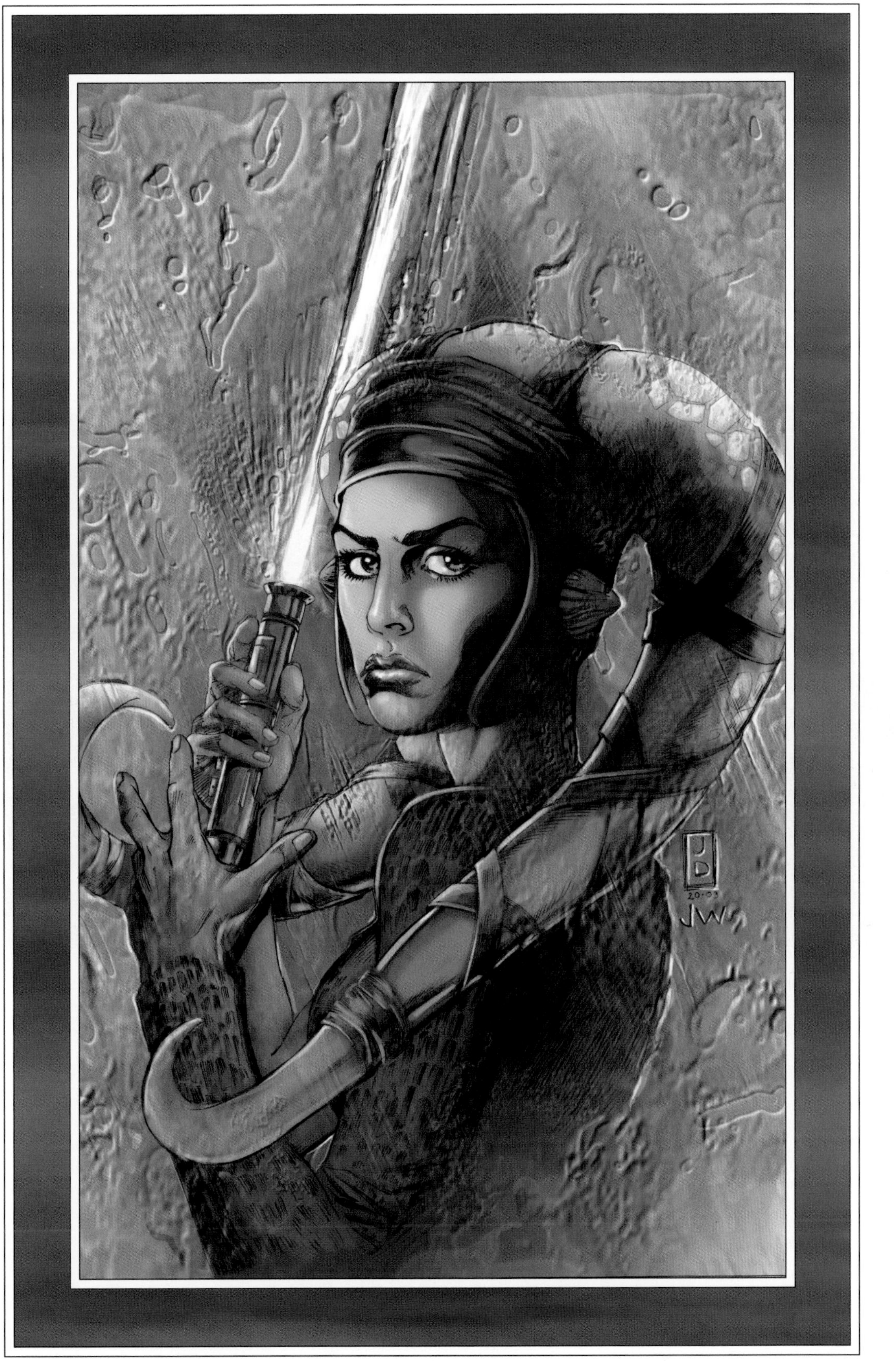

APPROXIMATELY SIX MONTHS AFTER THE BATTLE OF GEONOSIS...

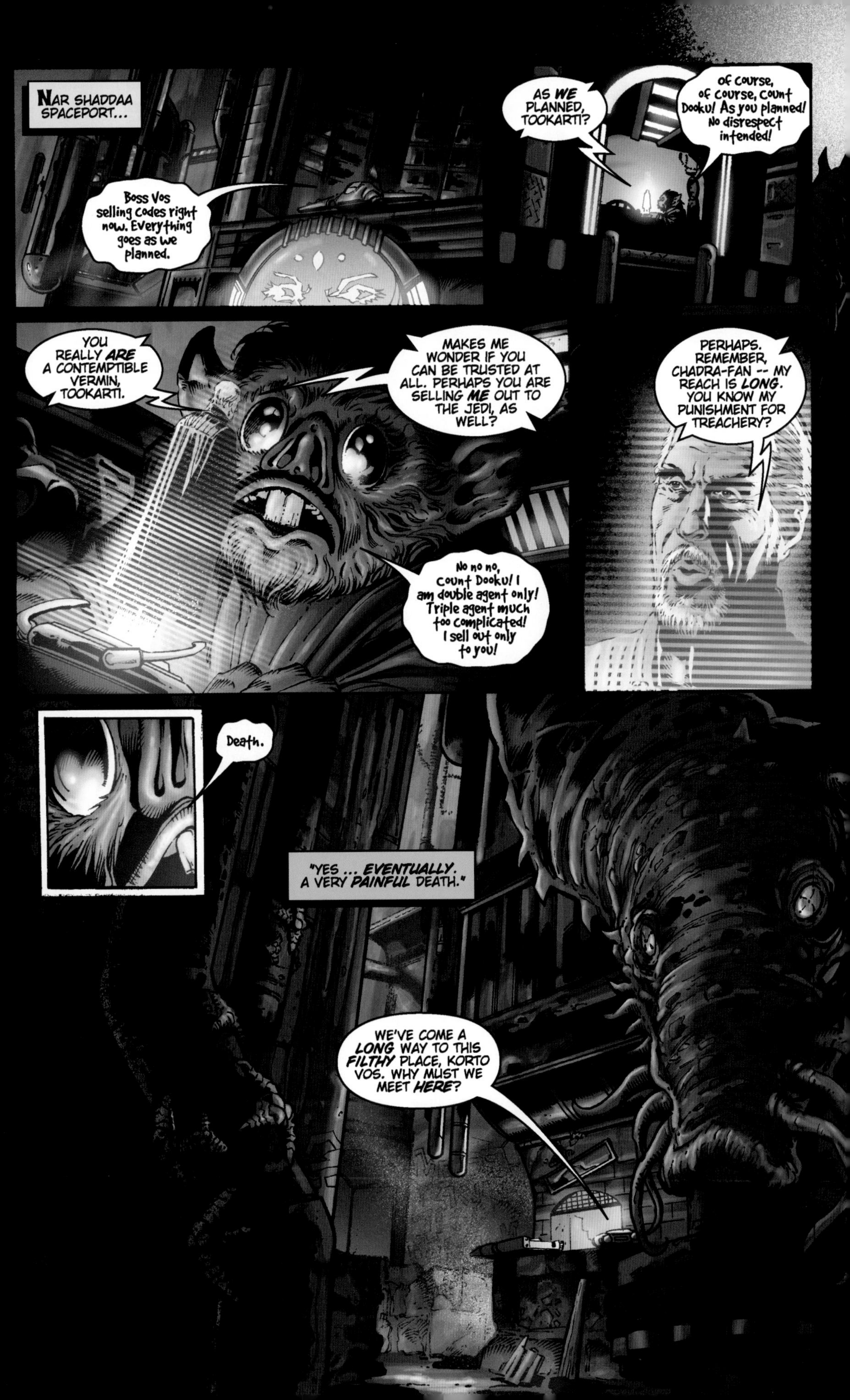
NAR SHADDAA SPACEPORT...
Boss Vos selling codes right now. Everything goes as we planned.
AS WE PLANNED, TOOKARTI?
Of course, of course, Count Dooku! As you planned! No disrespect intended!
YOU REALLY ARE A CONTEMPTIBLE VERMIN, TOOKARTI.
MAKES ME WONDER IF YOU CAN BE TRUSTED AT ALL. PERHAPS YOU ARE SELLING ME OUT TO THE JEDI, AS WELL?
No no no, Count Dooku! I am double agent only! Triple agent much too complicated! I sell out only to you!
PERHAPS. REMEMBER, CHADRA-FAN -- MY REACH IS LONG. YOU KNOW MY PUNISHMENT FOR TREACHERY?
Death.
"YES ... EVENTUALLY. A VERY PAINFUL DEATH."
WE'VE COME A LONG WAY TO THIS FILTHY PLACE, KORTO VOS. WHY MUST WE MEET HERE?

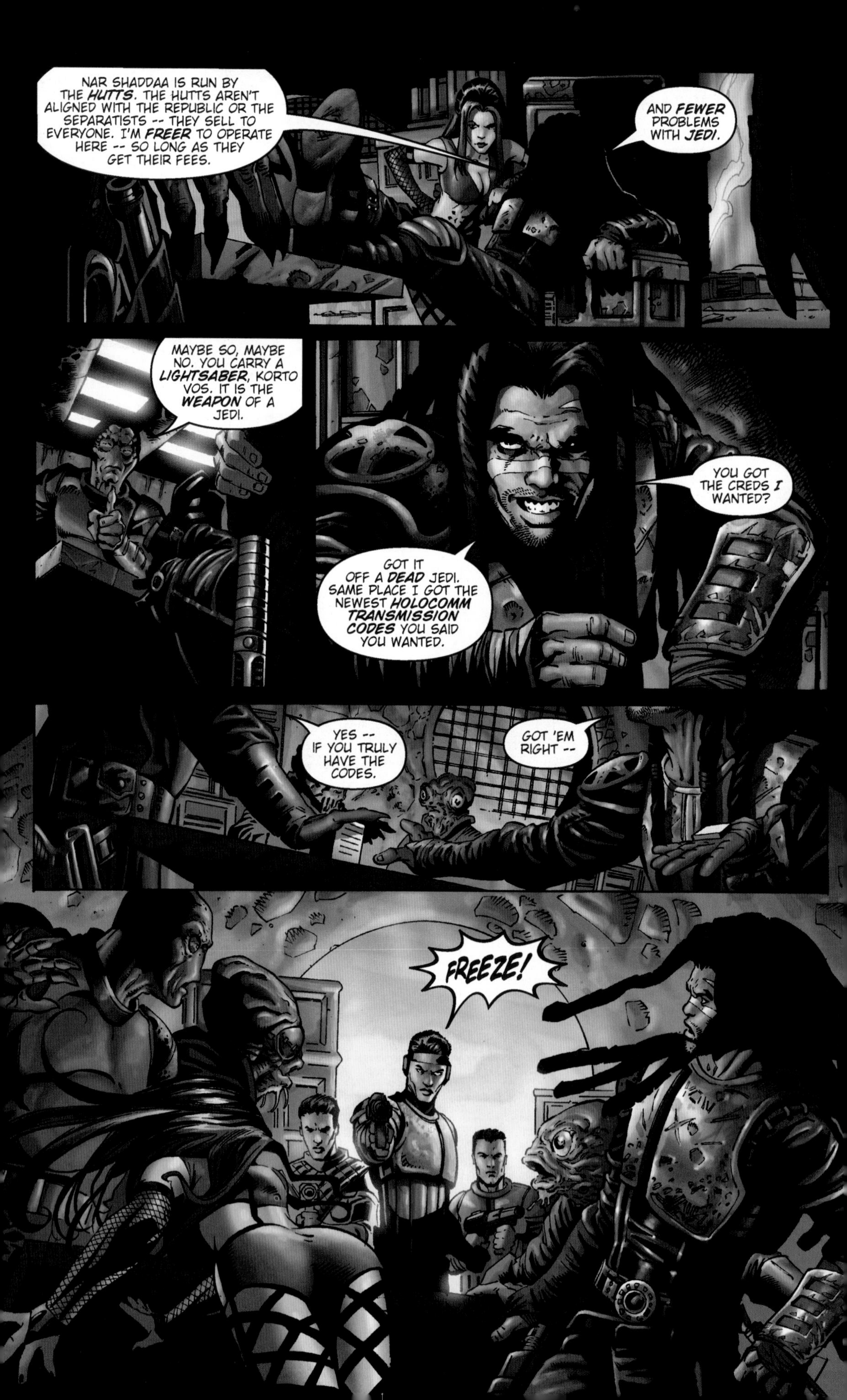
NAR SHADDAA IS RUN BY THE HUTTS. THE HUTTS AREN'T ALIGNED WITH THE REPUBLIC OR THE SEPARATISTS -- THEY SELL TO EVERYONE. I'M FREER TO OPERATE HERE -- SO LONG AS THEY GET THEIR FEES.
AND FEWER PROBLEMS WITH JEDI.
MAYBE SO, MAYBE NO. YOU CARRY A LIGHTSABER, KORTO VOS. IT IS THE WEAPON OF A JEDI.
GOT IT OFF A DEAD JEDI. SAME PLACE I GOT THE NEWEST HOLOCOMM TRANSMISSION CODES YOU SAID YOU WANTED.
YOU GOT THE CREDS I WANTED?
YES -- IF YOU TRULY HAVE THE CODES.
GOT 'EM RIGHT --
FREEZE!

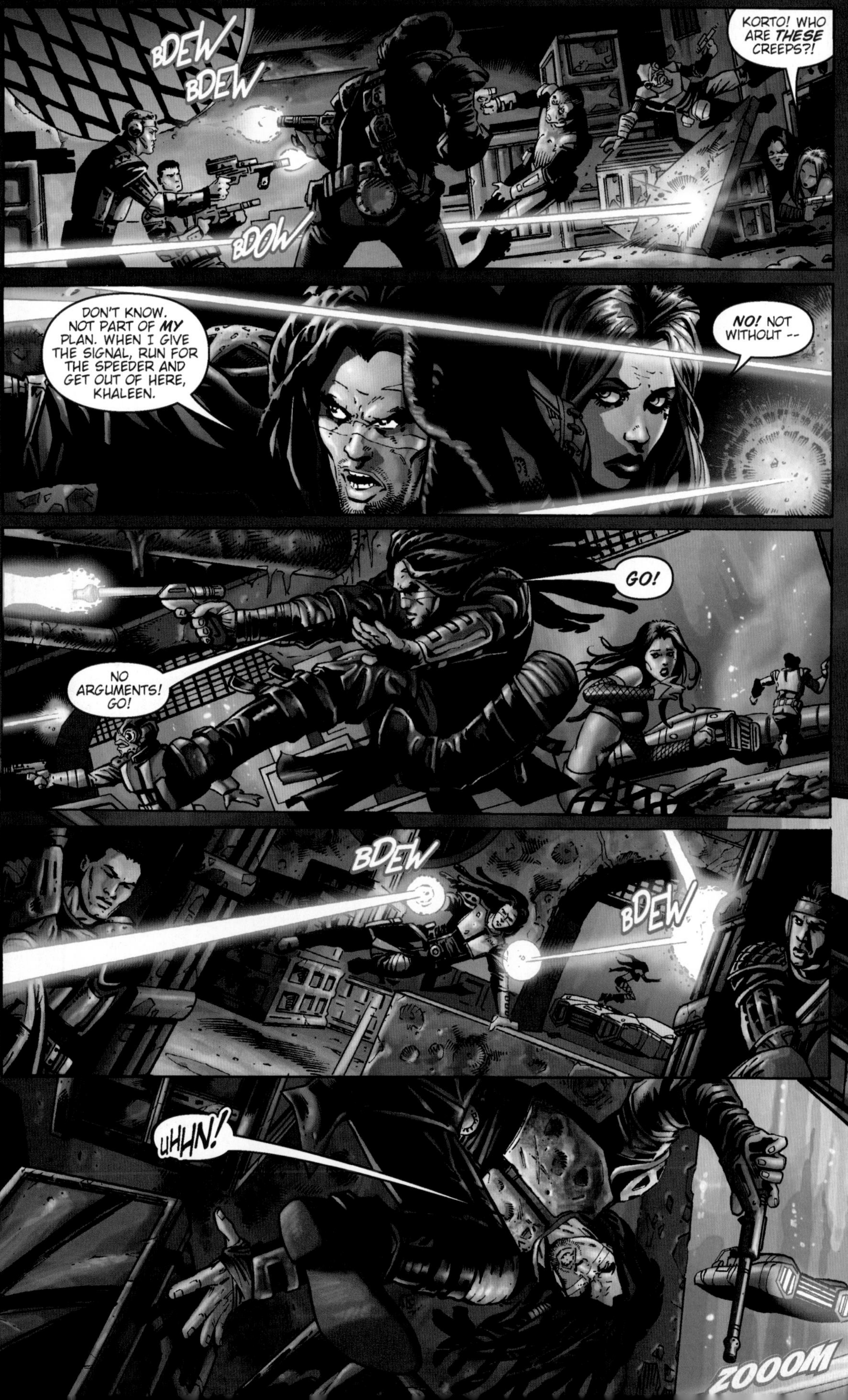
BDEW
BDEW
KORTO! WHO ARE *THESE* CREEPS?!
BDOW
DON'T KNOW. NOT PART OF *MY* PLAN. WHEN I GIVE THE SIGNAL, RUN FOR THE SPEEDER AND GET OUT OF HERE, KHALEEN.
NO! NOT WITHOUT --
GO!
NO ARGUMENTS! GO!
BDEW
BDEW
UHHN!
ZOOOM

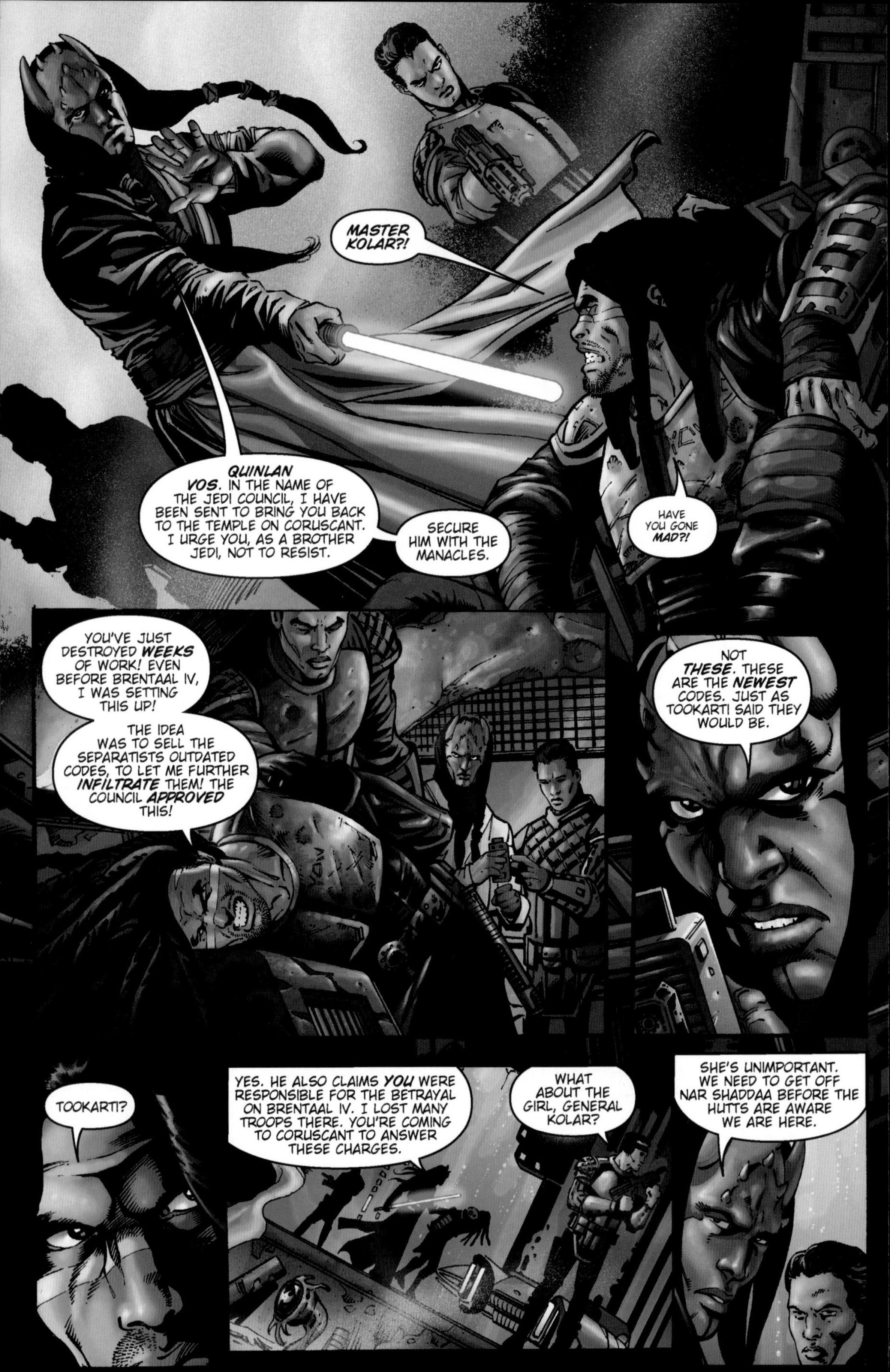
MASTER KOLAR?!
QUINLAN VOS. IN THE NAME OF THE JEDI COUNCIL, I HAVE BEEN SENT TO BRING YOU BACK TO THE TEMPLE ON CORUSCANT. I URGE YOU, AS A BROTHER JEDI, NOT TO RESIST.
SECURE HIM WITH THE MANACLES.
HAVE YOU GONE MAD?!
YOU'VE JUST DESTROYED WEEKS OF WORK! EVEN BEFORE BRENTAAL IV, I WAS SETTING THIS UP!
THE IDEA WAS TO SELL THE SEPARATISTS OUTDATED CODES, TO LET ME FURTHER INFILTRATE THEM! THE COUNCIL APPROVED THIS!
NOT THESE. THESE ARE THE NEWEST CODES. JUST AS TOOKARTI SAID THEY WOULD BE.
TOOKARTI?
YES. HE ALSO CLAIMS YOU WERE RESPONSIBLE FOR THE BETRAYAL ON BRENTAAL IV. I LOST MANY TROOPS THERE. YOU'RE COMING TO CORUSCANT TO ANSWER THESE CHARGES.
WHAT ABOUT THE GIRL, GENERAL KOLAR?
SHE'S UNIMPORTANT. WE NEED TO GET OFF NAR SHADDAA BEFORE THE HUTTS ARE AWARE WE ARE HERE.

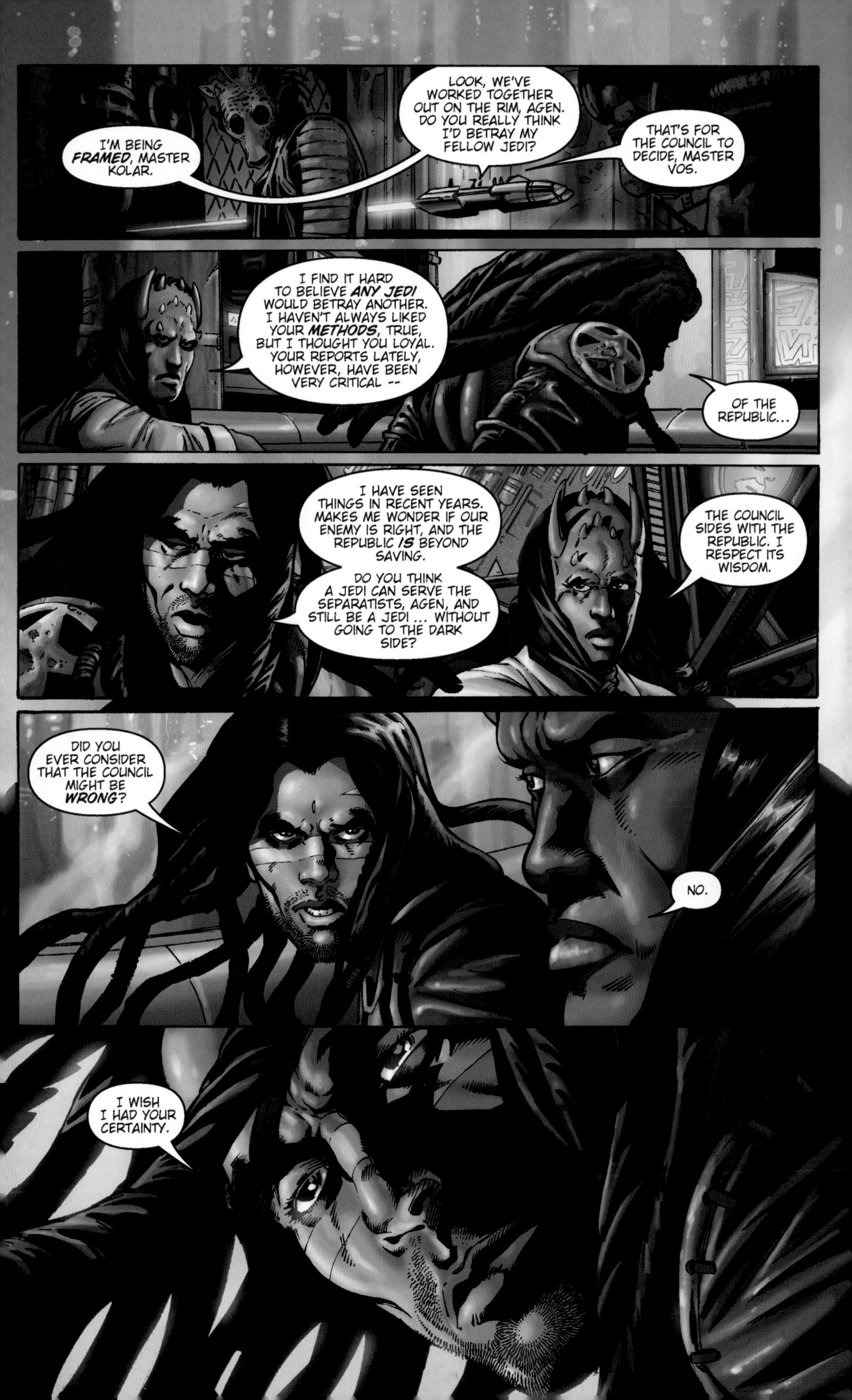
I'M BEING FRAMED, MASTER KOLAR.
LOOK, WE'VE WORKED TOGETHER OUT ON THE RIM, AGEN. DO YOU REALLY THINK I'D BETRAY MY FELLOW JEDI?
THAT'S FOR THE COUNCIL TO DECIDE, MASTER VOS.
I FIND IT HARD TO BELIEVE ANY JEDI WOULD BETRAY ANOTHER. I HAVEN'T ALWAYS LIKED YOUR METHODS, TRUE, BUT I THOUGHT YOU LOYAL. YOUR REPORTS LATELY, HOWEVER, HAVE BEEN VERY CRITICAL --
OF THE REPUBLIC...
I HAVE SEEN THINGS IN RECENT YEARS. MAKES ME WONDER IF OUR ENEMY IS RIGHT, AND THE REPUBLIC IS BEYOND SAVING.
DO YOU THINK A JEDI CAN SERVE THE SEPARATISTS, AGEN, AND STILL BE A JEDI ... WITHOUT GOING TO THE DARK SIDE?
THE COUNCIL SIDES WITH THE REPUBLIC. I RESPECT ITS WISDOM.
DID YOU EVER CONSIDER THAT THE COUNCIL MIGHT BE WRONG?
NO.
I WISH I HAD YOUR CERTAINTY.

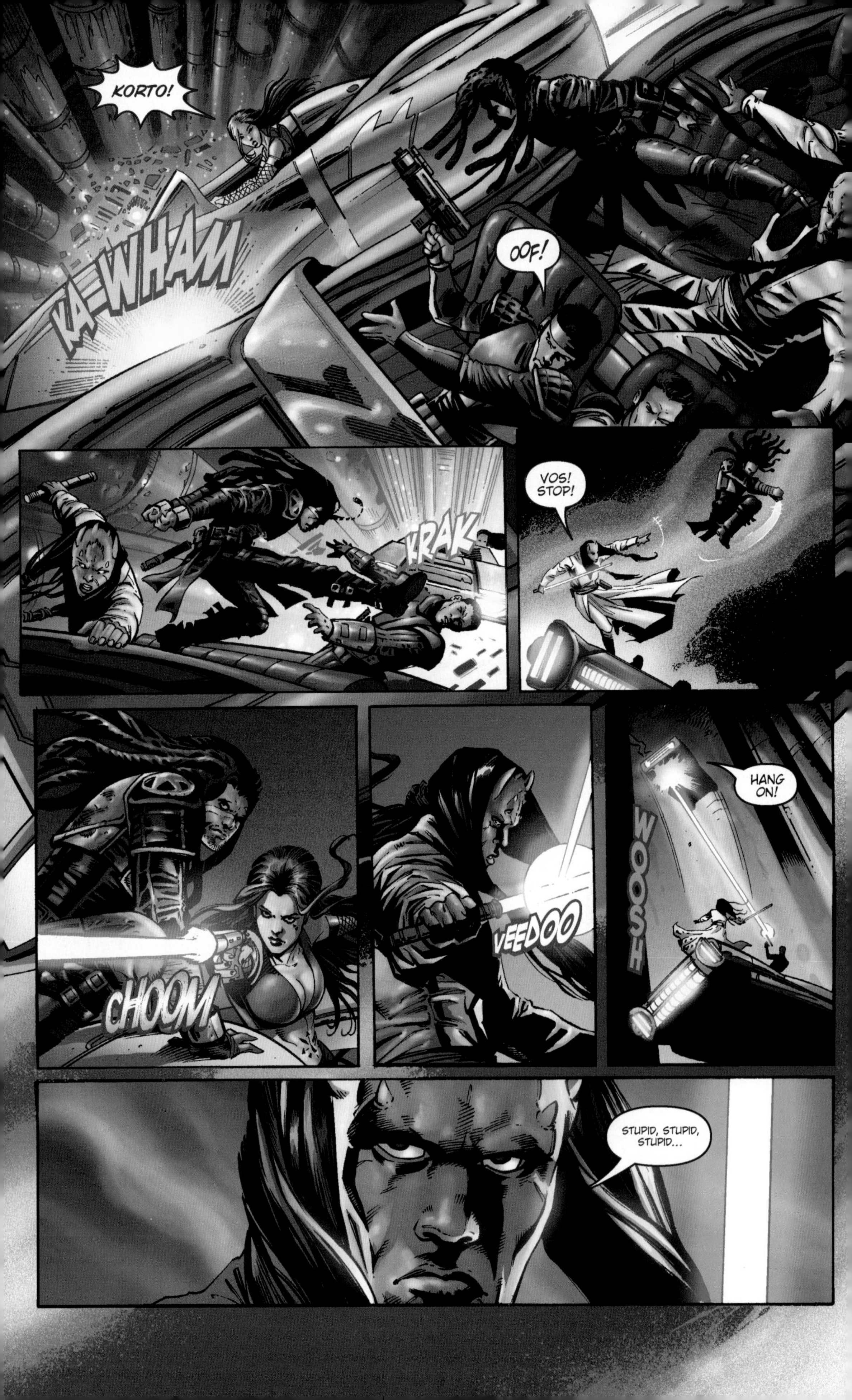
KORTO!
KA-WHAM
OOF!
KRAK
VOS! STOP!
CHOOM
VEEDOO
WOOSH
HANG ON!
STUPID, STUPID, STUPID...

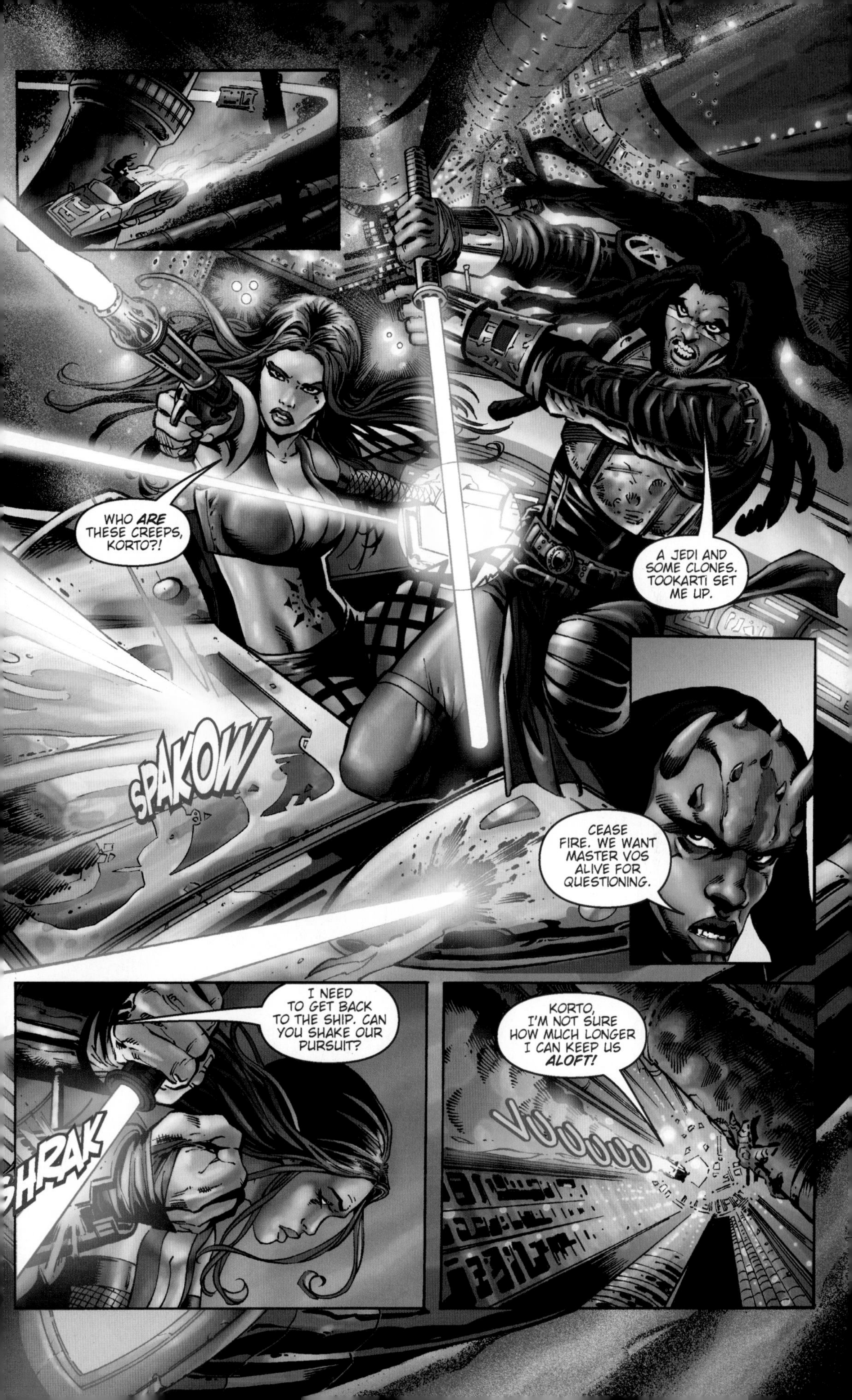
WHO ARE THESE CREEPS, KORTO?!
A JEDI AND SOME CLONES. TOOKARTI SET ME UP.
SPAKOW
CEASE FIRE. WE WANT MASTER VOS ALIVE FOR QUESTIONING.
I NEED TO GET BACK TO THE SHIP. CAN YOU SHAKE OUR PURSUIT?
SHRAK
KORTO, I'M NOT SURE HOW MUCH LONGER I CAN KEEP US ALOFT!
VOOOOOO

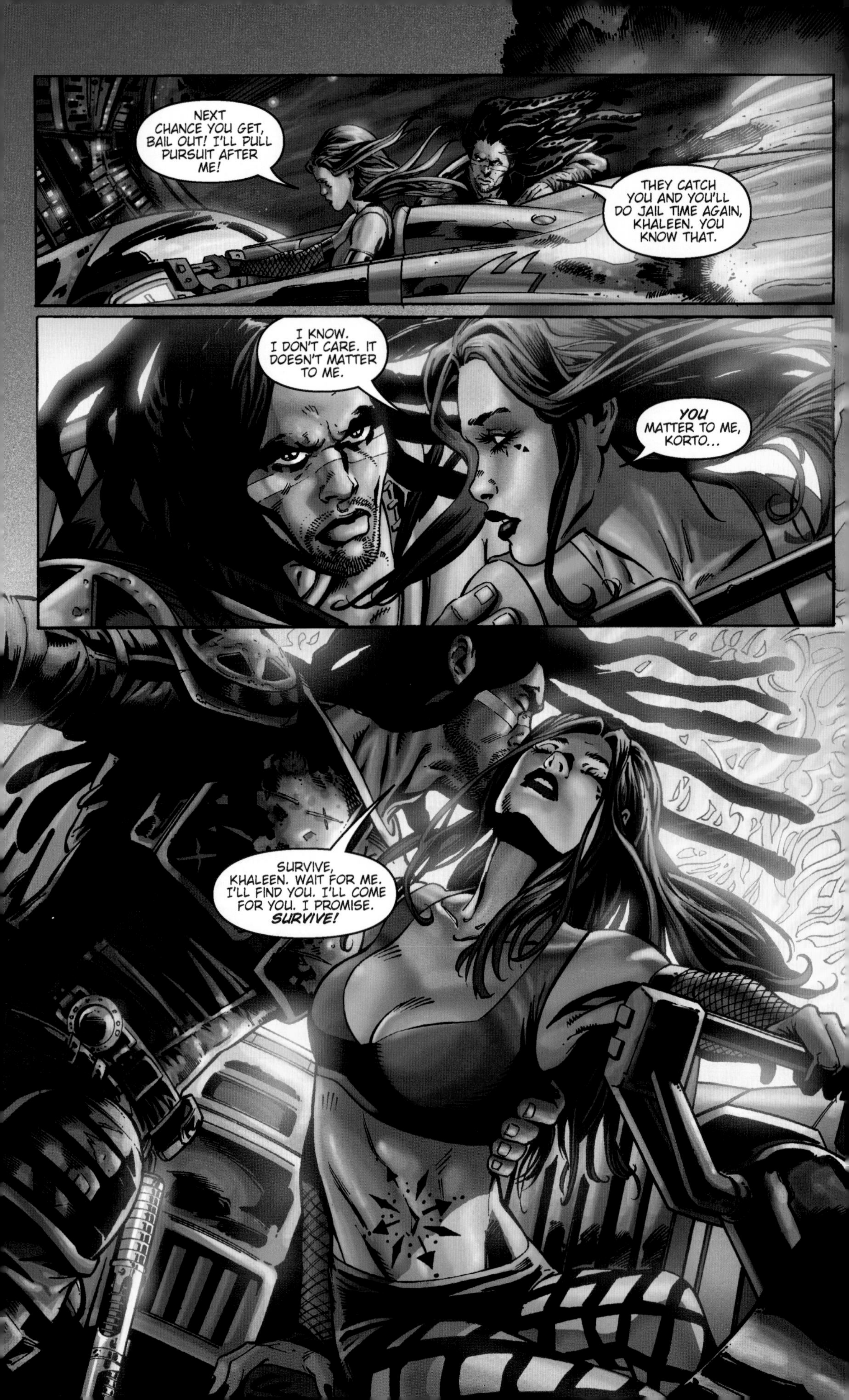
NEXT CHANCE YOU GET, BAIL OUT! I'LL PULL PURSUIT AFTER ME!
THEY CATCH YOU AND YOU'LL DO JAIL TIME AGAIN, KHALEEN. YOU KNOW THAT.
I KNOW. I DON'T CARE. IT DOESN'T MATTER TO ME.
YOU MATTER TO ME, KORTO...
SURVIVE, KHALEEN. WAIT FOR ME. I'LL FIND YOU. I'LL COME FOR YOU. I PROMISE. SURVIVE!

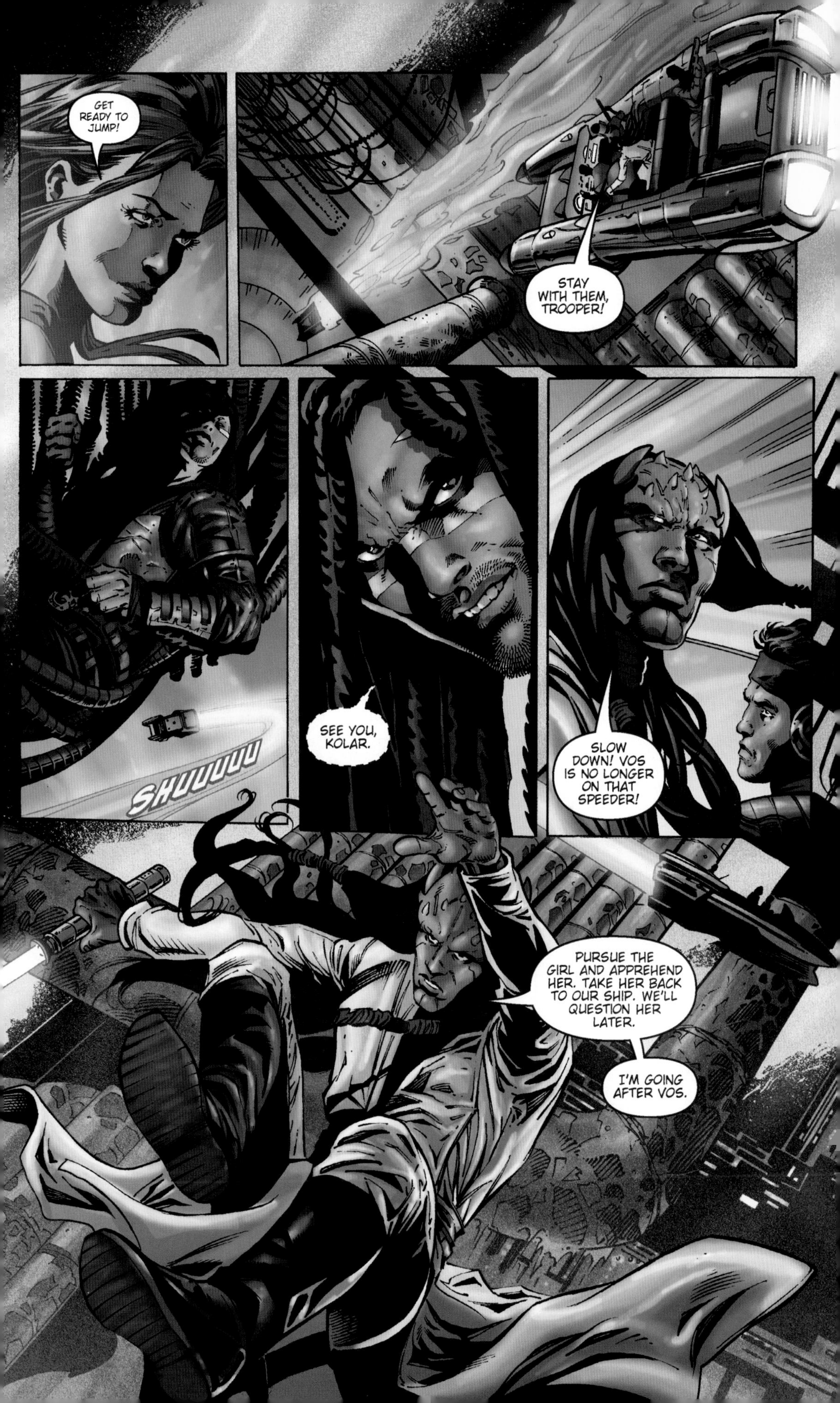
GET READY TO JUMP!
STAY WITH THEM, TROOPER!
SHUUUUU
SEE YOU, KOLAR.
SLOW DOWN! VOS IS NO LONGER ON THAT SPEEDER!
PURSUE THE GIRL AND APPREHEND HER. TAKE HER BACK TO OUR SHIP. WE'LL QUESTION HER LATER.
I'M GOING AFTER VOS.

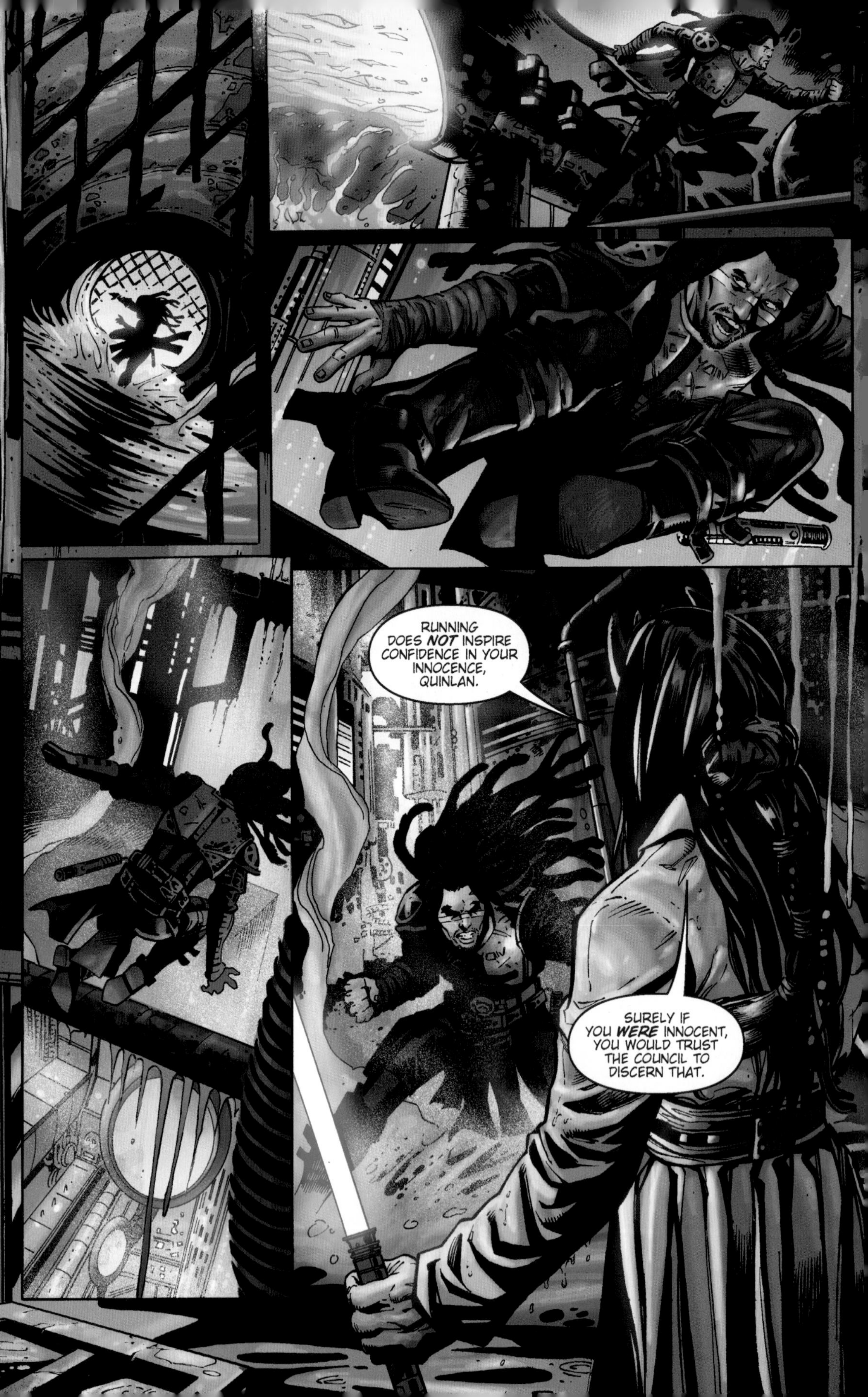
RUNNING DOES **NOT** INSPIRE CONFIDENCE IN YOUR INNOCENCE, QUINLAN.
SURELY IF YOU ***WERE*** INNOCENT, YOU WOULD TRUST THE COUNCIL TO DISCERN THAT.

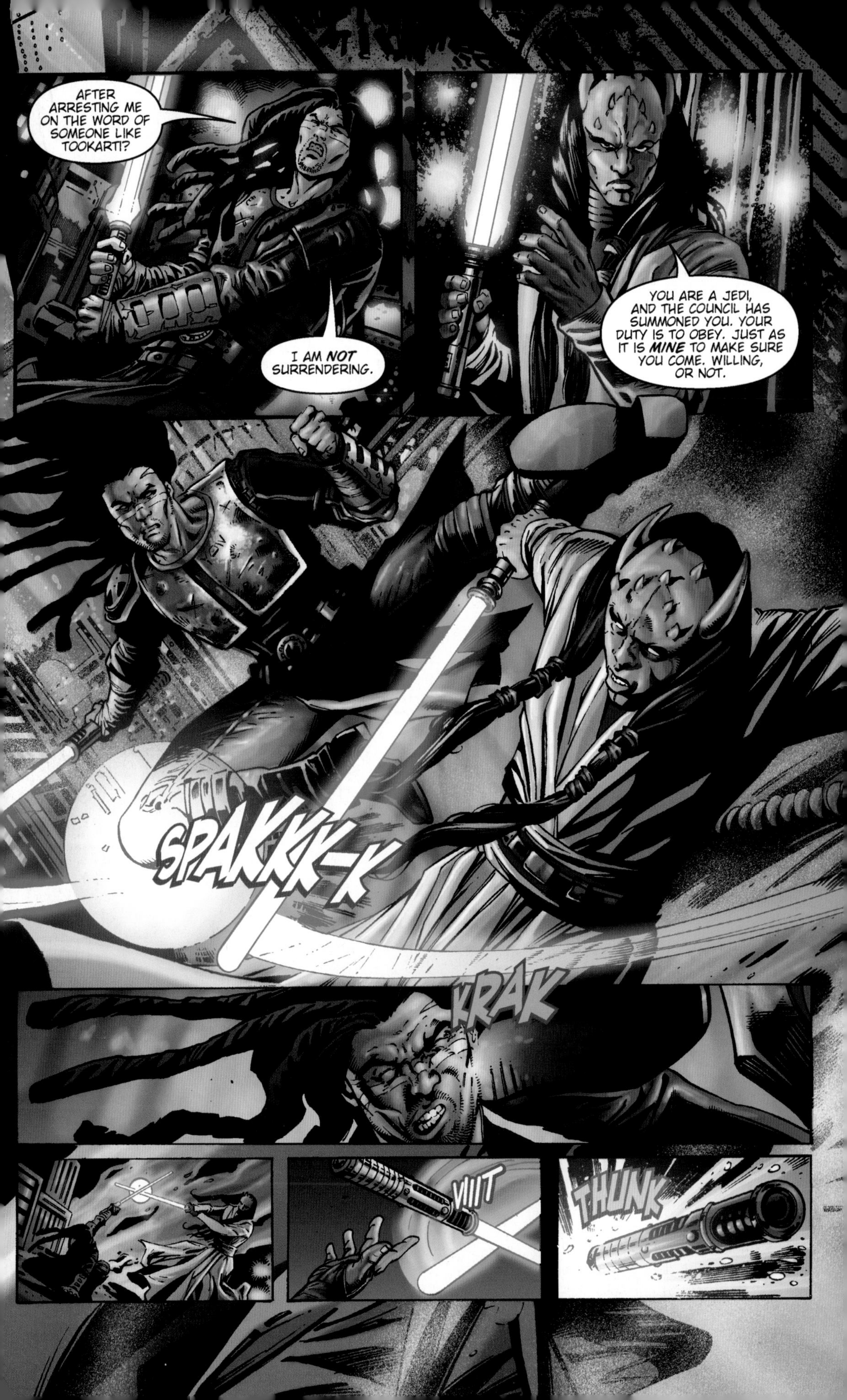
AFTER ARRESTING ME ON THE WORD OF SOMEONE LIKE TOOKARTI?
I AM NOT SURRENDERING.
YOU ARE A JEDI, AND THE COUNCIL HAS SUMMONED YOU. YOUR DUTY IS TO OBEY. JUST AS IT IS MINE TO MAKE SURE YOU COME. WILLING, OR NOT.
SPAKKK-K
KRAK
VIIIT
THUNK

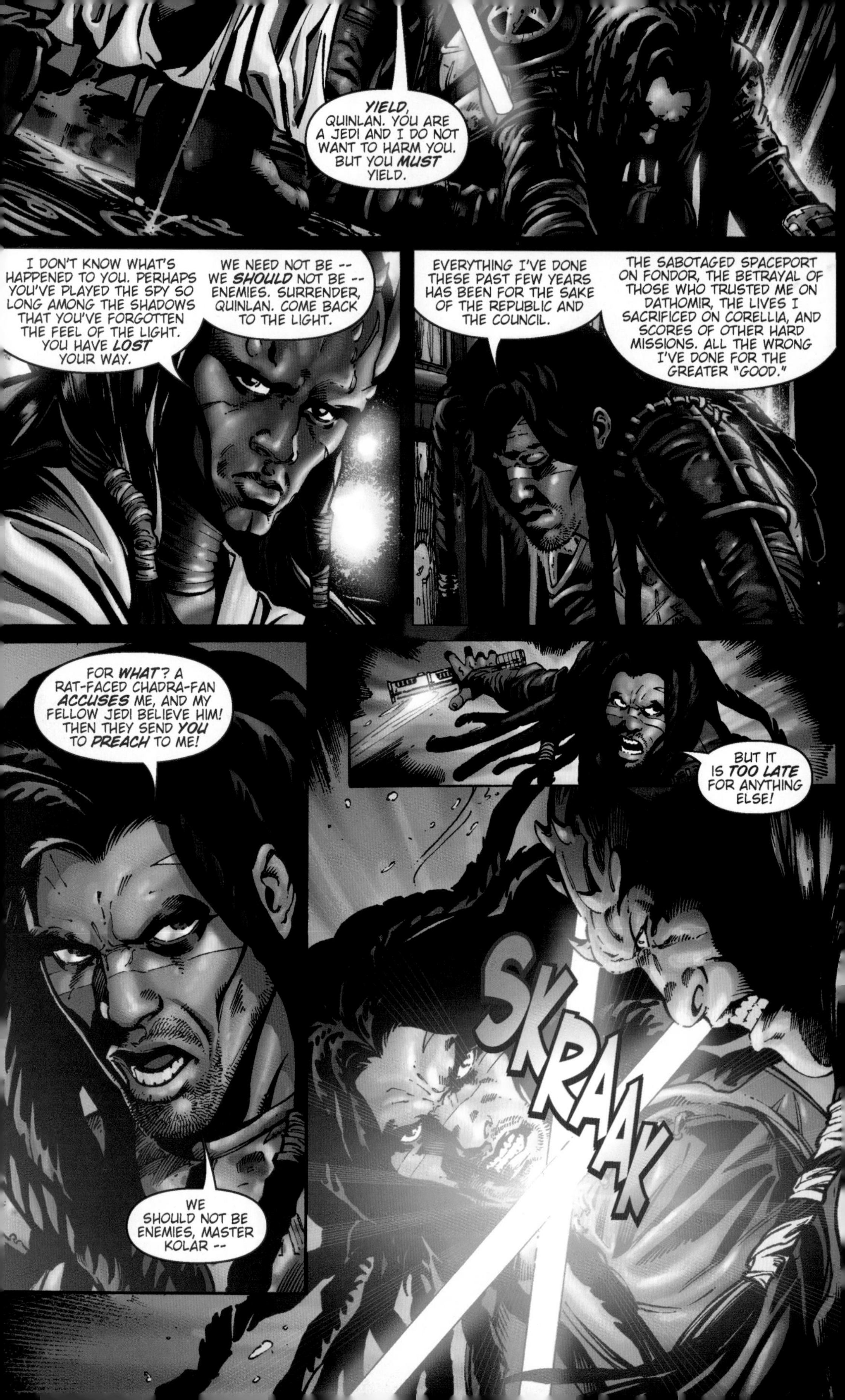
YIELD, QUINLAN. YOU ARE A JEDI AND I DO NOT WANT TO HARM YOU. BUT YOU MUST YIELD.
I DON'T KNOW WHAT'S HAPPENED TO YOU. PERHAPS YOU'VE PLAYED THE SPY SO LONG AMONG THE SHADOWS THAT YOU'VE FORGOTTEN THE FEEL OF THE LIGHT. YOU HAVE LOST YOUR WAY.
WE NEED NOT BE -- WE SHOULD NOT BE -- ENEMIES. SURRENDER, QUINLAN. COME BACK TO THE LIGHT.
EVERYTHING I'VE DONE THESE PAST FEW YEARS HAS BEEN FOR THE SAKE OF THE REPUBLIC AND THE COUNCIL.
THE SABOTAGED SPACEPORT ON FONDOR, THE BETRAYAL OF THOSE WHO TRUSTED ME ON DATHOMIR, THE LIVES I SACRIFICED ON CORELLIA, AND SCORES OF OTHER HARD MISSIONS. ALL THE WRONG I'VE DONE FOR THE GREATER "GOOD."
FOR WHAT? A RAT-FACED CHADRA-FAN ACCUSES ME, AND MY FELLOW JEDI BELIEVE HIM! THEN THEY SEND YOU TO PREACH TO ME!
WE SHOULD NOT BE ENEMIES, MASTER KOLAR --
BUT IT IS TOO LATE FOR ANYTHING ELSE!
SKRAAK

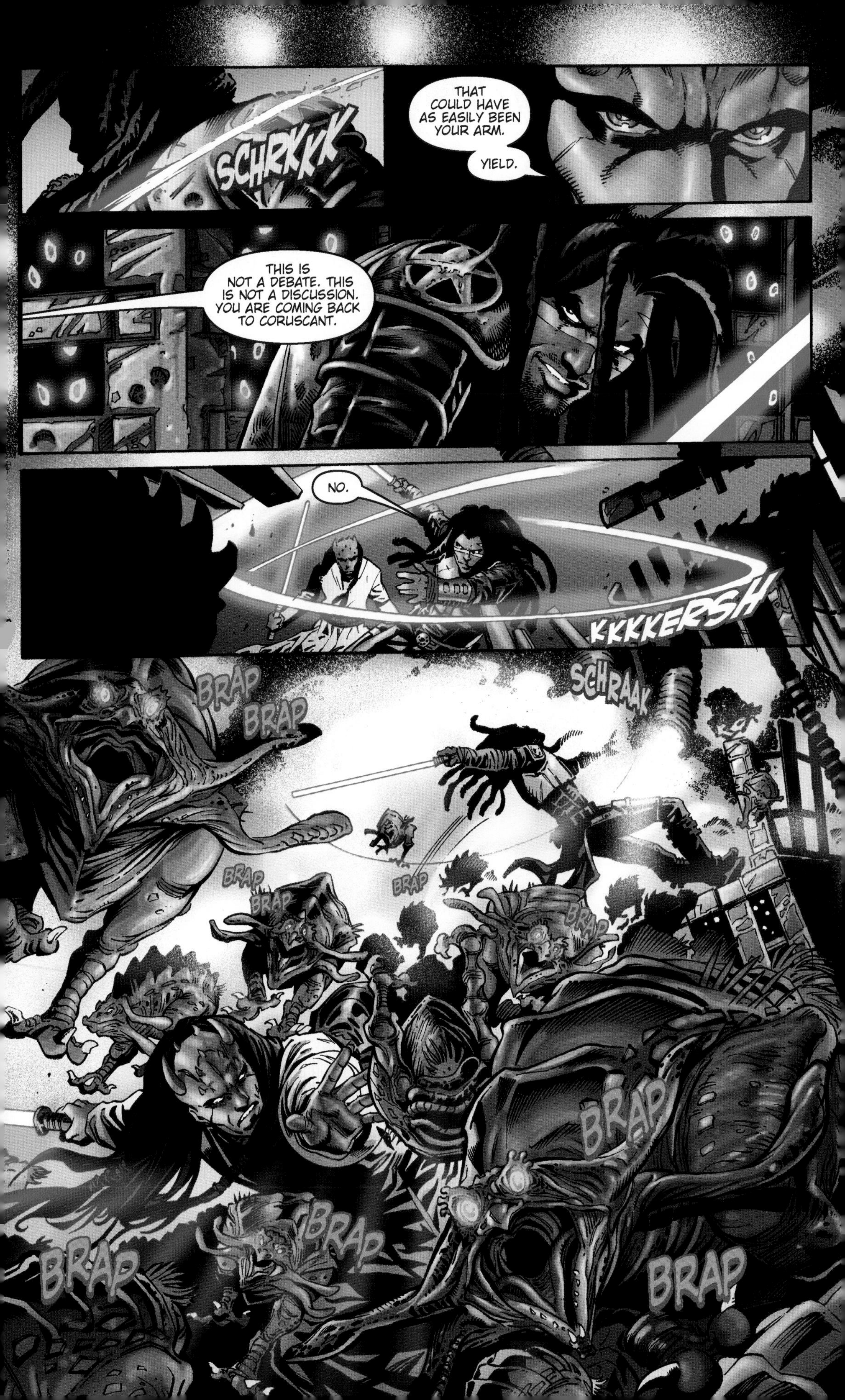
SCHRKKK
THAT COULD HAVE AS EASILY BEEN YOUR ARM.
YIELD.
THIS IS NOT A DEBATE. THIS IS NOT A DISCUSSION. YOU ARE COMING BACK TO CORUSCANT.
NO.
KKKKERSH
BRAP
BRAP
SCHRAAK
BRAP
BRAP
BRAP
BRAP
BRAP
BRAP
BRAP
BRAP

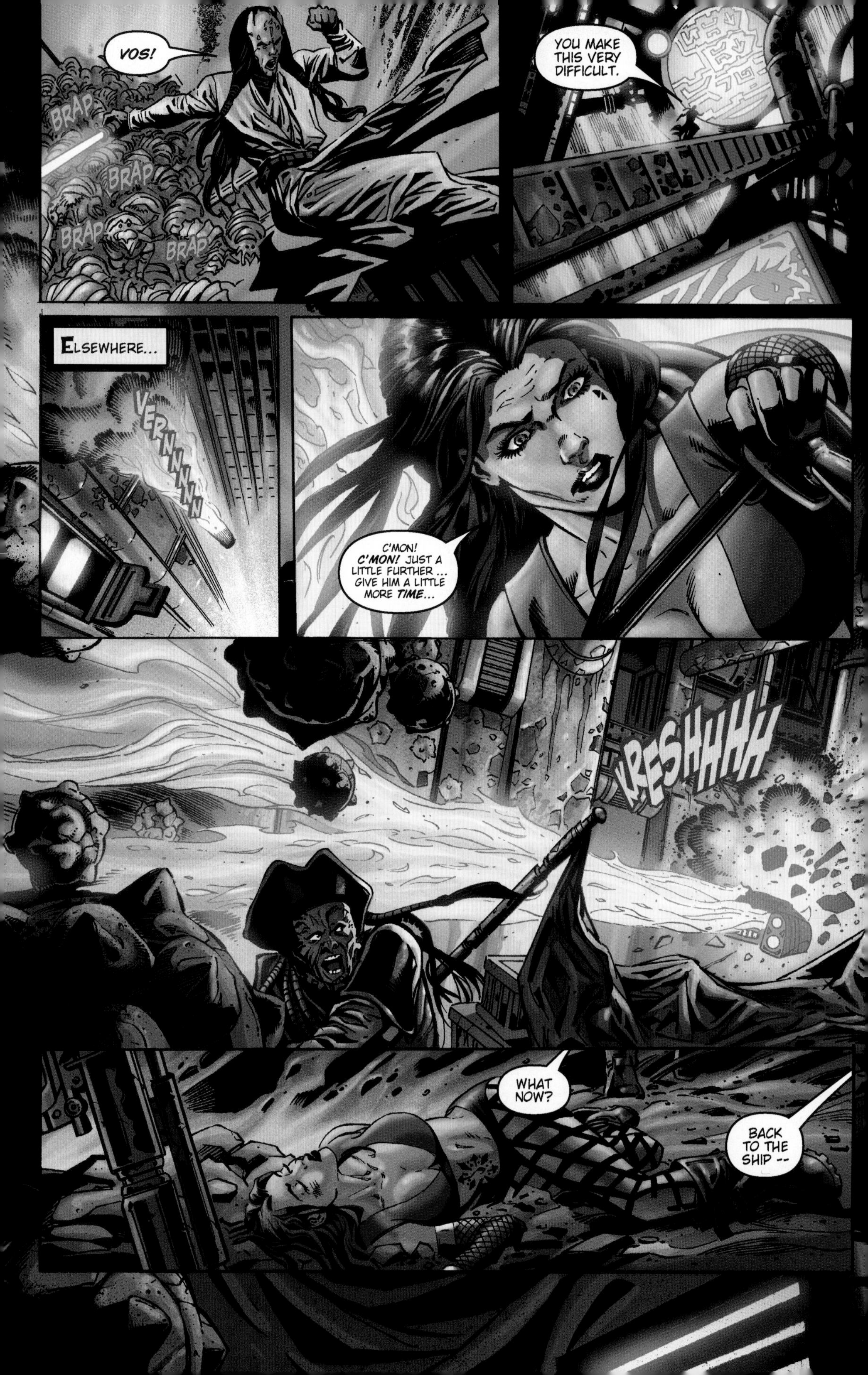
VOS!
BRAP
BRAP
BRAP
BRAP
YOU MAKE THIS VERY DIFFICULT.
ELSEWHERE...
VERNNNNN
C'MON! C'MON! JUST A LITTLE FURTHER... GIVE HIM A LITTLE MORE TIME...
VRESHHHH
WHAT NOW?
BACK TO THE SHIP --

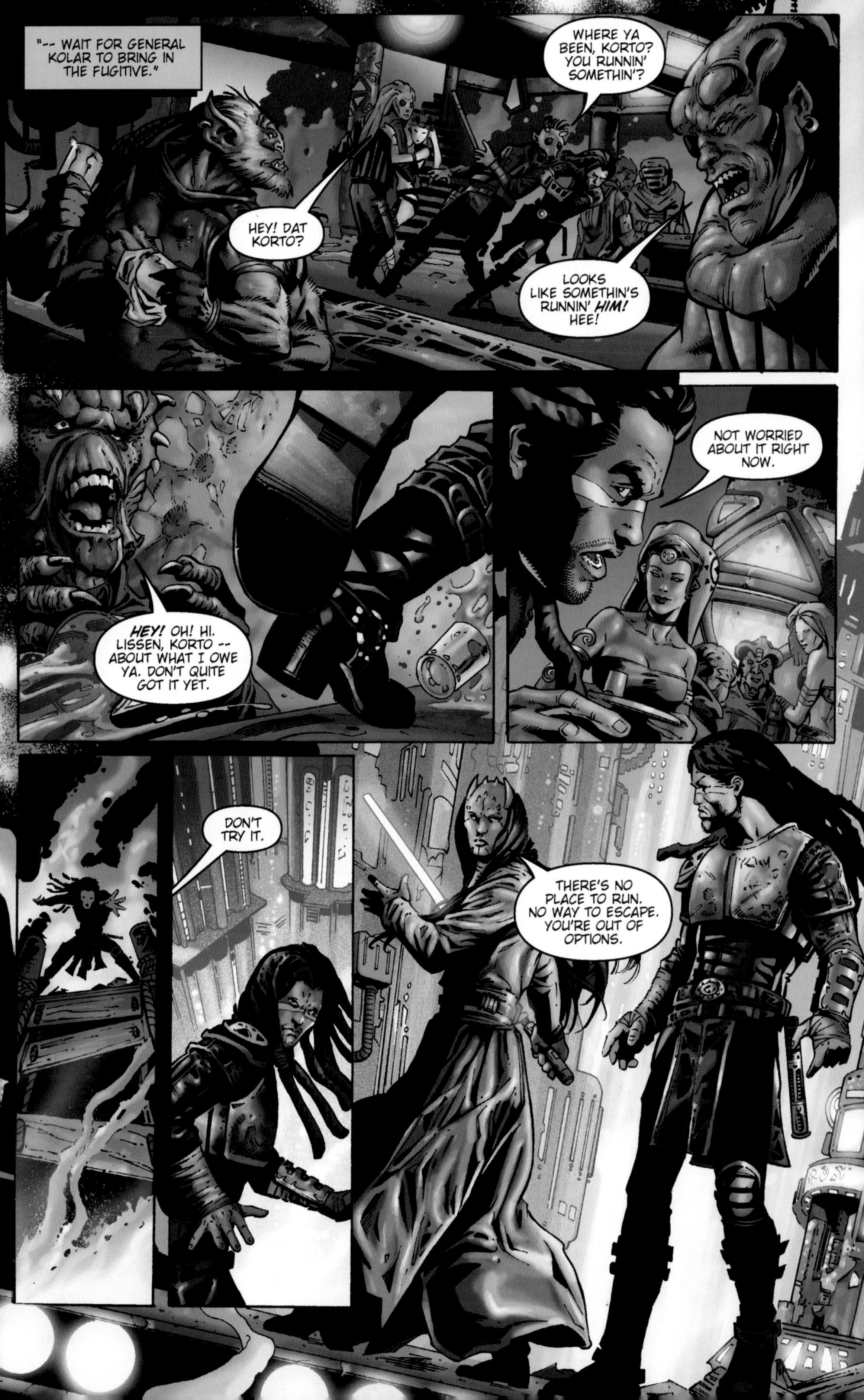
"-- WAIT FOR GENERAL KOLAR TO BRING IN THE FUGITIVE."
HEY! DAT KORTO?
WHERE YA BEEN, KORTO? YOU RUNNIN' SOMETHIN'?
LOOKS LIKE SOMETHIN'S RUNNIN' *HIM!* HEE!
HEY! OH! HI. LISSEN, KORTO -- ABOUT WHAT I OWE YA. DON'T QUITE GOT IT YET.
NOT WORRIED ABOUT IT RIGHT NOW.
DON'T TRY IT.
THERE'S NO PLACE TO RUN. NO WAY TO ESCAPE. YOU'RE OUT OF OPTIONS.

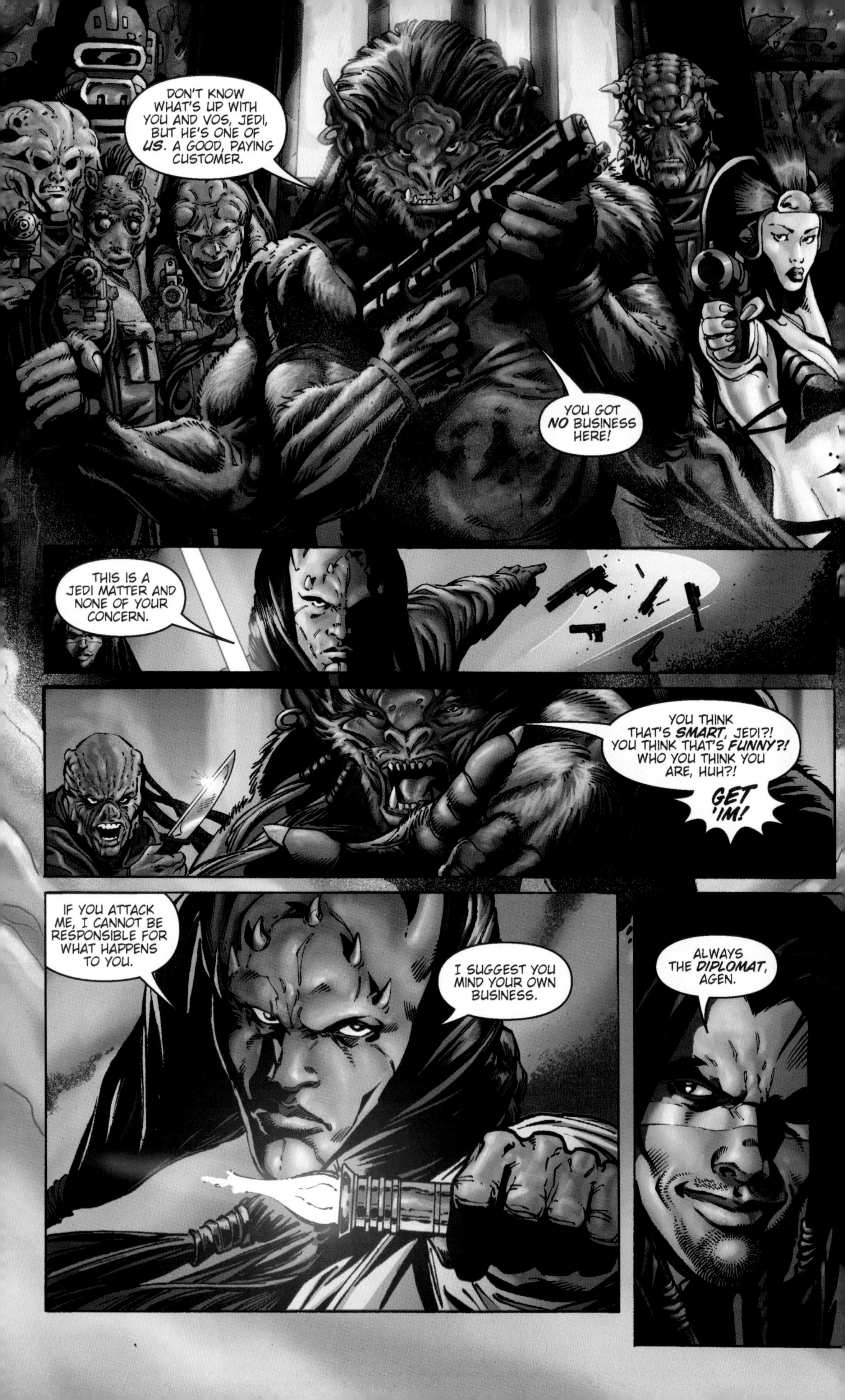
DON'T KNOW WHAT'S UP WITH YOU AND VOS, JEDI, BUT HE'S ONE OF ***US***. A GOOD, PAYING CUSTOMER.
YOU GOT ***NO*** BUSINESS HERE!
THIS IS A JEDI MATTER AND NONE OF YOUR CONCERN.
YOU THINK THAT'S ***SMART***, JEDI?! YOU THINK THAT'S ***FUNNY?!*** WHO YOU THINK YOU ARE, HUH?!
GET 'IM!
IF YOU ATTACK ME, I CANNOT BE RESPONSIBLE FOR WHAT HAPPENS TO YOU.
I SUGGEST YOU MIND YOUR OWN BUSINESS.
ALWAYS THE ***DIPLOMAT***, AGEN.

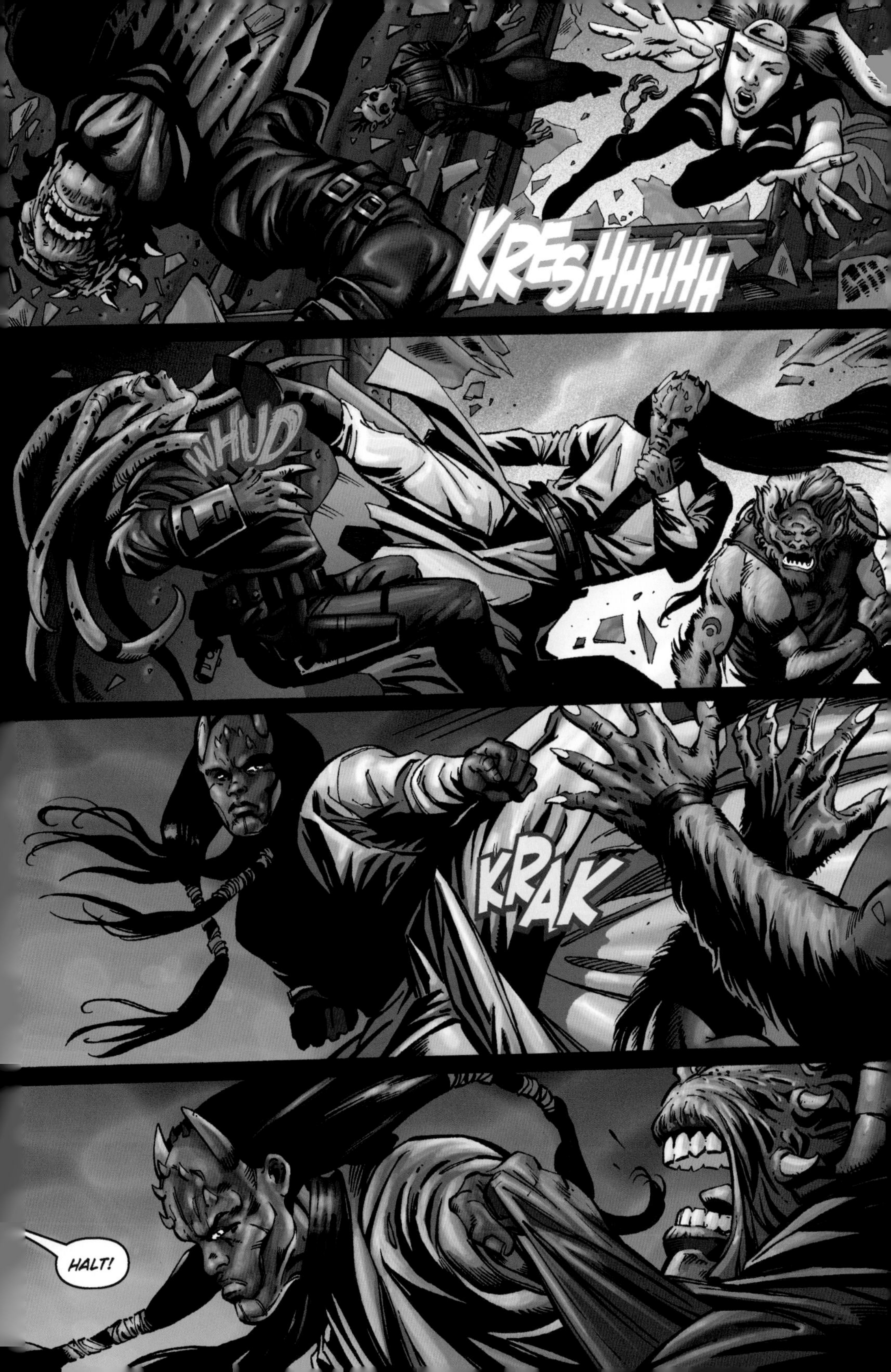
KRESHHHHH
WHUD
KRAK
HALT!

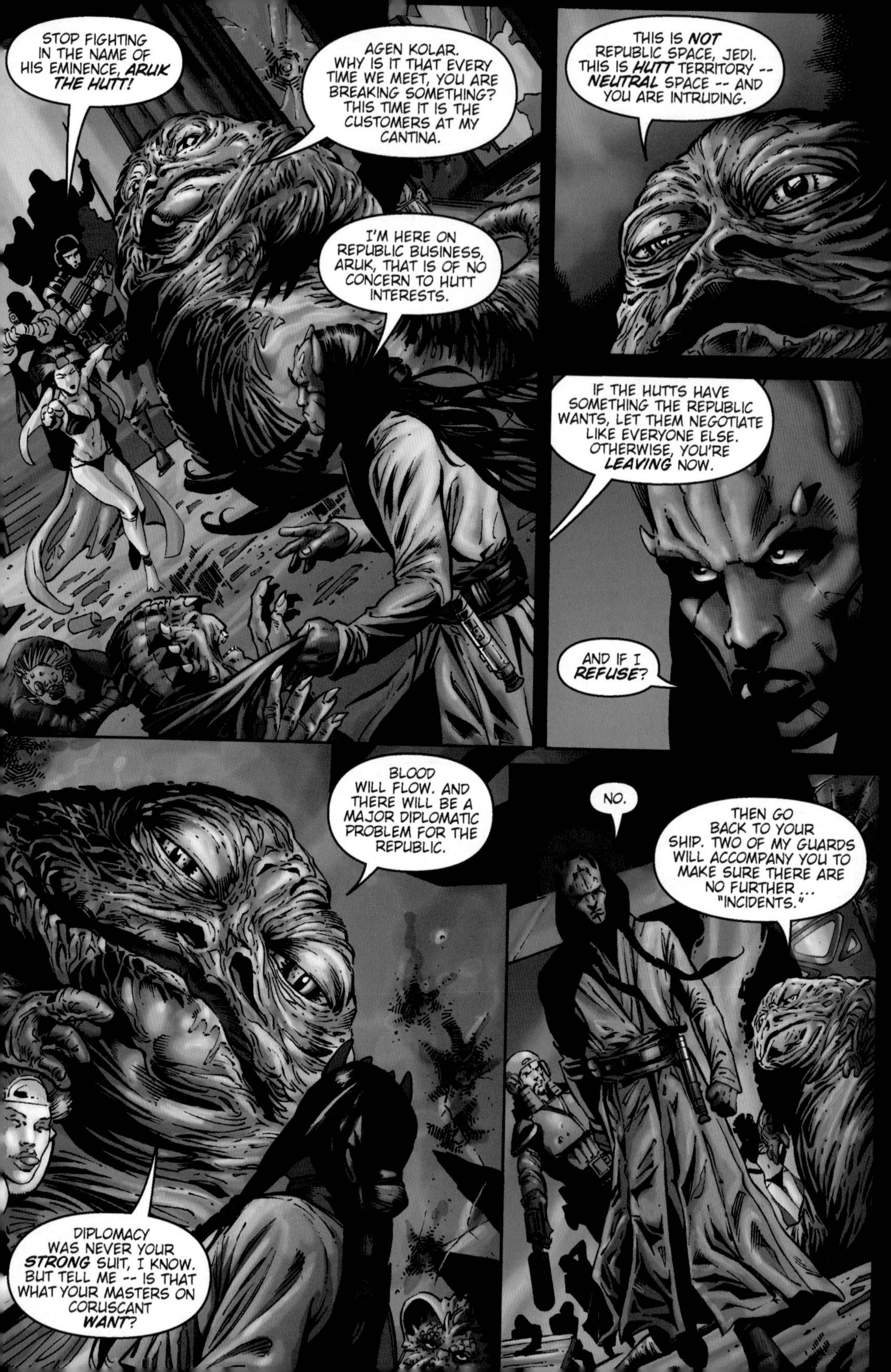
STOP FIGHTING IN THE NAME OF HIS EMINENCE, ARUK THE HUTT!
AGEN KOLAR. WHY IS IT THAT EVERY TIME WE MEET, YOU ARE BREAKING SOMETHING? THIS TIME IT IS THE CUSTOMERS AT MY CANTINA.
I'M HERE ON REPUBLIC BUSINESS, ARUK, THAT IS OF NO CONCERN TO HUTT INTERESTS.
THIS IS NOT REPUBLIC SPACE, JEDI. THIS IS HUTT TERRITORY -- NEUTRAL SPACE -- AND YOU ARE INTRUDING.
IF THE HUTTS HAVE SOMETHING THE REPUBLIC WANTS, LET THEM NEGOTIATE LIKE EVERYONE ELSE. OTHERWISE, YOU'RE LEAVING NOW.
AND IF I REFUSE?
BLOOD WILL FLOW. AND THERE WILL BE A MAJOR DIPLOMATIC PROBLEM FOR THE REPUBLIC.
DIPLOMACY WAS NEVER YOUR STRONG SUIT, I KNOW. BUT TELL ME -- IS THAT WHAT YOUR MASTERS ON CORUSCANT WANT?
NO.
THEN GO BACK TO YOUR SHIP. TWO OF MY GUARDS WILL ACCOMPANY YOU TO MAKE SURE THERE ARE NO FURTHER ... "INCIDENTS."

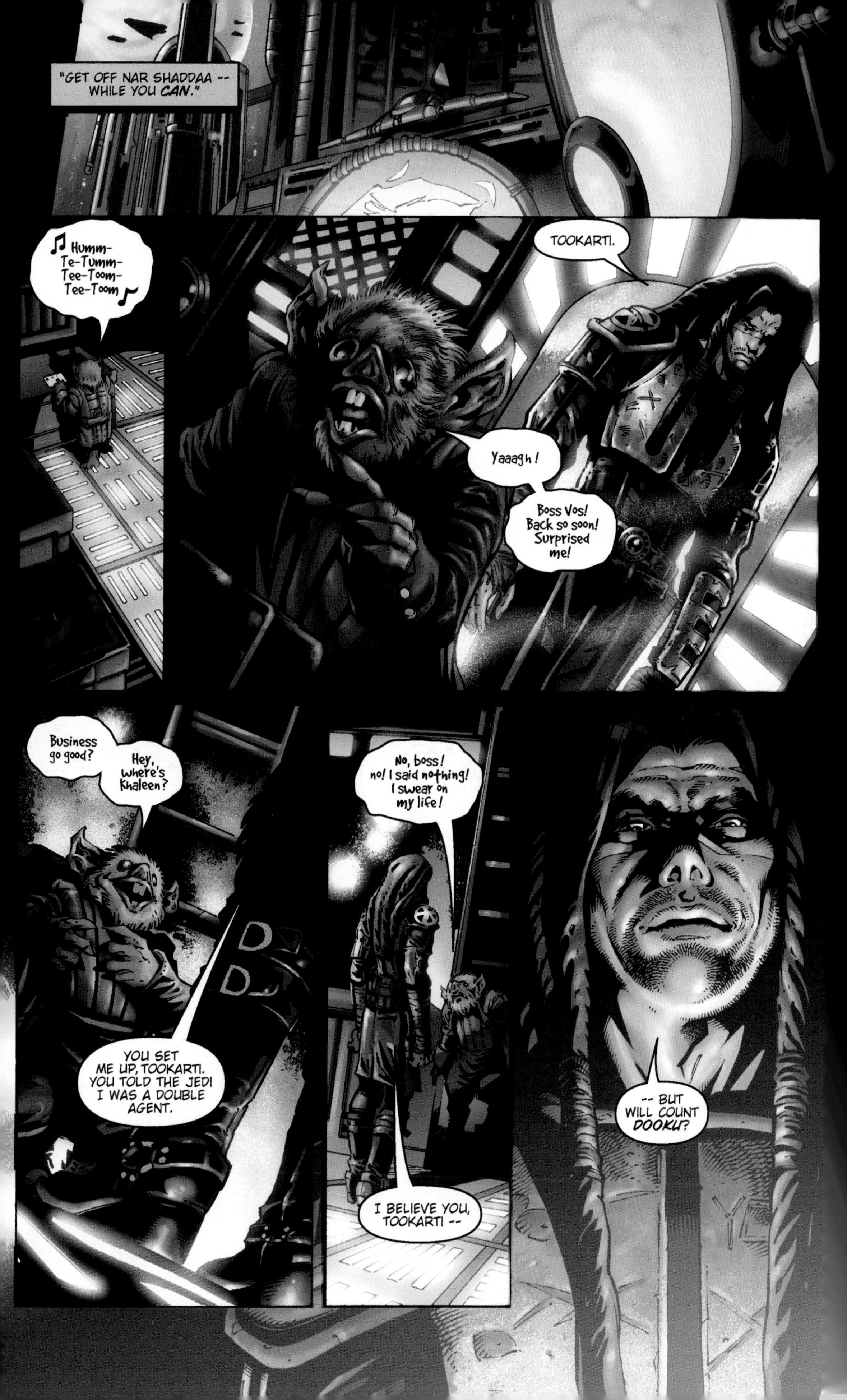
"GET OFF NAR SHADDAA -- WHILE YOU CAN."
Humm-Te-Tumm-Tee-Toom-Tee-Toom
TOOKARTI.
Yaaagh!
Boss Vos! Back so soon! Surprised me!
Business go good?
Hey, where's Khaleen?
YOU SET ME UP, TOOKARTI. YOU TOLD THE JEDI I WAS A DOUBLE AGENT.
No, boss! no! I said nothing! I swear on my life!
I BELIEVE YOU, TOOKARTI --
-- BUT WILL COUNT DOOKU?

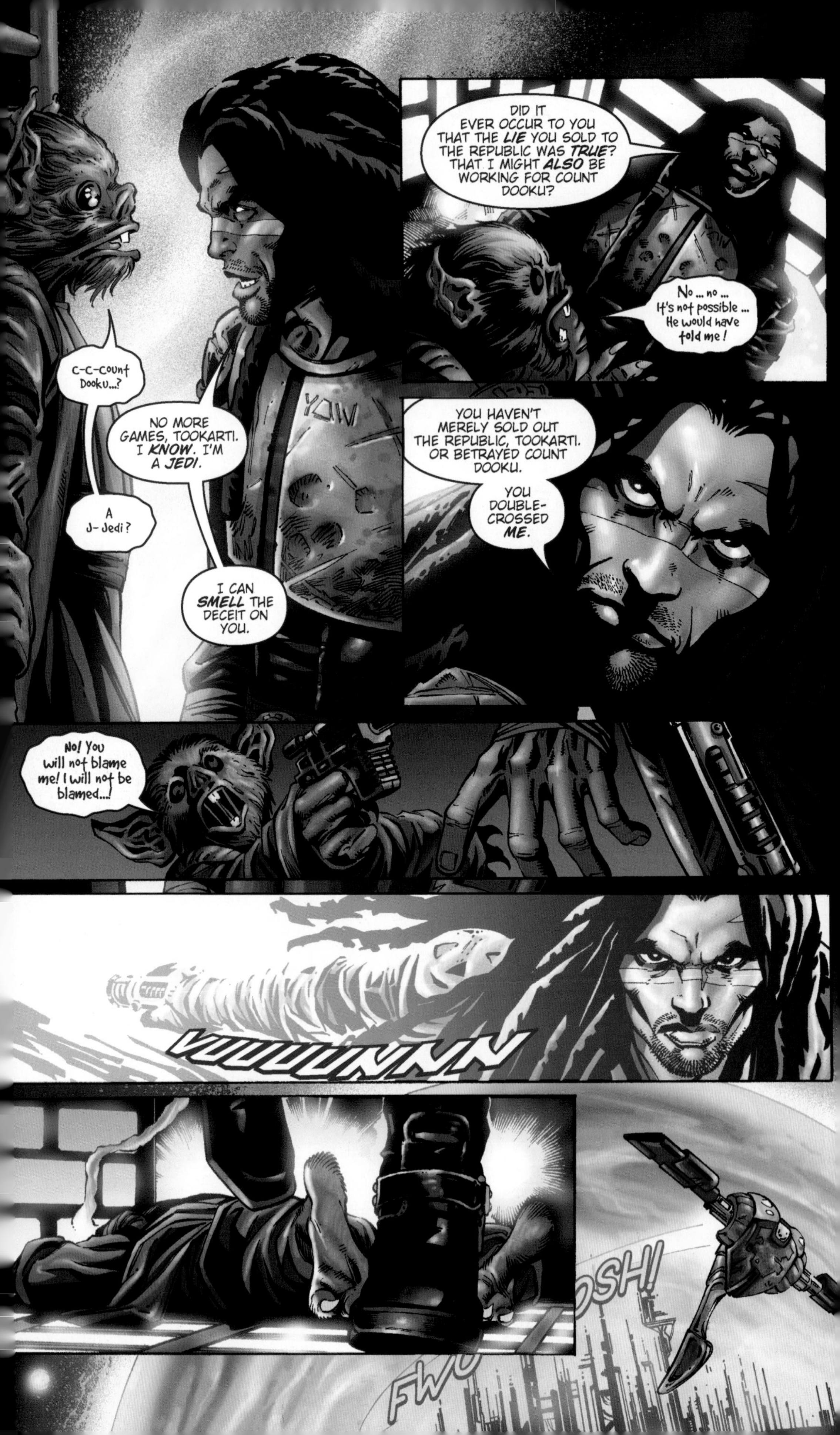
DID IT EVER OCCUR TO YOU THAT THE LIE YOU SOLD TO THE REPUBLIC WAS TRUE? THAT I MIGHT ALSO BE WORKING FOR COUNT DOOKU?
No ... no ... It's not possible ... He would have told me!
C-C-Count Dooku...?
NO MORE GAMES, TOOKARTI. I KNOW. I'M A JEDI.
A J-Jedi?
I CAN SMELL THE DECEIT ON YOU.
YOU HAVEN'T MERELY SOLD OUT THE REPUBLIC, TOOKARTI. OR BETRAYED COUNT DOOKU.
YOU DOUBLE-CROSSED ME.
No! You will not blame me! I will not be blamed...!
VUUUUNNN
FWO
OSH!

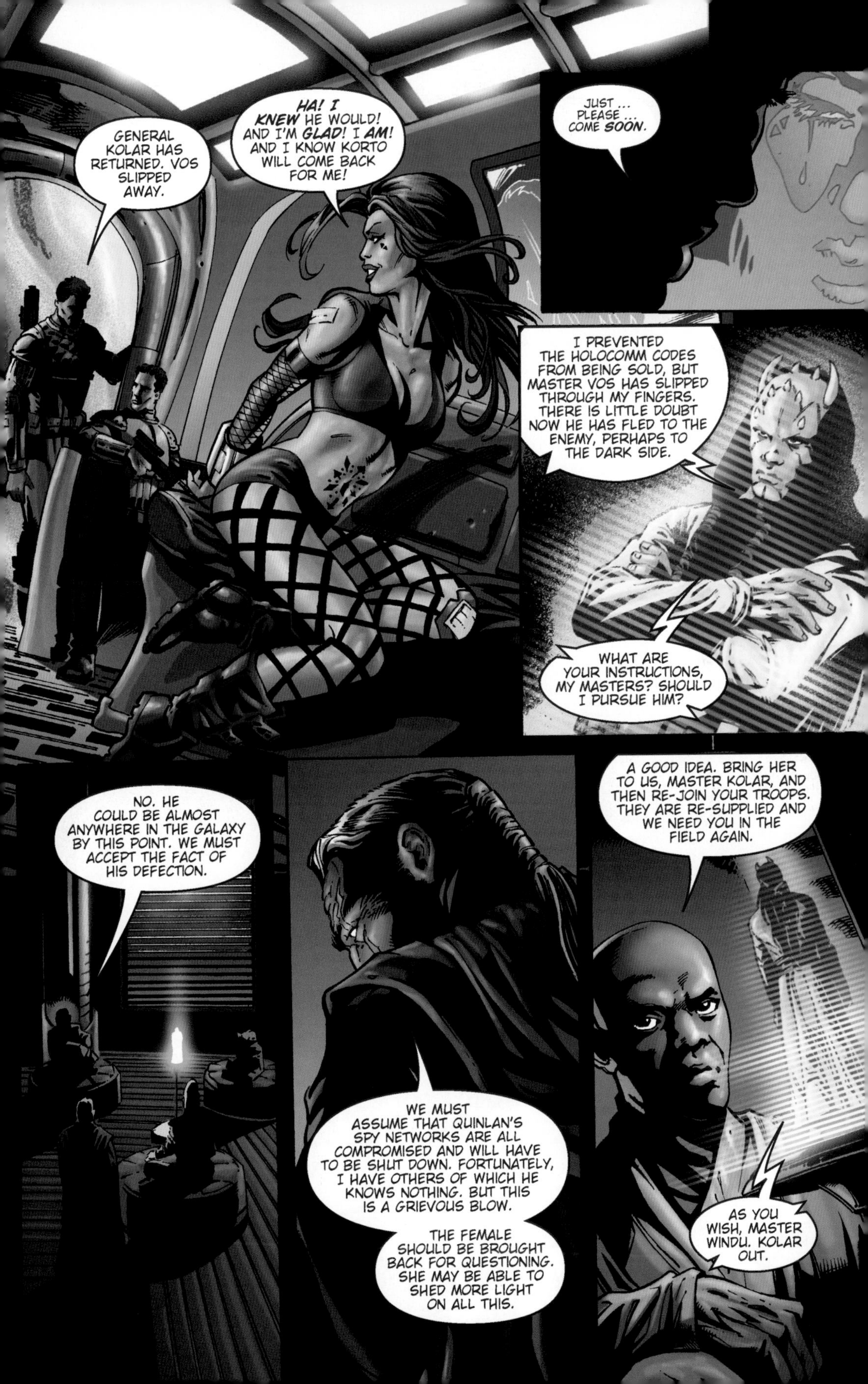
GENERAL KOLAR HAS RETURNED. VOS SLIPPED AWAY.
HA! I KNEW HE WOULD! AND I'M GLAD! I AM! AND I KNOW KORTO WILL COME BACK FOR ME!
JUST ... PLEASE ... COME SOON.
I PREVENTED THE HOLOCOMM CODES FROM BEING SOLD, BUT MASTER VOS HAS SLIPPED THROUGH MY FINGERS. THERE IS LITTLE DOUBT NOW HE HAS FLED TO THE ENEMY, PERHAPS TO THE DARK SIDE.
WHAT ARE YOUR INSTRUCTIONS, MY MASTERS? SHOULD I PURSUE HIM?
NO. HE COULD BE ALMOST ANYWHERE IN THE GALAXY BY THIS POINT. WE MUST ACCEPT THE FACT OF HIS DEFECTION.
WE MUST ASSUME THAT QUINLAN'S SPY NETWORKS ARE ALL COMPROMISED AND WILL HAVE TO BE SHUT DOWN. FORTUNATELY, I HAVE OTHERS OF WHICH HE KNOWS NOTHING. BUT THIS IS A GRIEVOUS BLOW.
THE FEMALE SHOULD BE BROUGHT BACK FOR QUESTIONING. SHE MAY BE ABLE TO SHED MORE LIGHT ON ALL THIS.
A GOOD IDEA. BRING HER TO US, MASTER KOLAR, AND THEN RE-JOIN YOUR TROOPS. THEY ARE RE-SUPPLIED AND WE NEED YOU IN THE FIELD AGAIN.
AS YOU WISH, MASTER WINDU. KOLAR OUT.

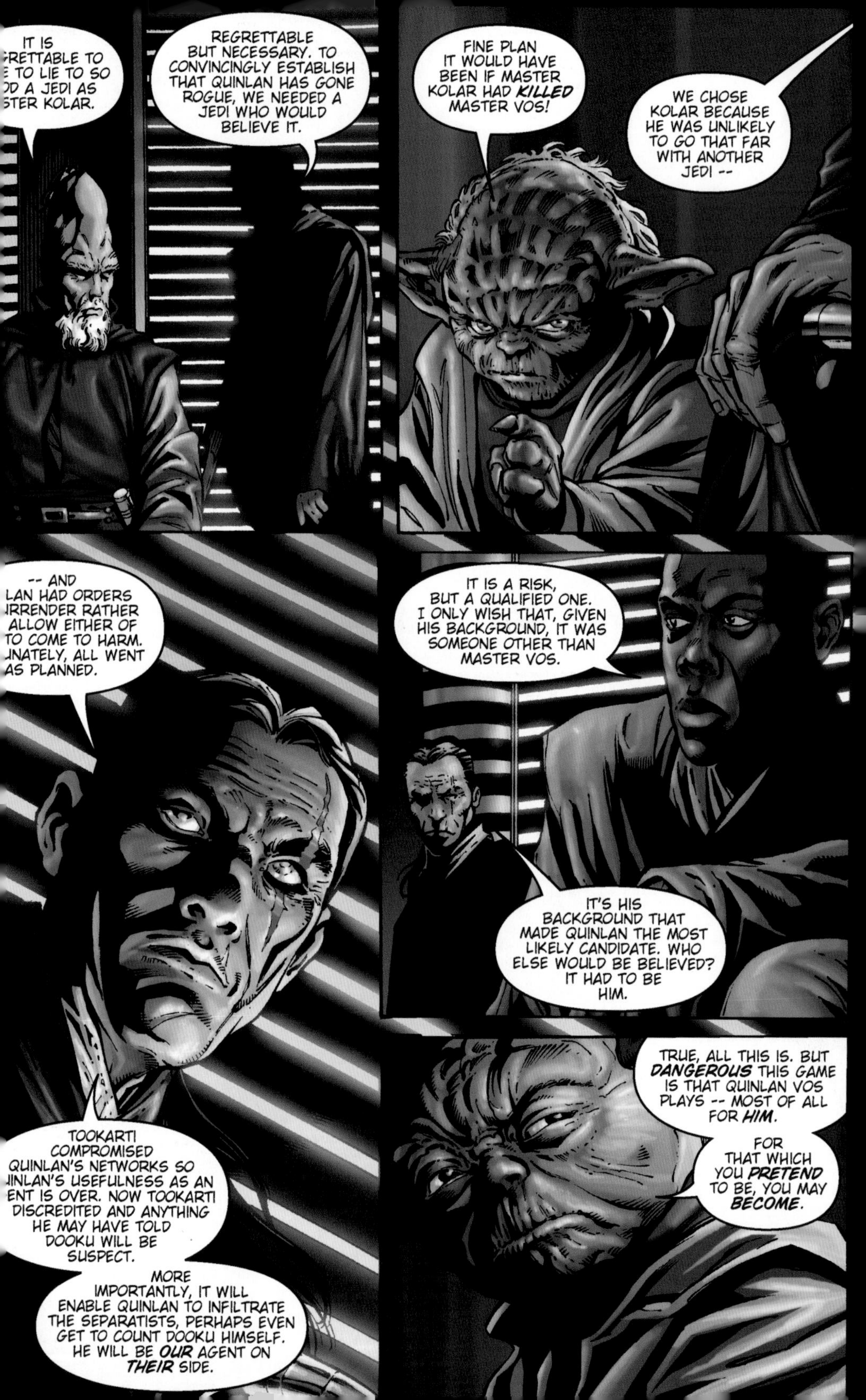
IT IS GRETTABLE TO E TO LIE TO SO OD A JEDI AS STER KOLAR.
REGRETTABLE BUT NECESSARY. TO CONVINCINGLY ESTABLISH THAT QUINLAN HAS GONE ROGUE, WE NEEDED A JEDI WHO WOULD BELIEVE IT.
FINE PLAN IT WOULD HAVE BEEN IF MASTER KOLAR HAD ***KILLED*** MASTER VOS!
WE CHOSE KOLAR BECAUSE HE WAS UNLIKELY TO GO THAT FAR WITH ANOTHER JEDI --
-- AND LAN HAD ORDERS RRENDER RATHER ALLOW EITHER OF TO COME TO HARM. UNATELY, ALL WENT AS PLANNED.
IT IS A RISK, BUT A QUALIFIED ONE. I ONLY WISH THAT, GIVEN HIS BACKGROUND, IT WAS SOMEONE OTHER THAN MASTER VOS.
IT'S HIS BACKGROUND THAT MADE QUINLAN THE MOST LIKELY CANDIDATE. WHO ELSE WOULD BE BELIEVED? IT HAD TO BE HIM.
TOOKARTI COMPROMISED QUINLAN'S NETWORKS SO UINLAN'S USEFULNESS AS AN ENT IS OVER. NOW TOOKARTI DISCREDITED AND ANYTHING HE MAY HAVE TOLD DOOKU WILL BE SUSPECT.
MORE IMPORTANTLY, IT WILL ENABLE QUINLAN TO INFILTRATE THE SEPARATISTS, PERHAPS EVEN GET TO COUNT DOOKU HIMSELF. HE WILL BE ***OUR*** AGENT ON ***THEIR*** SIDE.
TRUE, ALL THIS IS. BUT ***DANGEROUS*** THIS GAME IS THAT QUINLAN VOS PLAYS -- MOST OF ALL FOR ***HIM***.
FOR THAT WHICH YOU ***PRETEND*** TO BE, YOU MAY ***BECOME***.

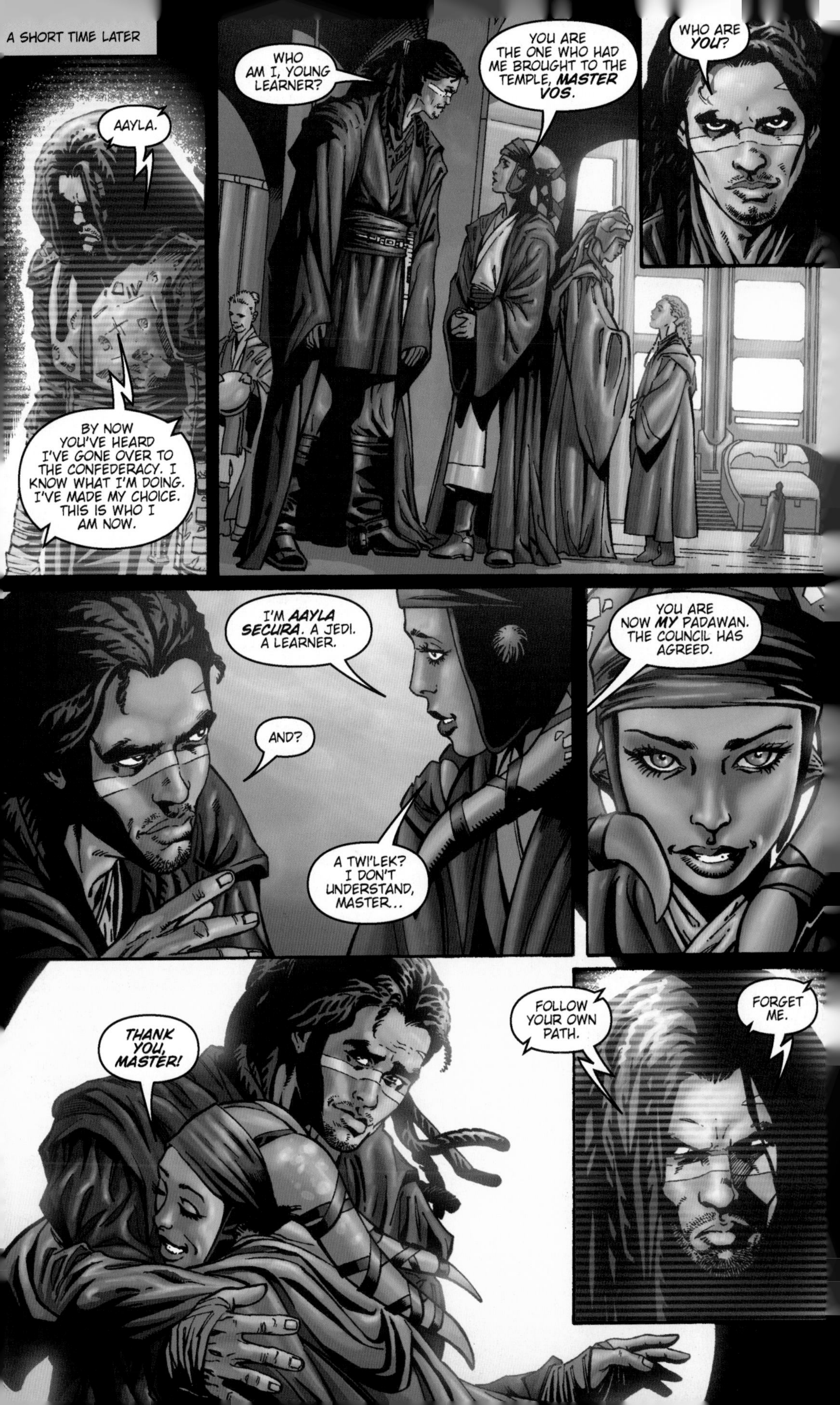
A SHORT TIME LATER
AAYLA.
BY NOW YOU'VE HEARD I'VE GONE OVER TO THE CONFEDERACY. I KNOW WHAT I'M DOING. I'VE MADE MY CHOICE. THIS IS WHO I AM NOW.
WHO AM I, YOUNG LEARNER?
YOU ARE THE ONE WHO HAD ME BROUGHT TO THE TEMPLE, MASTER VOS.
WHO ARE YOU?
I'M AAYLA SECURA. A JEDI. A LEARNER.
AND?
A TWI'LEK? I DON'T UNDERSTAND, MASTER...
YOU ARE NOW MY PADAWAN. THE COUNCIL HAS AGREED.
THANK YOU, MASTER!
FOLLOW YOUR OWN PATH.
FORGET ME.

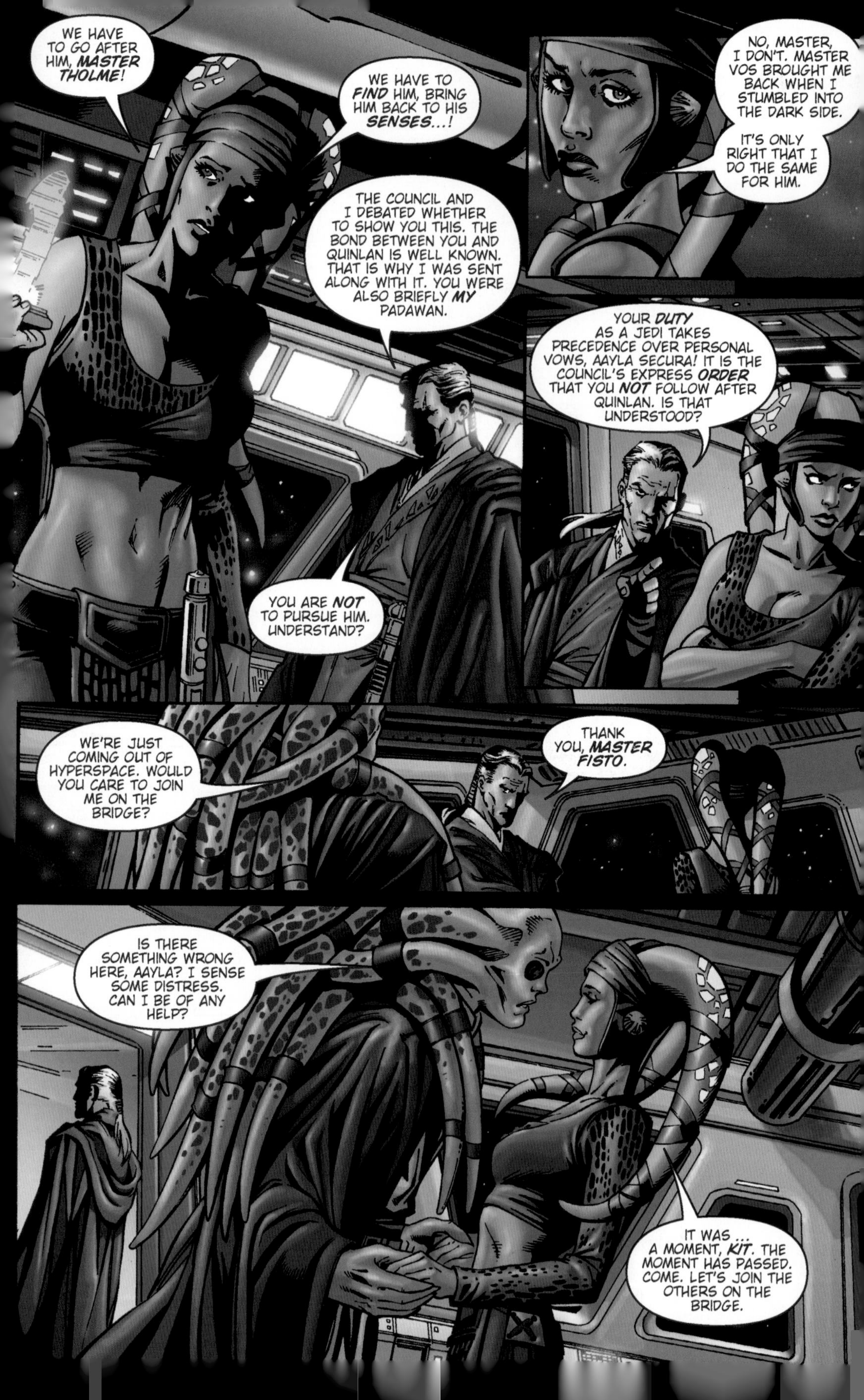
WE HAVE TO GO AFTER HIM, MASTER THOLME!
WE HAVE TO FIND HIM, BRING HIM BACK TO HIS SENSES...!
THE COUNCIL AND I DEBATED WHETHER TO SHOW YOU THIS. THE BOND BETWEEN YOU AND QUINLAN IS WELL KNOWN. THAT IS WHY I WAS SENT ALONG WITH IT. YOU WERE ALSO BRIEFLY MY PADAWAN.
YOU ARE NOT TO PURSUE HIM. UNDERSTAND?
NO, MASTER, I DON'T. MASTER VOS BROUGHT ME BACK WHEN I STUMBLED INTO THE DARK SIDE.
IT'S ONLY RIGHT THAT I DO THE SAME FOR HIM.
YOUR DUTY AS A JEDI TAKES PRECEDENCE OVER PERSONAL VOWS, AAYLA SECURA! IT IS THE COUNCIL'S EXPRESS ORDER THAT YOU NOT FOLLOW AFTER QUINLAN. IS THAT UNDERSTOOD?
WE'RE JUST COMING OUT OF HYPERSPACE. WOULD YOU CARE TO JOIN ME ON THE BRIDGE?
THANK YOU, MASTER FISTO.
IS THERE SOMETHING WRONG HERE, AAYLA? I SENSE SOME DISTRESS. CAN I BE OF ANY HELP?
IT WAS ... A MOMENT, KIT. THE MOMENT HAS PASSED. COME. LET'S JOIN THE OTHERS ON THE BRIDGE.

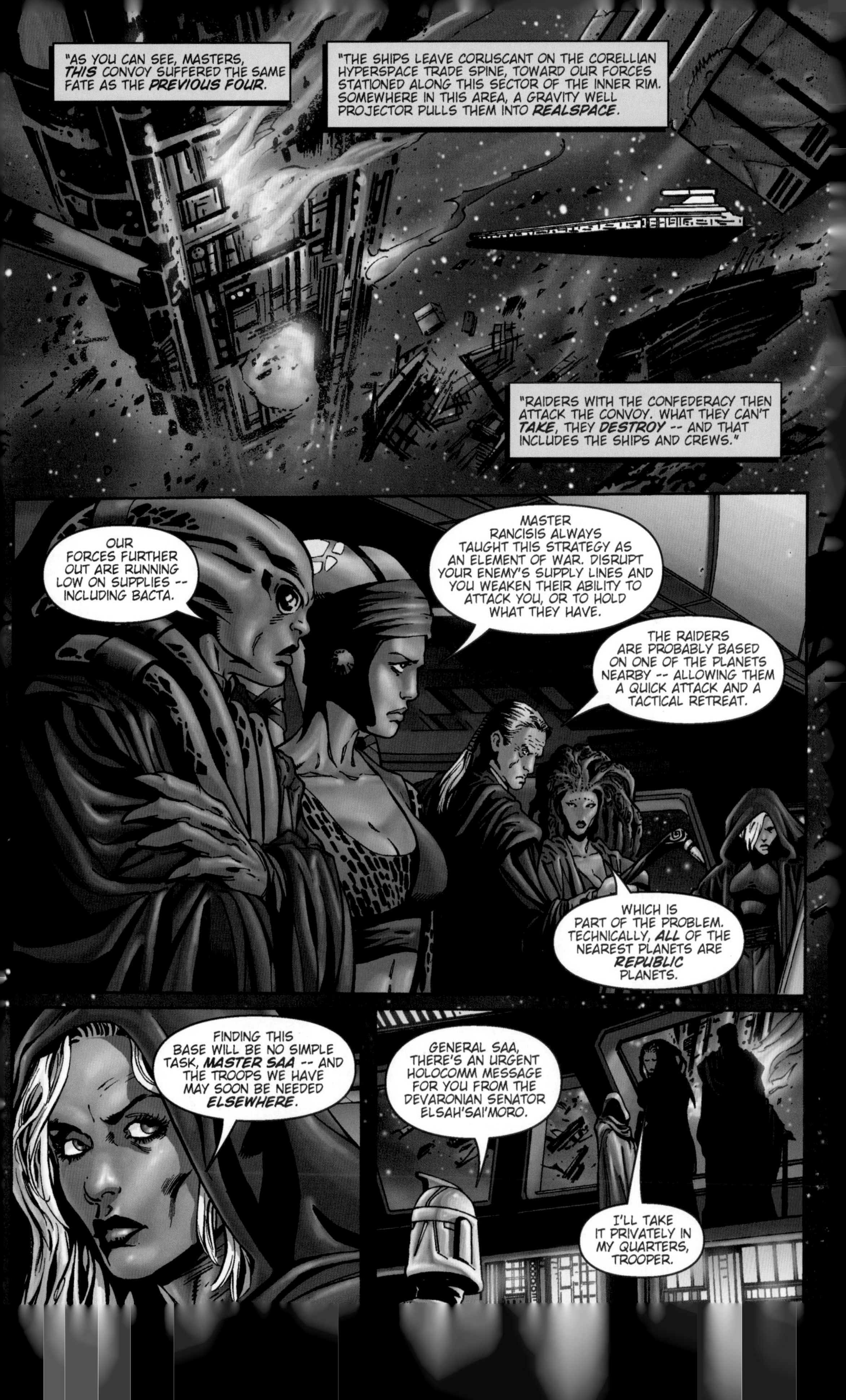

"AS YOU CAN SEE, MASTERS, THIS CONVOY SUFFERED THE SAME FATE AS THE PREVIOUS FOUR.
"THE SHIPS LEAVE CORUSCANT ON THE CORELLIAN HYPERSPACE TRADE SPINE, TOWARD OUR FORCES STATIONED ALONG THIS SECTOR OF THE INNER RIM. SOMEWHERE IN THIS AREA, A GRAVITY WELL PROJECTOR PULLS THEM INTO REALSPACE.
"RAIDERS WITH THE CONFEDERACY THEN ATTACK THE CONVOY. WHAT THEY CAN'T TAKE, THEY DESTROY -- AND THAT INCLUDES THE SHIPS AND CREWS."
OUR FORCES FURTHER OUT ARE RUNNING LOW ON SUPPLIES -- INCLUDING BACTA.
MASTER RANCISIS ALWAYS TAUGHT THIS STRATEGY AS AN ELEMENT OF WAR. DISRUPT YOUR ENEMY'S SUPPLY LINES AND YOU WEAKEN THEIR ABILITY TO ATTACK YOU, OR TO HOLD WHAT THEY HAVE.
THE RAIDERS ARE PROBABLY BASED ON ONE OF THE PLANETS NEARBY -- ALLOWING THEM A QUICK ATTACK AND A TACTICAL RETREAT.
WHICH IS PART OF THE PROBLEM. TECHNICALLY, ALL OF THE NEAREST PLANETS ARE REPUBLIC PLANETS.
FINDING THIS BASE WILL BE NO SIMPLE TASK, MASTER SAA -- AND THE TROOPS WE HAVE MAY SOON BE NEEDED ELSEWHERE.
GENERAL SAA, THERE'S AN URGENT HOLOCOMM MESSAGE FOR YOU FROM THE DEVARONIAN SENATOR ELSAH'SAI'MORO.
I'LL TAKE IT PRIVATELY IN MY QUARTERS, TROOPER.

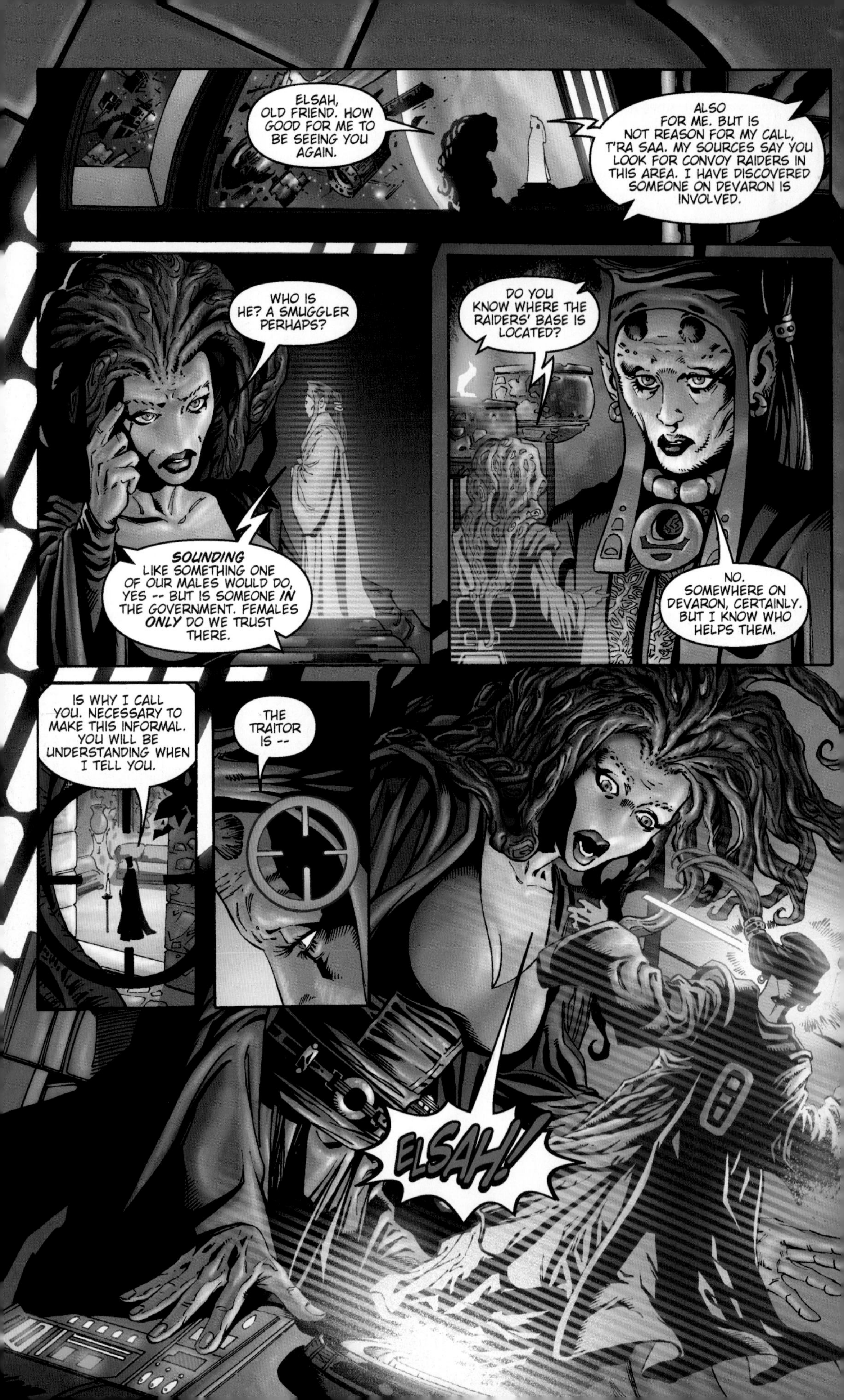
ELSAH, OLD FRIEND. HOW GOOD FOR ME TO BE SEEING YOU AGAIN.
ALSO FOR ME. BUT IS NOT REASON FOR MY CALL, T'RA SAA. MY SOURCES SAY YOU LOOK FOR CONVOY RAIDERS IN THIS AREA. I HAVE DISCOVERED SOMEONE ON DEVARON IS INVOLVED.
WHO IS HE? A SMUGGLER PERHAPS?
SOUNDING LIKE SOMETHING ONE OF OUR MALES WOULD DO, YES -- BUT IS SOMEONE IN THE GOVERNMENT. FEMALES ONLY DO WE TRUST THERE.
DO YOU KNOW WHERE THE RAIDERS' BASE IS LOCATED?
NO. SOMEWHERE ON DEVARON, CERTAINLY. BUT I KNOW WHO HELPS THEM.
IS WHY I CALL YOU. NECESSARY TO MAKE THIS INFORMAL. YOU WILL BE UNDERSTANDING WHEN I TELL YOU.
THE TRAITOR IS --
ELSAH!

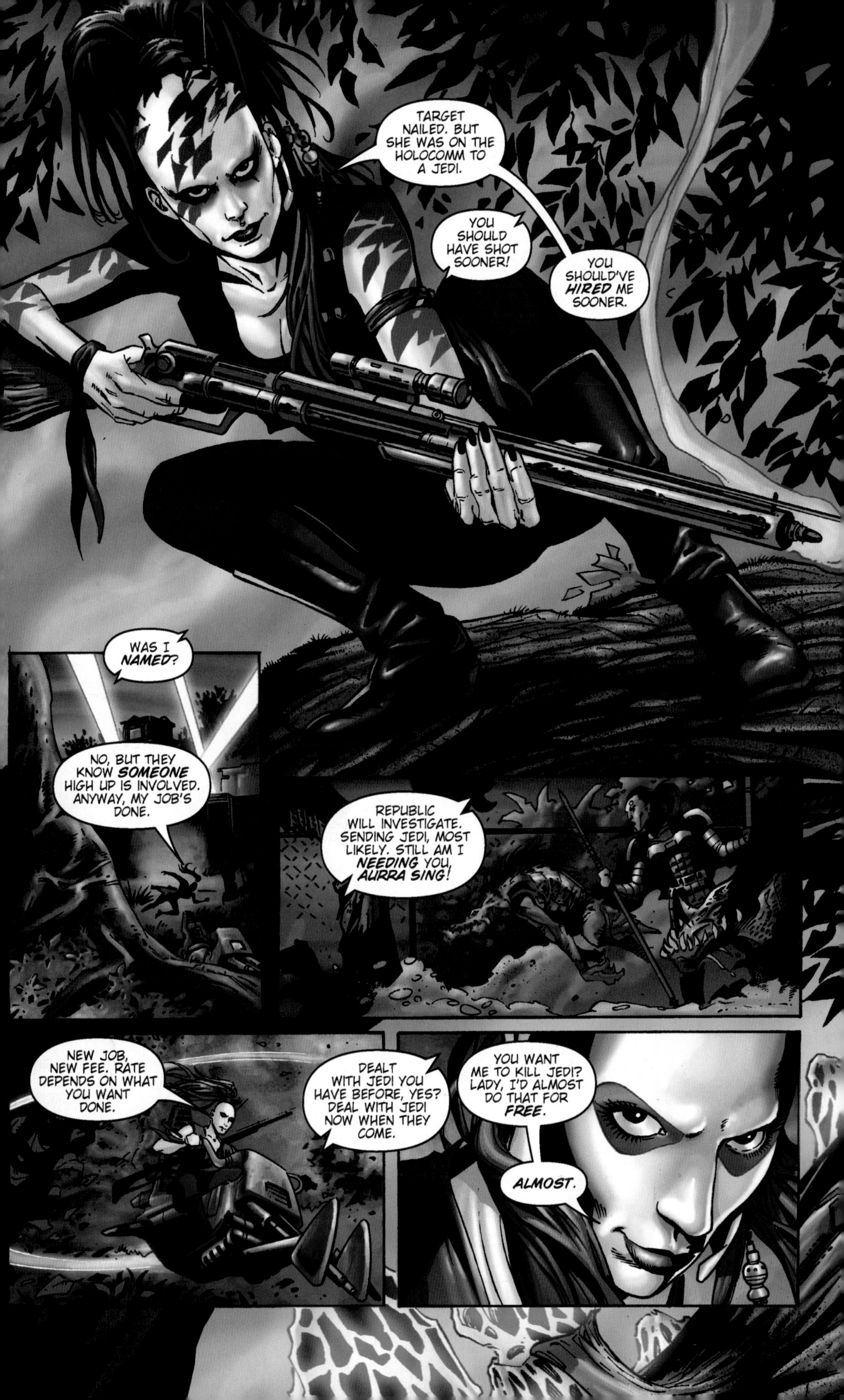
TARGET NAILED. BUT SHE WAS ON THE HOLOCOMM TO A JEDI.
YOU SHOULD HAVE SHOT SOONER!
YOU SHOULD'VE HIRED ME SOONER.
WAS I NAMED?
NO, BUT THEY KNOW SOMEONE HIGH UP IS INVOLVED. ANYWAY, MY JOB'S DONE.
REPUBLIC WILL INVESTIGATE. SENDING JEDI, MOST LIKELY. STILL AM I NEEDING YOU, AURRA SING!
NEW JOB, NEW FEE. RATE DEPENDS ON WHAT YOU WANT DONE.
DEALT WITH JEDI YOU HAVE BEFORE, YES? DEAL WITH JEDI NOW WHEN THEY COME.
YOU WANT ME TO KILL JEDI? LADY, I'D ALMOST DO THAT FOR FREE.
ALMOST.

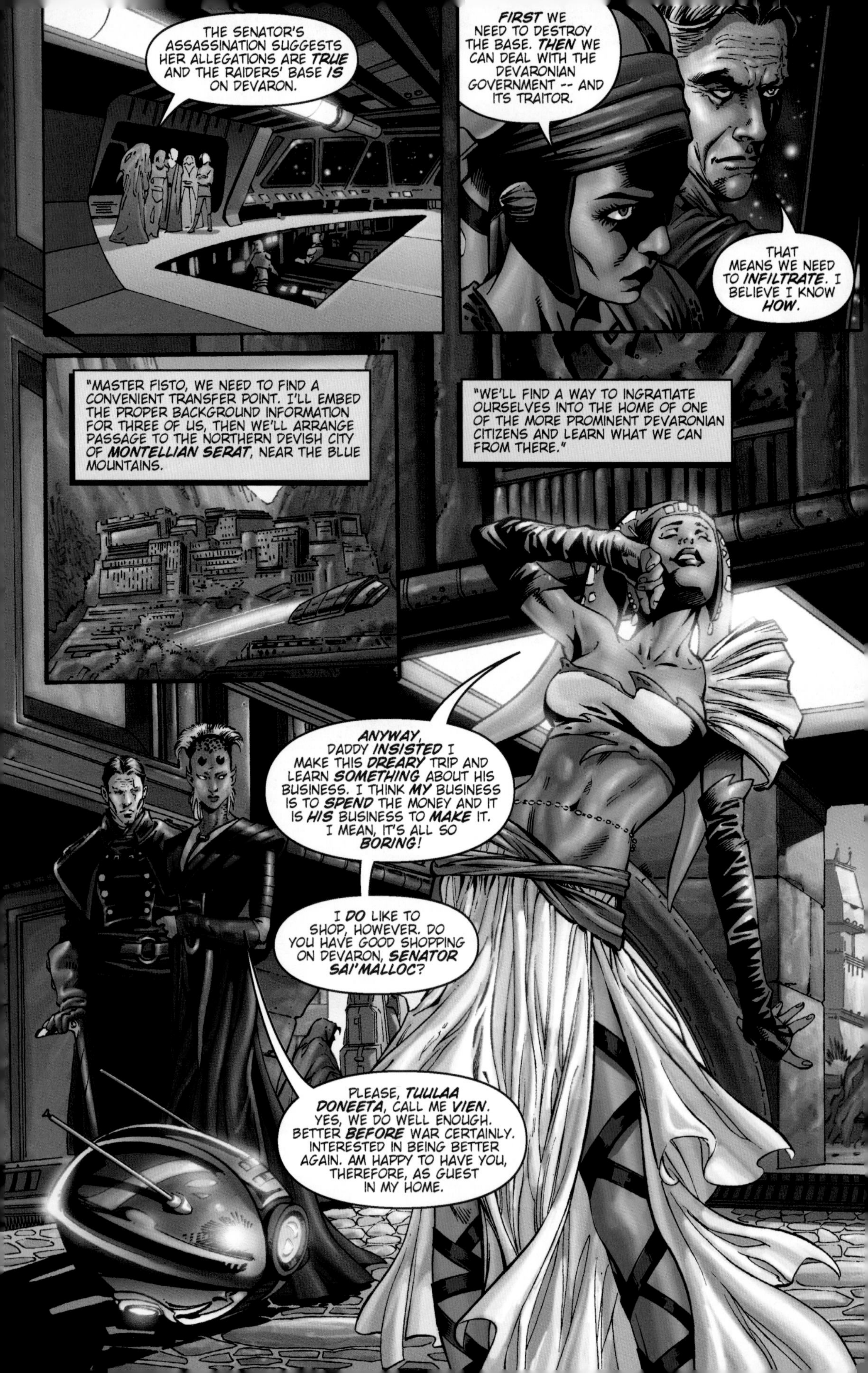
THE SENATOR'S ASSASSINATION SUGGESTS HER ALLEGATIONS ARE TRUE AND THE RAIDERS' BASE IS ON DEVARON.
FIRST WE NEED TO DESTROY THE BASE. THEN WE CAN DEAL WITH THE DEVARONIAN GOVERNMENT -- AND ITS TRAITOR.
THAT MEANS WE NEED TO INFILTRATE. I BELIEVE I KNOW HOW.
"MASTER FISTO, WE NEED TO FIND A CONVENIENT TRANSFER POINT. I'LL EMBED THE PROPER BACKGROUND INFORMATION FOR THREE OF US, THEN WE'LL ARRANGE PASSAGE TO THE NORTHERN DEVISH CITY OF MONTELLIAN SERAT, NEAR THE BLUE MOUNTAINS.
"WE'LL FIND A WAY TO INGRATIATE OURSELVES INTO THE HOME OF ONE OF THE MORE PROMINENT DEVARONIAN CITIZENS AND LEARN WHAT WE CAN FROM THERE."
ANYWAY, DADDY INSISTED I MAKE THIS DREARY TRIP AND LEARN SOMETHING ABOUT HIS BUSINESS. I THINK MY BUSINESS IS TO SPEND THE MONEY AND IT IS HIS BUSINESS TO MAKE IT. I MEAN, IT'S ALL SO BORING!
I DO LIKE TO SHOP, HOWEVER. DO YOU HAVE GOOD SHOPPING ON DEVARON, SENATOR SAI'MALLOC?
PLEASE, TUULAA DONEETA, CALL ME VIEN. YES, WE DO WELL ENOUGH. BETTER BEFORE WAR CERTAINLY. INTERESTED IN BEING BETTER AGAIN. AM HAPPY TO HAVE YOU, THEREFORE, AS GUEST IN MY HOME.

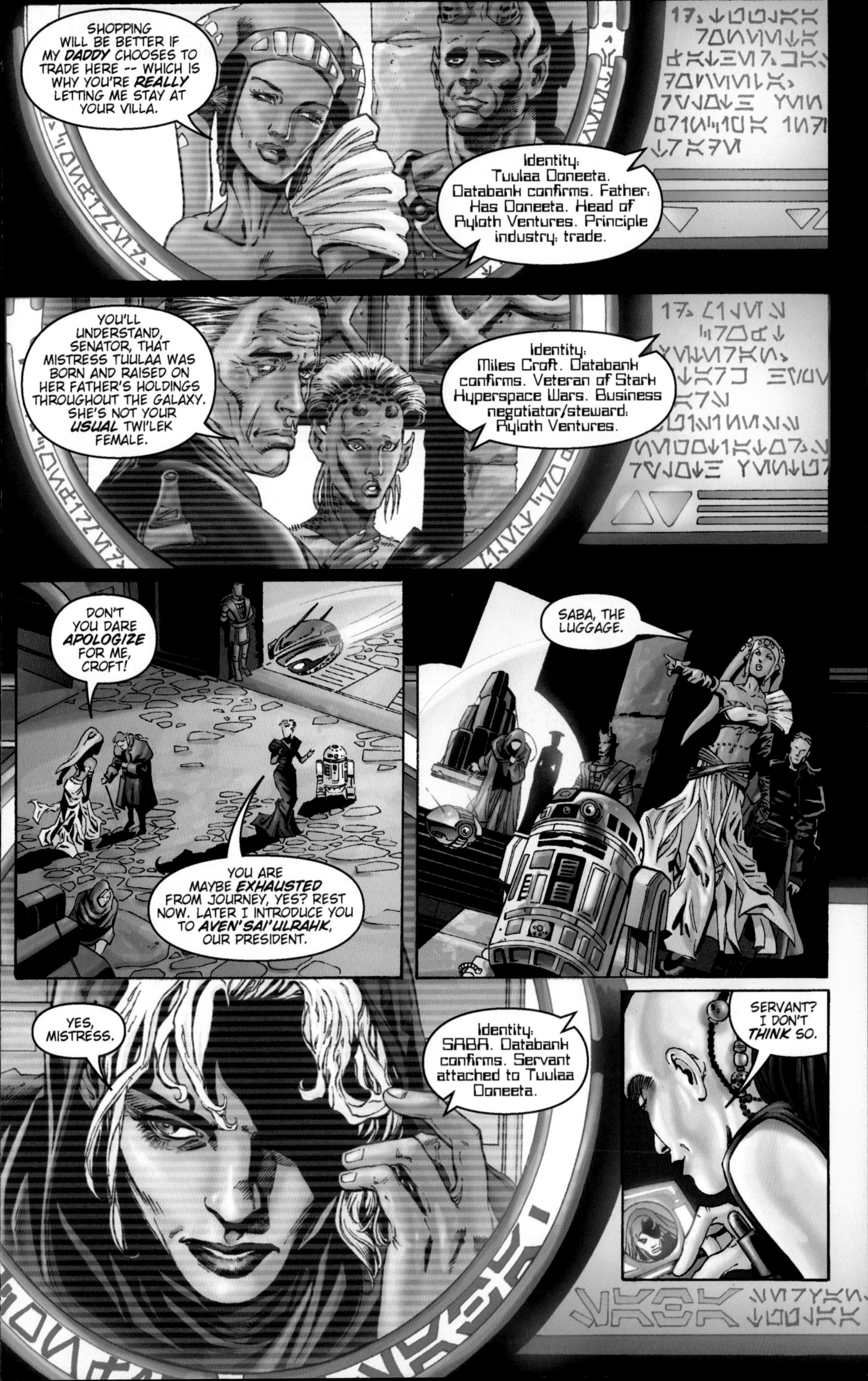
SHOPPING WILL BE BETTER IF MY DADDY CHOOSES TO TRADE HERE -- WHICH IS WHY YOU'RE REALLY LETTING ME STAY AT YOUR VILLA.
Identity: Tuulaa Doneeta. Databank confirms. Father: Has Doneeta. Head of Ryloth Ventures. Principle industry: trade.
YOU'LL UNDERSTAND, SENATOR, THAT MISTRESS TUULAA WAS BORN AND RAISED ON HER FATHER'S HOLDINGS THROUGHOUT THE GALAXY. SHE'S NOT YOUR USUAL TWI'LEK FEMALE.
Identity: Miles Croft. Databank confirms. Veteran of Stark Hyperspace Wars. Business negotiator/steward: Ryloth Ventures.
DON'T YOU DARE APOLOGIZE FOR ME, CROFT!
YOU ARE MAYBE EXHAUSTED FROM JOURNEY, YES? REST NOW. LATER I INTRODUCE YOU TO AVEN'SAI'ULRAHK, OUR PRESIDENT.
SABA, THE LUGGAGE.
YES, MISTRESS.
Identity: SABA. Databank confirms. Servant attached to Tuulaa Doneeta.
SERVANT? I DON'T THINK SO.

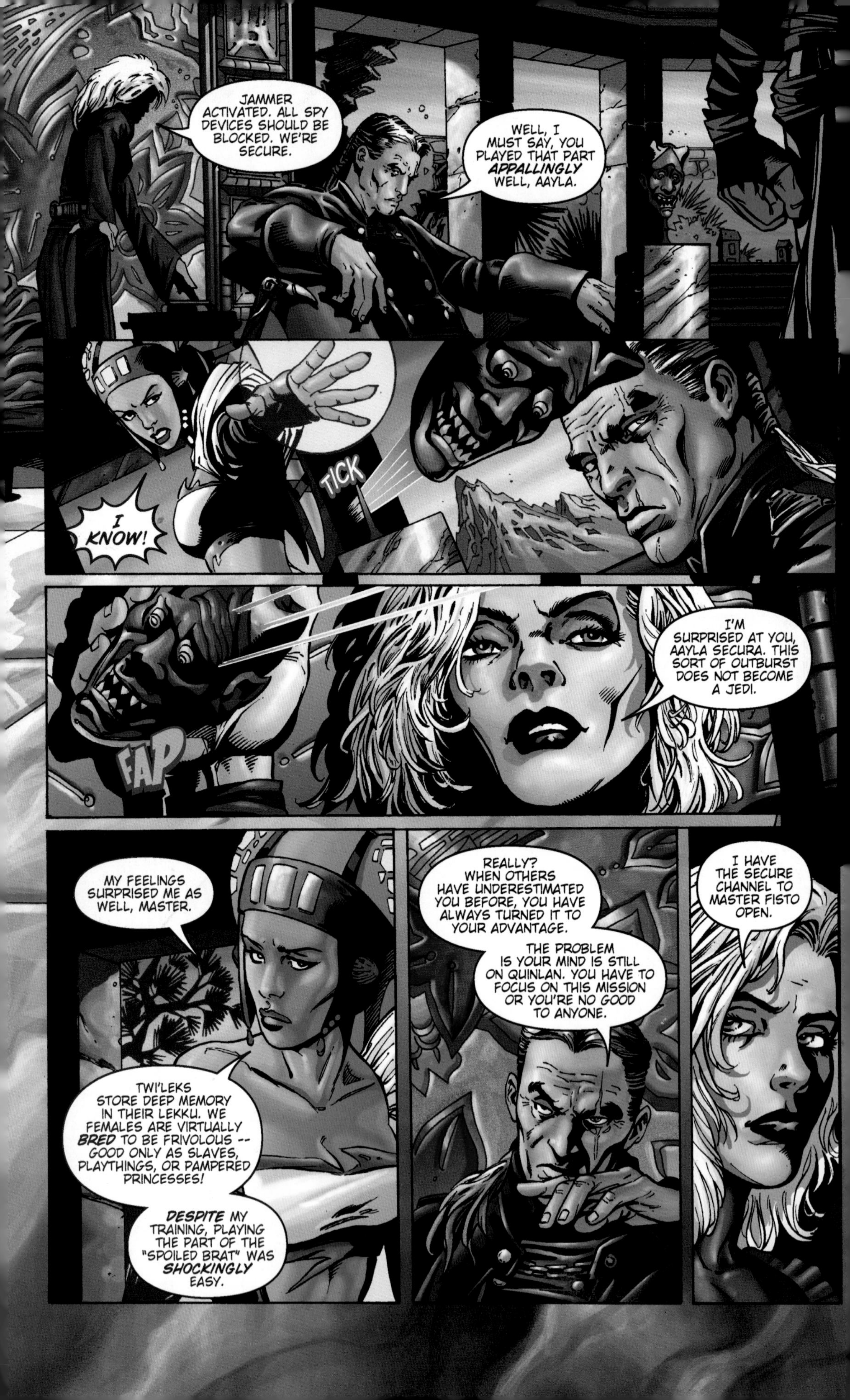
JAMMER ACTIVATED. ALL SPY DEVICES SHOULD BE BLOCKED. WE'RE SECURE.
WELL, I MUST SAY, YOU PLAYED THAT PART APPALLINGLY WELL, AAYLA.
I KNOW!
TICK
FAP
I'M SURPRISED AT YOU, AAYLA SECURA. THIS SORT OF OUTBURST DOES NOT BECOME A JEDI.
MY FEELINGS SURPRISED ME AS WELL, MASTER.
TWI'LEKS STORE DEEP MEMORY IN THEIR LEKKU. WE FEMALES ARE VIRTUALLY BRED TO BE FRIVOLOUS -- GOOD ONLY AS SLAVES, PLAYTHINGS, OR PAMPERED PRINCESSES!
DESPITE MY TRAINING, PLAYING THE PART OF THE "SPOILED BRAT" WAS SHOCKINGLY EASY.
REALLY? WHEN OTHERS HAVE UNDERESTIMATED YOU BEFORE, YOU HAVE ALWAYS TURNED IT TO YOUR ADVANTAGE.
THE PROBLEM IS YOUR MIND IS STILL ON QUINLAN. YOU HAVE TO FOCUS ON THIS MISSION OR YOU'RE NO GOOD TO ANYONE.
I HAVE THE SECURE CHANNEL TO MASTER FISTO OPEN.

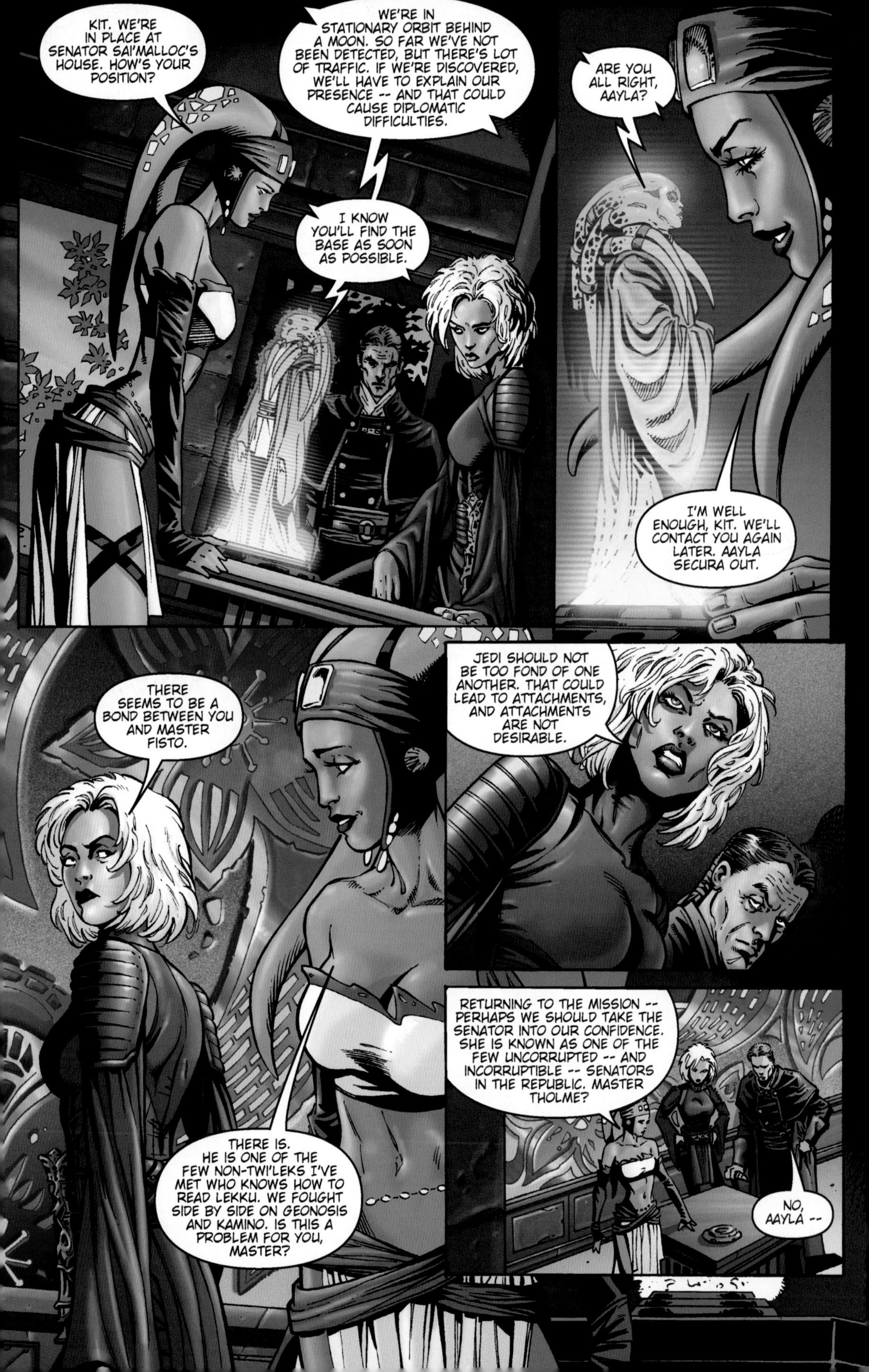

KIT. WE'RE IN PLACE AT SENATOR SAI'MALLOC'S HOUSE. HOW'S YOUR POSITION?
WE'RE IN STATIONARY ORBIT BEHIND A MOON. SO FAR WE'VE NOT BEEN DETECTED, BUT THERE'S LOT OF TRAFFIC. IF WE'RE DISCOVERED, WE'LL HAVE TO EXPLAIN OUR PRESENCE -- AND THAT COULD CAUSE DIPLOMATIC DIFFICULTIES.
I KNOW YOU'LL FIND THE BASE AS SOON AS POSSIBLE.
ARE YOU ALL RIGHT, AAYLA?
I'M WELL ENOUGH, KIT. WE'LL CONTACT YOU AGAIN LATER. AAYLA SECURA OUT.
THERE SEEMS TO BE A BOND BETWEEN YOU AND MASTER FISTO.
THERE IS. HE IS ONE OF THE FEW NON-TWI'LEKS I'VE MET WHO KNOWS HOW TO READ LEKKU. WE FOUGHT SIDE BY SIDE ON GEONOSIS AND KAMINO. IS THIS A PROBLEM FOR YOU, MASTER?
JEDI SHOULD NOT BE TOO FOND OF ONE ANOTHER. THAT COULD LEAD TO ATTACHMENTS, AND ATTACHMENTS ARE NOT DESIRABLE.
RETURNING TO THE MISSION -- PERHAPS WE SHOULD TAKE THE SENATOR INTO OUR CONFIDENCE. SHE IS KNOWN AS ONE OF THE FEW UNCORRUPTED -- AND INCORRUPTIBLE -- SENATORS IN THE REPUBLIC. MASTER THOLME?
NO, AAYLA --

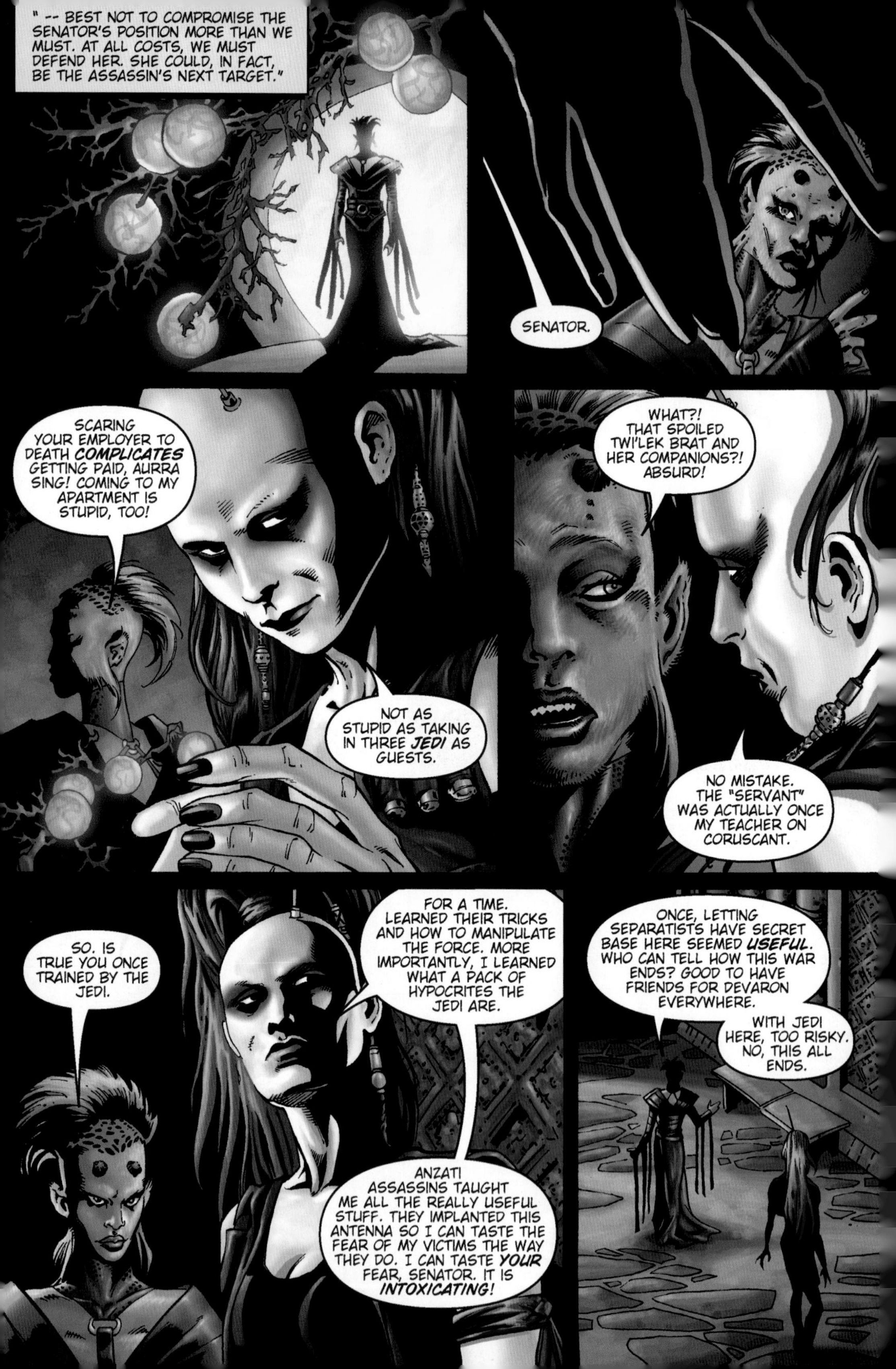
"-- BEST NOT TO COMPROMISE THE SENATOR'S POSITION MORE THAN WE MUST. AT ALL COSTS, WE MUST DEFEND HER. SHE COULD, IN FACT, BE THE ASSASSIN'S NEXT TARGET."
SENATOR.
SCARING YOUR EMPLOYER TO DEATH COMPLICATES GETTING PAID, AURRA SING! COMING TO MY APARTMENT IS STUPID, TOO!
NOT AS STUPID AS TAKING IN THREE JEDI AS GUESTS.
WHAT?! THAT SPOILED TWI'LEK BRAT AND HER COMPANIONS?! ABSURD!
NO MISTAKE. THE "SERVANT" WAS ACTUALLY ONCE MY TEACHER ON CORUSCANT.
SO. IS TRUE YOU ONCE TRAINED BY THE JEDI.
FOR A TIME. LEARNED THEIR TRICKS AND HOW TO MANIPULATE THE FORCE. MORE IMPORTANTLY, I LEARNED WHAT A PACK OF HYPOCRITES THE JEDI ARE.
ANZATI ASSASSINS TAUGHT ME ALL THE REALLY USEFUL STUFF. THEY IMPLANTED THIS ANTENNA SO I CAN TASTE THE FEAR OF MY VICTIMS THE WAY THEY DO. I CAN TASTE YOUR FEAR, SENATOR. IT IS INTOXICATING!
ONCE, LETTING SEPARATISTS HAVE SECRET BASE HERE SEEMED USEFUL. WHO CAN TELL HOW THIS WAR ENDS? GOOD TO HAVE FRIENDS FOR DEVARON EVERYWHERE.
WITH JEDI HERE, TOO RISKY. NO, THIS ALL ENDS.

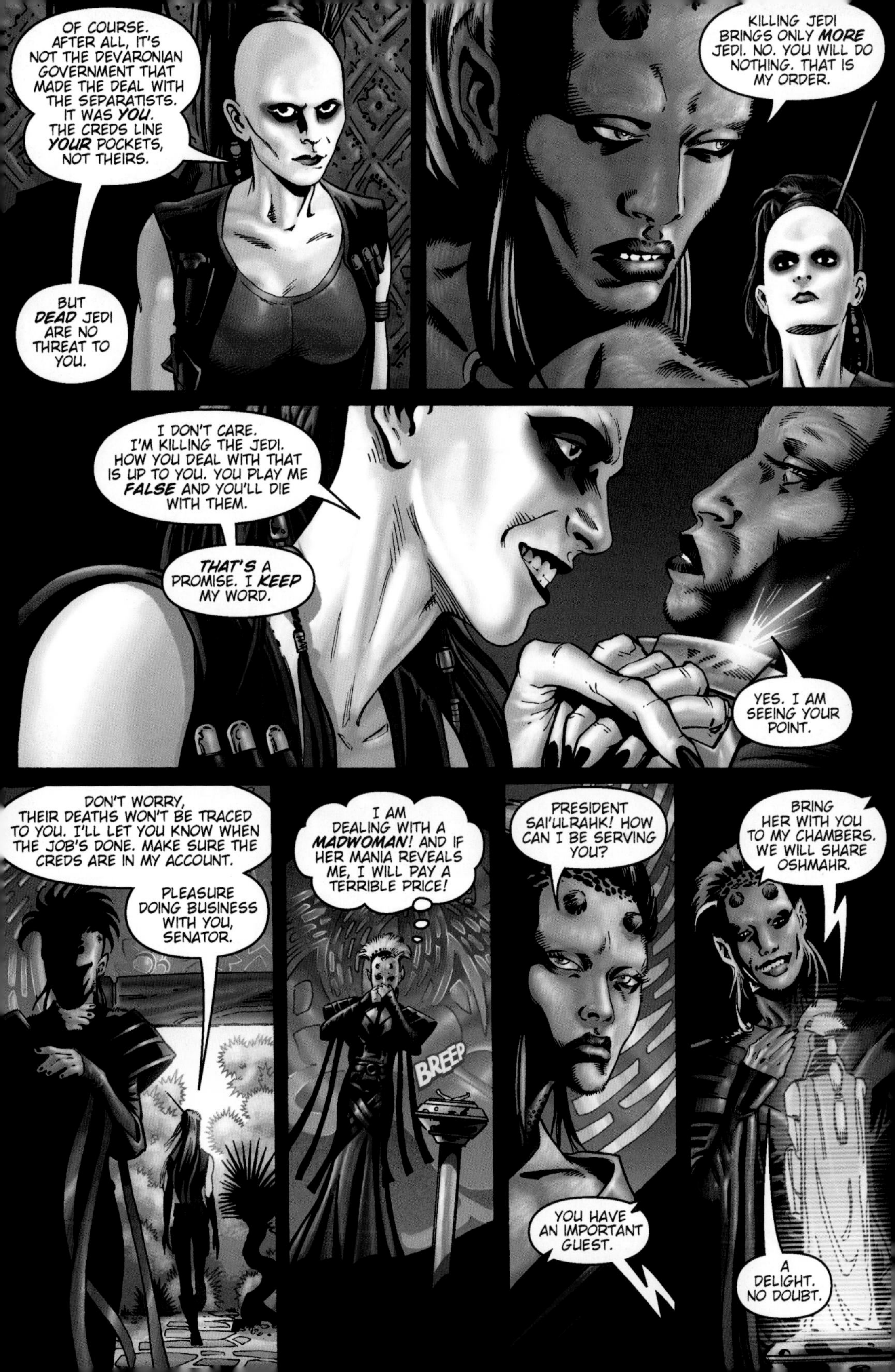
OF COURSE. AFTER ALL, IT'S NOT THE DEVARONIAN GOVERNMENT THAT MADE THE DEAL WITH THE SEPARATISTS. IT WAS YOU. THE CREDS LINE YOUR POCKETS, NOT THEIRS.
BUT DEAD JEDI ARE NO THREAT TO YOU.
KILLING JEDI BRINGS ONLY MORE JEDI. NO. YOU WILL DO NOTHING. THAT IS MY ORDER.
I DON'T CARE. I'M KILLING THE JEDI. HOW YOU DEAL WITH THAT IS UP TO YOU. YOU PLAY ME FALSE AND YOU'LL DIE WITH THEM.
THAT'S A PROMISE. I KEEP MY WORD.
YES. I AM SEEING YOUR POINT.
DON'T WORRY, THEIR DEATHS WON'T BE TRACED TO YOU. I'LL LET YOU KNOW WHEN THE JOB'S DONE. MAKE SURE THE CREDS ARE IN MY ACCOUNT.
PLEASURE DOING BUSINESS WITH YOU, SENATOR.
I AM DEALING WITH A MADWOMAN! AND IF HER MANIA REVEALS ME, I WILL PAY A TERRIBLE PRICE!
BREEP
PRESIDENT SAI'ULRAHK! HOW CAN I BE SERVING YOU?
YOU HAVE AN IMPORTANT GUEST.
BRING HER WITH YOU TO MY CHAMBERS. WE WILL SHARE OSHMAHR.
A DELIGHT. NO DOUBT.

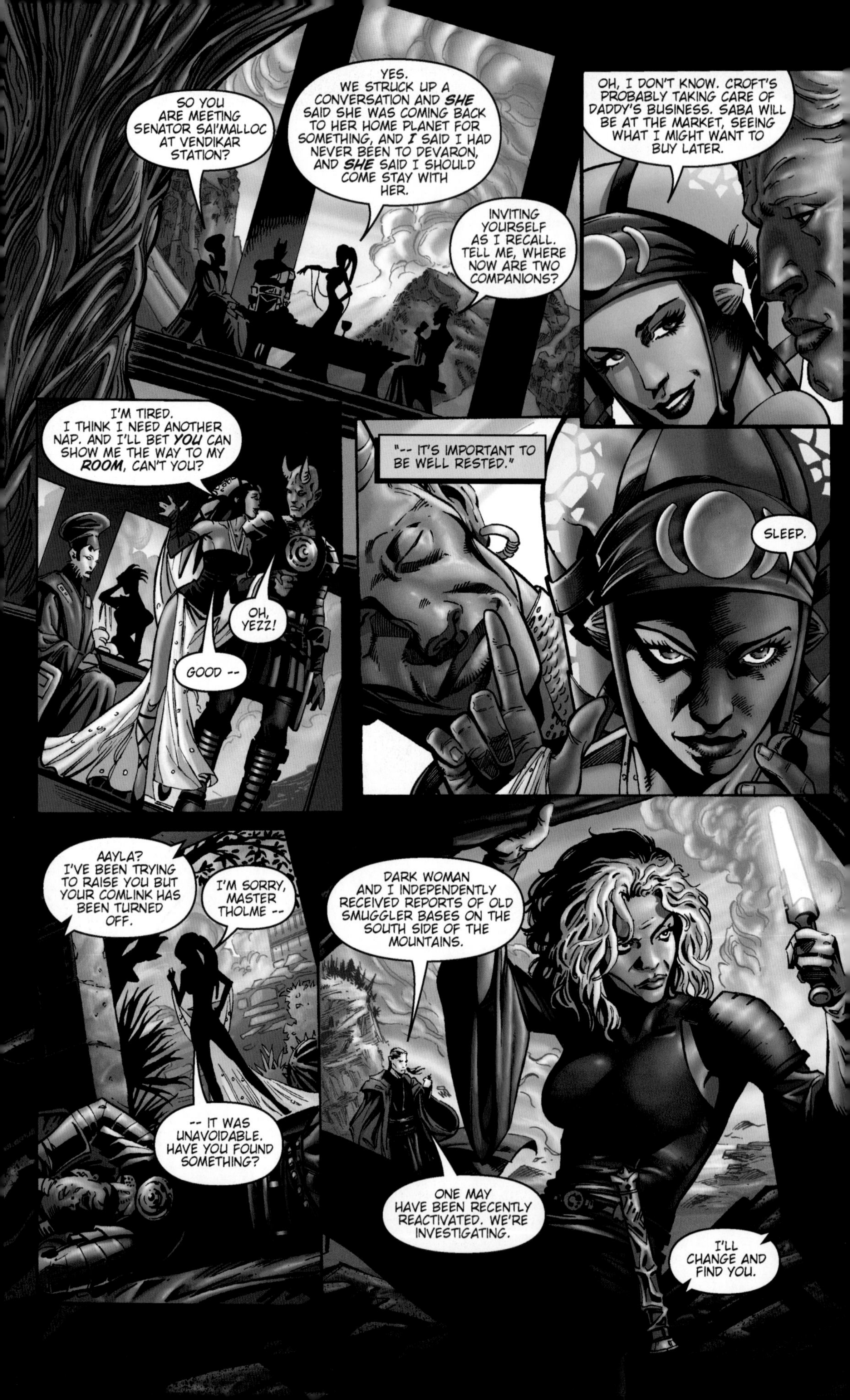

SO YOU ARE MEETING SENATOR SAI'MALLOC AT VENDIKAR STATION?
YES. WE STRUCK UP A CONVERSATION AND SHE SAID SHE WAS COMING BACK TO HER HOME PLANET FOR SOMETHING, AND I SAID I HAD NEVER BEEN TO DEVARON, AND SHE SAID I SHOULD COME STAY WITH HER.
INVITING YOURSELF AS I RECALL. TELL ME, WHERE NOW ARE TWO COMPANIONS?
OH, I DON'T KNOW. CROFT'S PROBABLY TAKING CARE OF DADDY'S BUSINESS. SABA WILL BE AT THE MARKET, SEEING WHAT I MIGHT WANT TO BUY LATER.
I'M TIRED. I THINK I NEED ANOTHER NAP. AND I'LL BET YOU CAN SHOW ME THE WAY TO MY ROOM, CAN'T YOU?
OH, YEZZ!
GOOD --
"-- IT'S IMPORTANT TO BE WELL RESTED."
SLEEP.
AAYLA? I'VE BEEN TRYING TO RAISE YOU BUT YOUR COMLINK HAS BEEN TURNED OFF.
I'M SORRY, MASTER THOLME --
-- IT WAS UNAVOIDABLE. HAVE YOU FOUND SOMETHING?
DARK WOMAN AND I INDEPENDENTLY RECEIVED REPORTS OF OLD SMUGGLER BASES ON THE SOUTH SIDE OF THE MOUNTAINS.
ONE MAY HAVE BEEN RECENTLY REACTIVATED. WE'RE INVESTIGATING.
I'LL CHANGE AND FIND YOU.

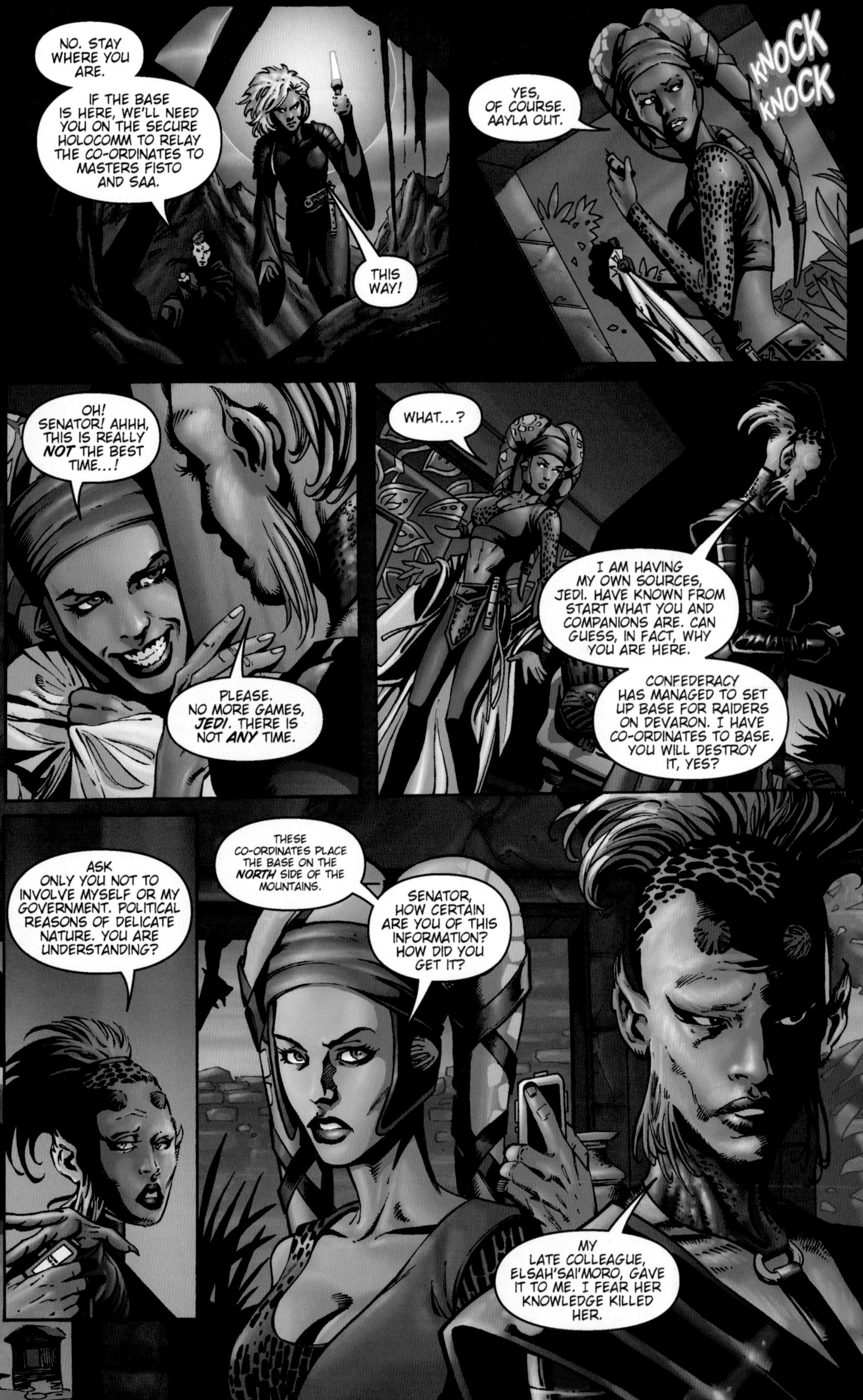
NO. STAY WHERE YOU ARE.
IF THE BASE IS HERE, WE'LL NEED YOU ON THE SECURE HOLOCOMM TO RELAY THE CO-ORDINATES TO MASTERS FISTO AND SAA.
THIS WAY!
KNOCK KNOCK
YES, OF COURSE. AAYLA OUT.
OH! SENATOR! AHHH, THIS IS REALLY NOT THE BEST TIME...!
PLEASE. NO MORE GAMES, JEDI. THERE IS NOT ANY TIME.
WHAT...?
I AM HAVING MY OWN SOURCES, JEDI. HAVE KNOWN FROM START WHAT YOU AND COMPANIONS ARE. CAN GUESS, IN FACT, WHY YOU ARE HERE.
CONFEDERACY HAS MANAGED TO SET UP BASE FOR RAIDERS ON DEVARON. I HAVE CO-ORDINATES TO BASE. YOU WILL DESTROY IT, YES?
ASK ONLY YOU NOT TO INVOLVE MYSELF OR MY GOVERNMENT. POLITICAL REASONS OF DELICATE NATURE. YOU ARE UNDERSTANDING?
THESE CO-ORDINATES PLACE THE BASE ON THE NORTH SIDE OF THE MOUNTAINS.
SENATOR, HOW CERTAIN ARE YOU OF THIS INFORMATION? HOW DID YOU GET IT?
MY LATE COLLEAGUE, ELSAH'SAI'MORO, GAVE IT TO ME. I FEAR HER KNOWLEDGE KILLED HER.

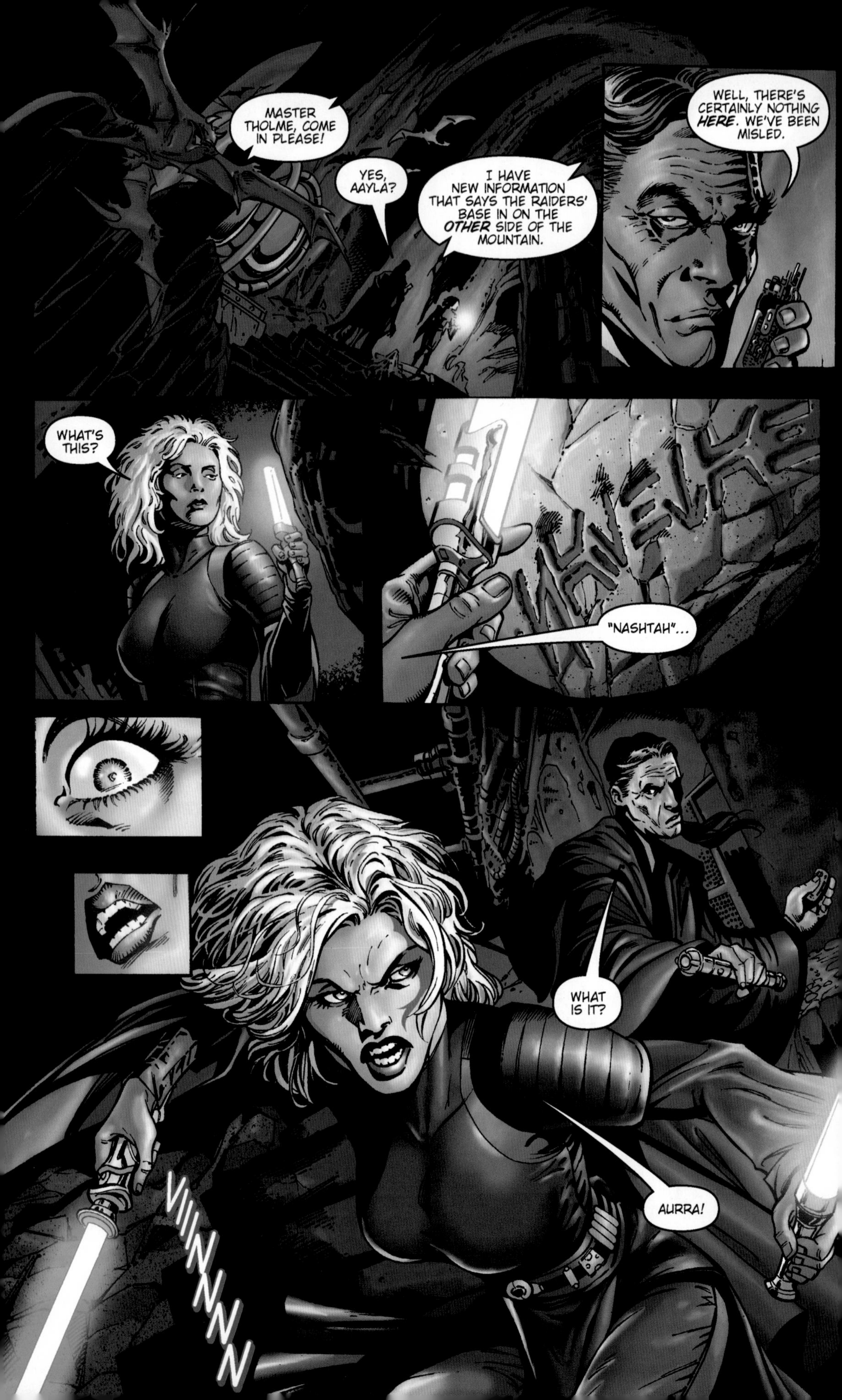
MASTER THOLME, COME IN PLEASE!
YES, AAYLA?
I HAVE NEW INFORMATION THAT SAYS THE RAIDERS' BASE IN ON THE OTHER SIDE OF THE MOUNTAIN.
WELL, THERE'S CERTAINLY NOTHING HERE. WE'VE BEEN MISLED.
WHAT'S THIS?
"NASHTAH"...
WHAT IS IT?
AURRA!
VIIINNNN

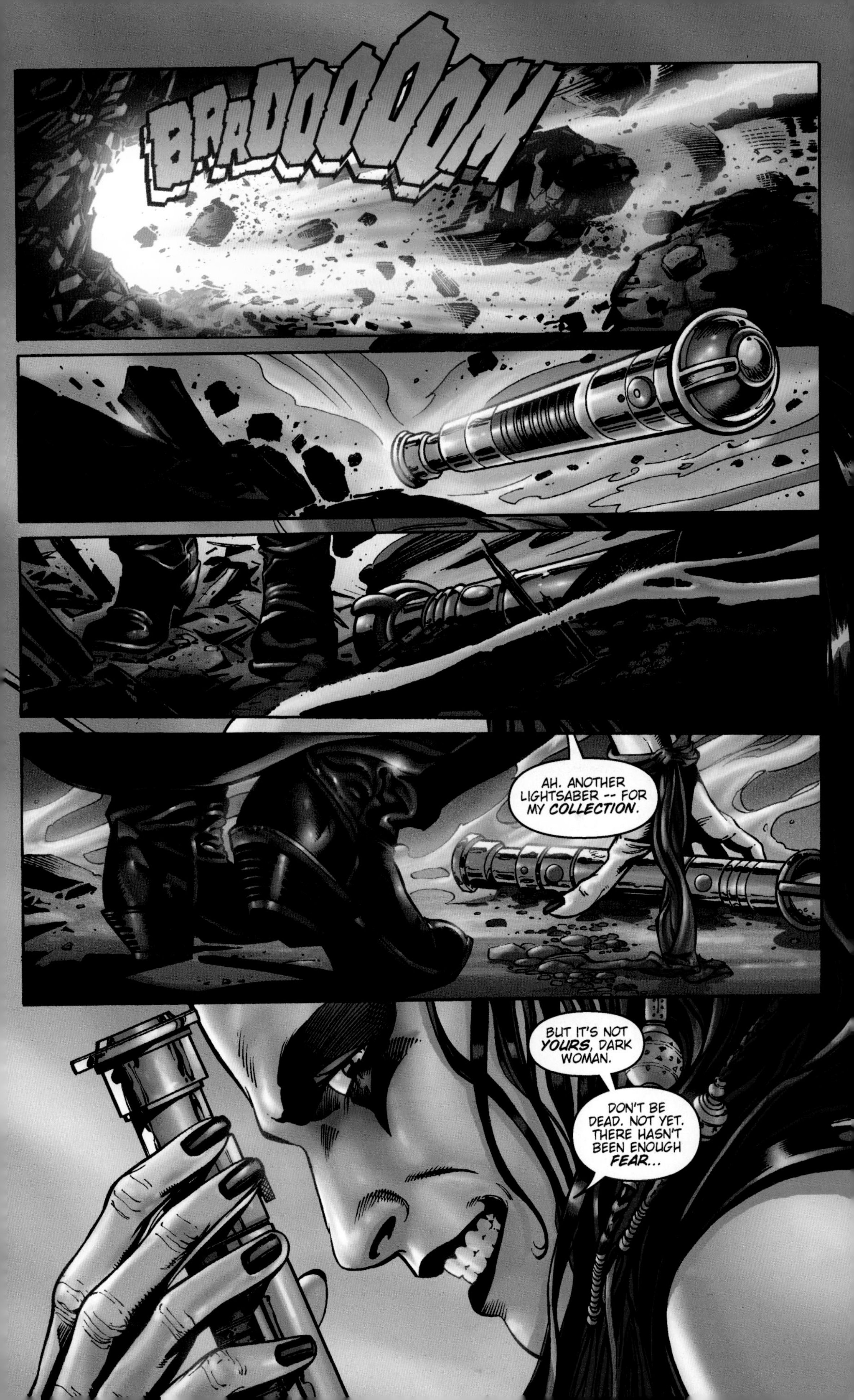
BRADOOOOOM
AH. ANOTHER LIGHTSABER -- FOR MY COLLECTION.
BUT IT'S NOT YOURS, DARK WOMAN.
DON'T BE DEAD. NOT YET. THERE HASN'T BEEN ENOUGH FEAR...

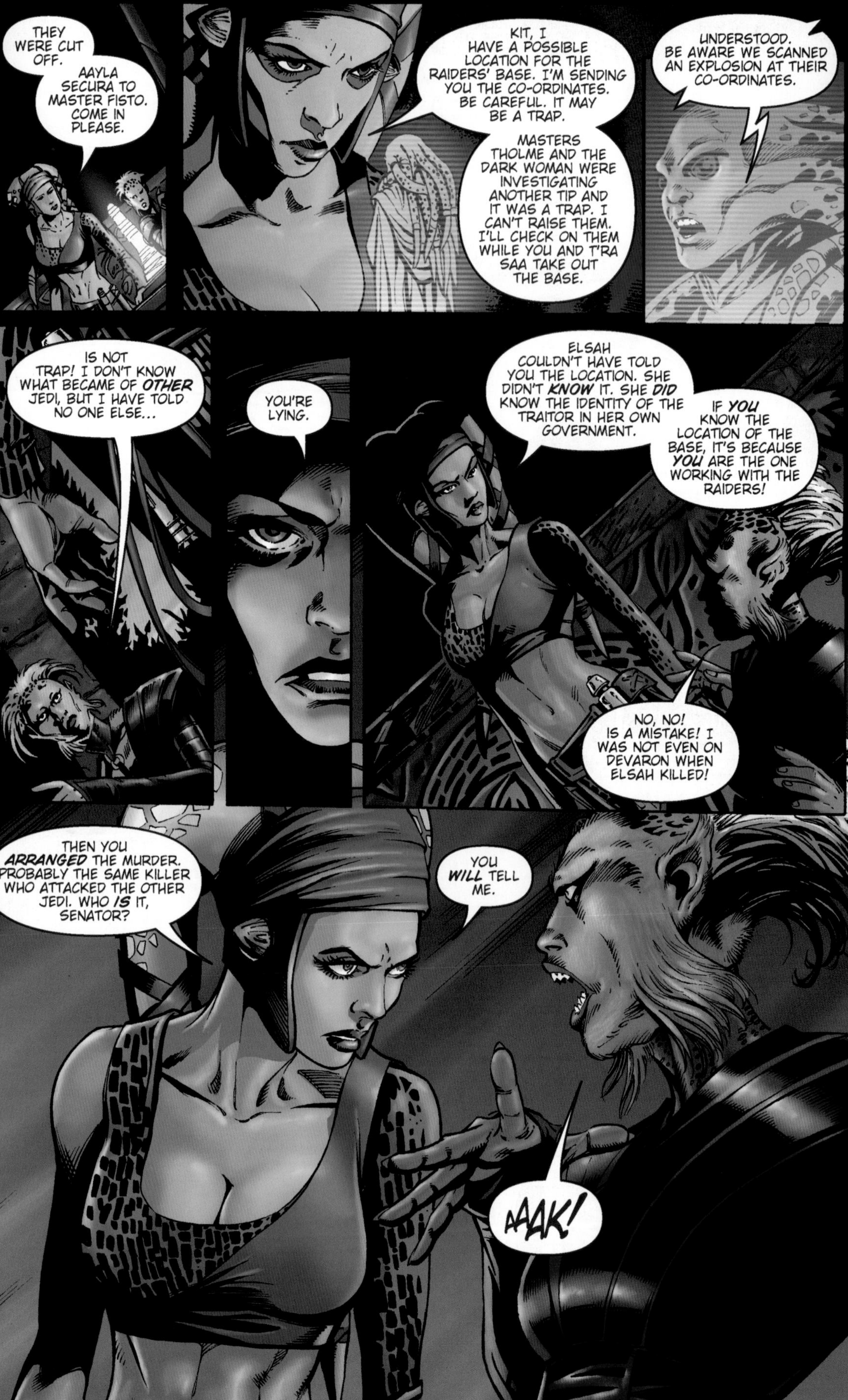
THEY WERE CUT OFF.
AAYLA SECURA TO MASTER FISTO. COME IN PLEASE.
KIT, I HAVE A POSSIBLE LOCATION FOR THE RAIDERS' BASE. I'M SENDING YOU THE CO-ORDINATES. BE CAREFUL. IT MAY BE A TRAP.
MASTERS THOLME AND THE DARK WOMAN WERE INVESTIGATING ANOTHER TIP AND IT WAS A TRAP. I CAN'T RAISE THEM. I'LL CHECK ON THEM WHILE YOU AND T'RA SAA TAKE OUT THE BASE.
UNDERSTOOD. BE AWARE WE SCANNED AN EXPLOSION AT THEIR CO-ORDINATES.
IS NOT TRAP! I DON'T KNOW WHAT BECAME OF *OTHER* JEDI, BUT I HAVE TOLD NO ONE ELSE...
YOU'RE LYING.
ELSAH COULDN'T HAVE TOLD YOU THE LOCATION. SHE DIDN'T *KNOW* IT. SHE *DID* KNOW THE IDENTITY OF THE TRAITOR IN HER OWN GOVERNMENT.
IF *YOU* KNOW THE LOCATION OF THE BASE, IT'S BECAUSE *YOU* ARE THE ONE WORKING WITH THE RAIDERS!
NO, NO! IS A MISTAKE! I WAS NOT EVEN ON DEVARON WHEN ELSAH KILLED!
THEN YOU *ARRANGED* THE MURDER. PROBABLY THE SAME KILLER WHO ATTACKED THE OTHER JEDI. WHO *IS* IT, SENATOR?
YOU *WILL* TELL ME.
AAAK!

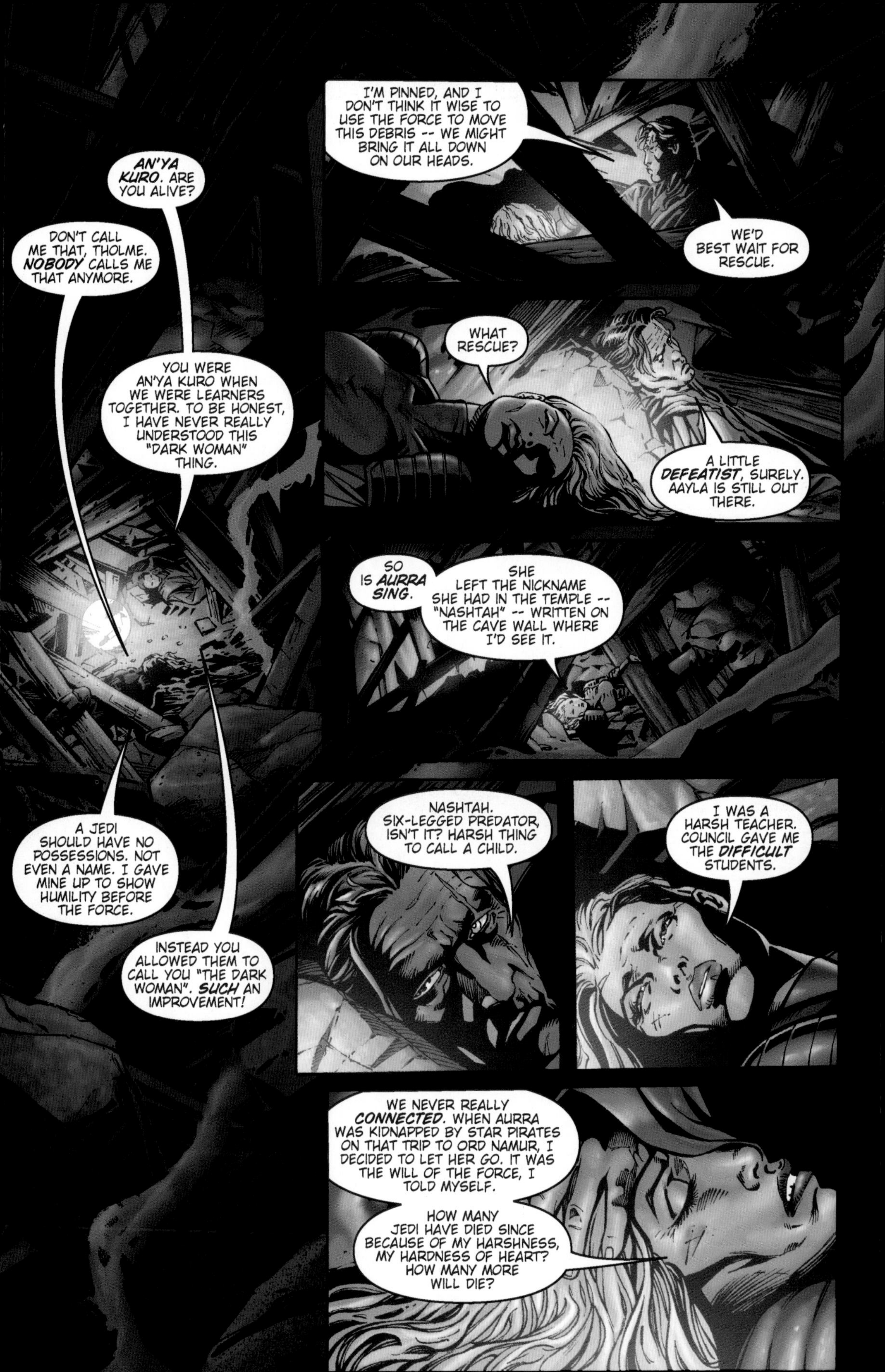
AN'YA KURO. ARE YOU ALIVE?
DON'T CALL ME THAT, THOLME. NOBODY CALLS ME THAT ANYMORE.
YOU WERE AN'YA KURO WHEN WE WERE LEARNERS TOGETHER. TO BE HONEST, I HAVE NEVER REALLY UNDERSTOOD THIS "DARK WOMAN" THING.
A JEDI SHOULD HAVE NO POSSESSIONS. NOT EVEN A NAME. I GAVE MINE UP TO SHOW HUMILITY BEFORE THE FORCE.
INSTEAD YOU ALLOWED THEM TO CALL YOU "THE DARK WOMAN". SUCH AN IMPROVEMENT!
I'M PINNED, AND I DON'T THINK IT WISE TO USE THE FORCE TO MOVE THIS DEBRIS -- WE MIGHT BRING IT ALL DOWN ON OUR HEADS.
WE'D BEST WAIT FOR RESCUE.
WHAT RESCUE?
A LITTLE DEFEATIST, SURELY. AAYLA IS STILL OUT THERE.
SO IS AURRA SING.
SHE LEFT THE NICKNAME SHE HAD IN THE TEMPLE -- "NASHTAH" -- WRITTEN ON THE CAVE WALL WHERE I'D SEE IT.
NASHTAH. SIX-LEGGED PREDATOR, ISN'T IT? HARSH THING TO CALL A CHILD.
I WAS A HARSH TEACHER. COUNCIL GAVE ME THE DIFFICULT STUDENTS.
WE NEVER REALLY CONNECTED. WHEN AURRA WAS KIDNAPPED BY STAR PIRATES ON THAT TRIP TO ORD NAMUR, I DECIDED TO LET HER GO. IT WAS THE WILL OF THE FORCE, I TOLD MYSELF.
HOW MANY JEDI HAVE DIED SINCE BECAUSE OF MY HARSHNESS, MY HARDNESS OF HEART? HOW MANY MORE WILL DIE?

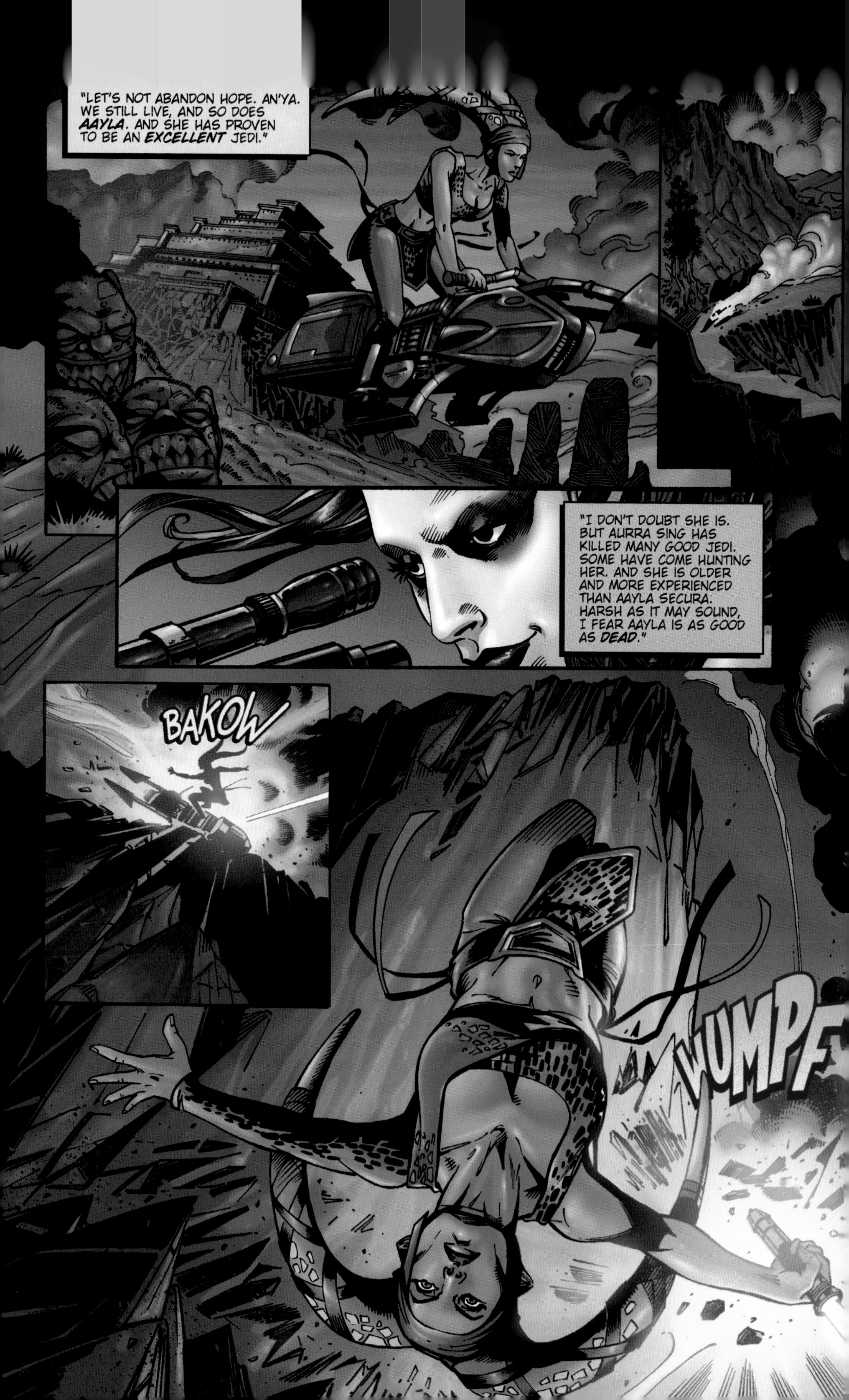
"LET'S NOT ABANDON HOPE. AN'YA. WE STILL LIVE, AND SO DOES **AAYLA**. AND SHE HAS PROVEN TO BE AN **EXCELLENT** JEDI."
"I DON'T DOUBT SHE IS. BUT AURRA SING HAS KILLED MANY GOOD JEDI. SOME HAVE COME HUNTING HER. AND SHE IS OLDER AND MORE EXPERIENCED THAN AAYLA SECURA. HARSH AS IT MAY SOUND, I FEAR AAYLA IS AS GOOD AS **DEAD**."
BAKOW
WUMPF

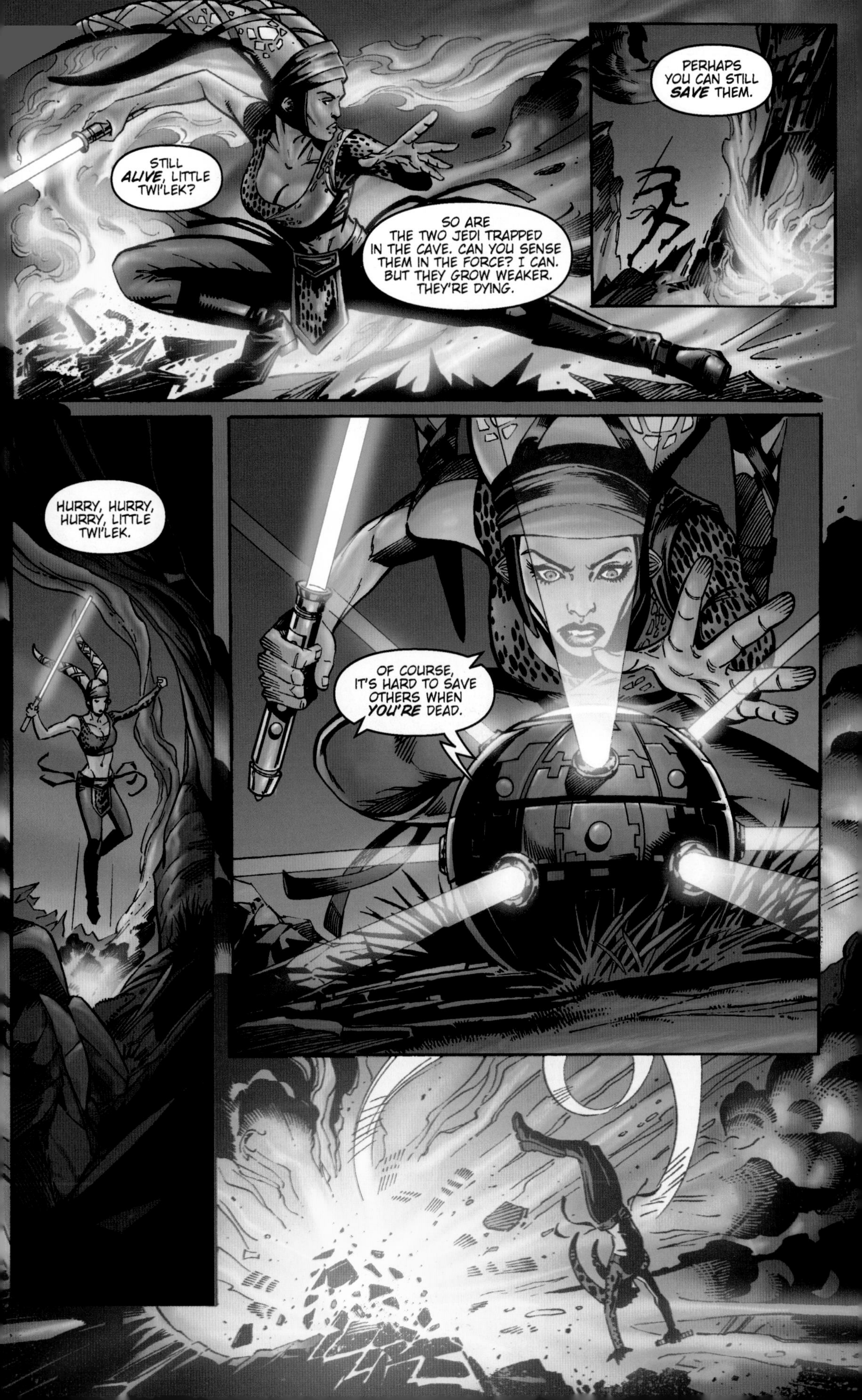
STILL ALIVE, LITTLE TWI'LEK?
SO ARE THE TWO JEDI TRAPPED IN THE CAVE. CAN YOU SENSE THEM IN THE FORCE? I CAN. BUT THEY GROW WEAKER. THEY'RE DYING.
PERHAPS YOU CAN STILL SAVE THEM.
HURRY, HURRY, HURRY, LITTLE TWI'LEK.
OF COURSE, IT'S HARD TO SAVE OTHERS WHEN YOU'RE DEAD.

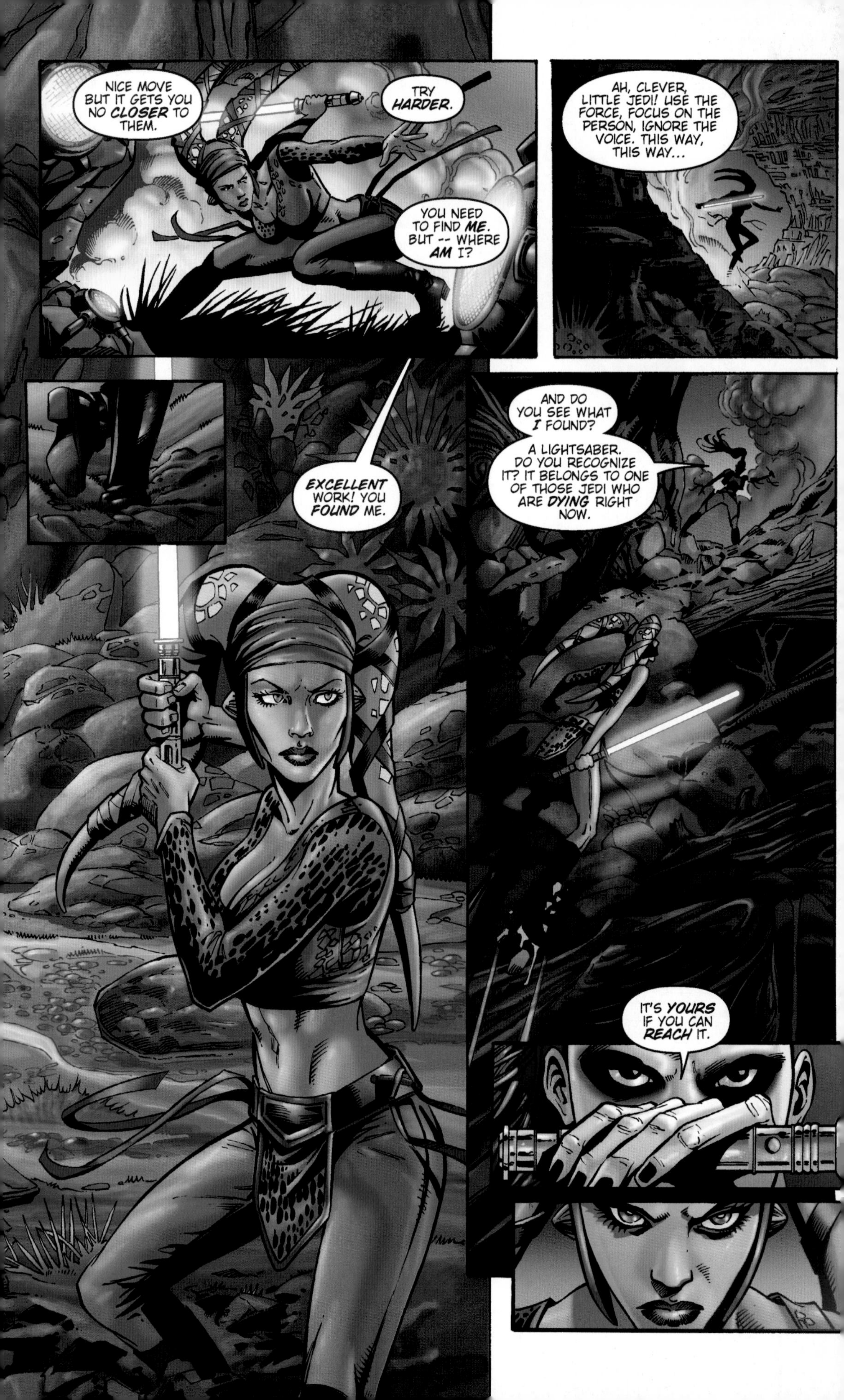
NICE MOVE BUT IT GETS YOU NO CLOSER TO THEM.
TRY HARDER.
YOU NEED TO FIND ME. BUT -- WHERE AM I?
AH, CLEVER, LITTLE JEDI! USE THE FORCE, FOCUS ON THE PERSON, IGNORE THE VOICE. THIS WAY, THIS WAY...
EXCELLENT WORK! YOU FOUND ME.
AND DO YOU SEE WHAT I FOUND?
A LIGHTSABER. DO YOU RECOGNIZE IT? IT BELONGS TO ONE OF THOSE JEDI WHO ARE DYING RIGHT NOW.
IT'S YOURS IF YOU CAN REACH IT.

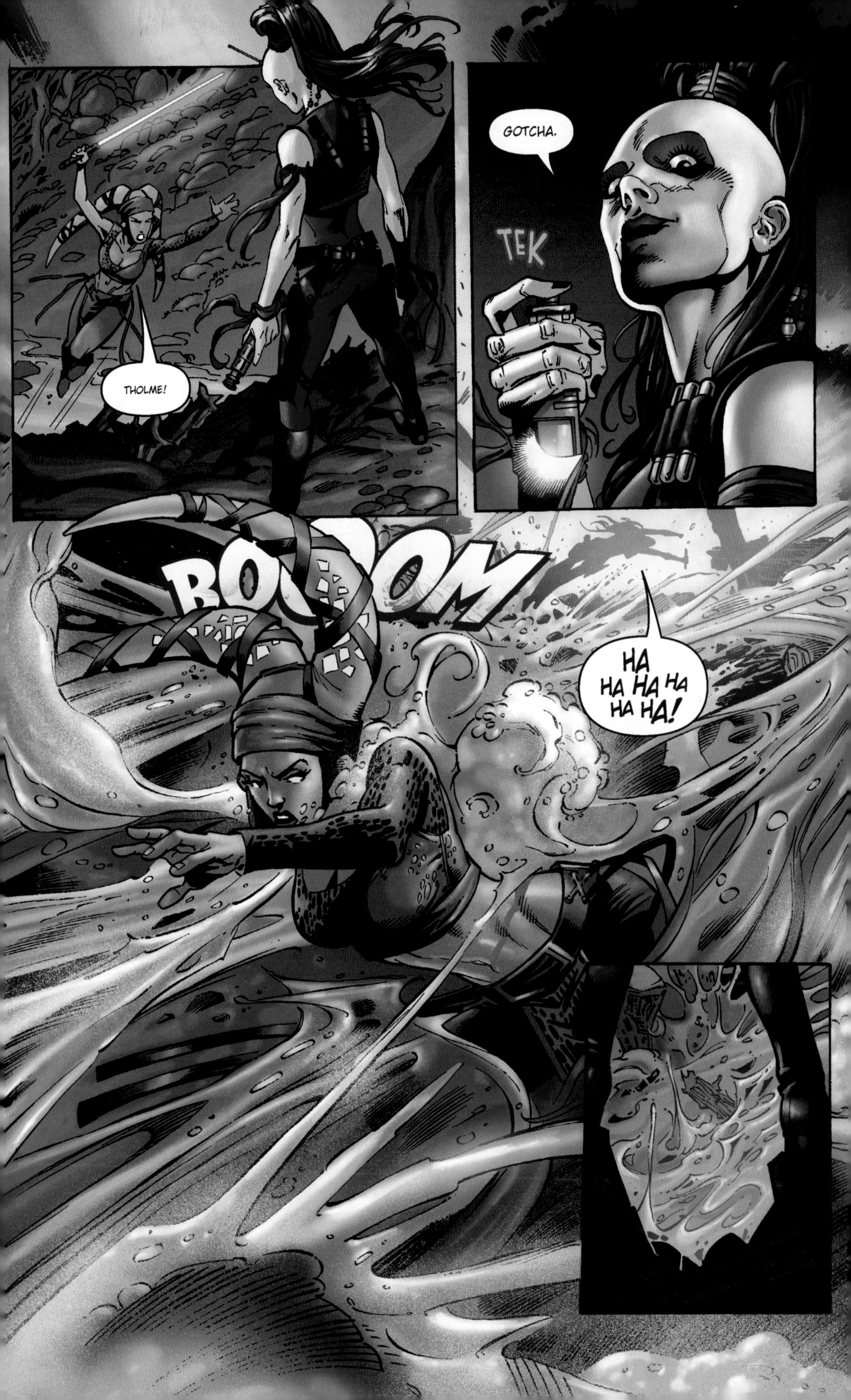
THOLME!
GOTCHA.
TEK
BOOOM
HA HA HA HA HA HA!

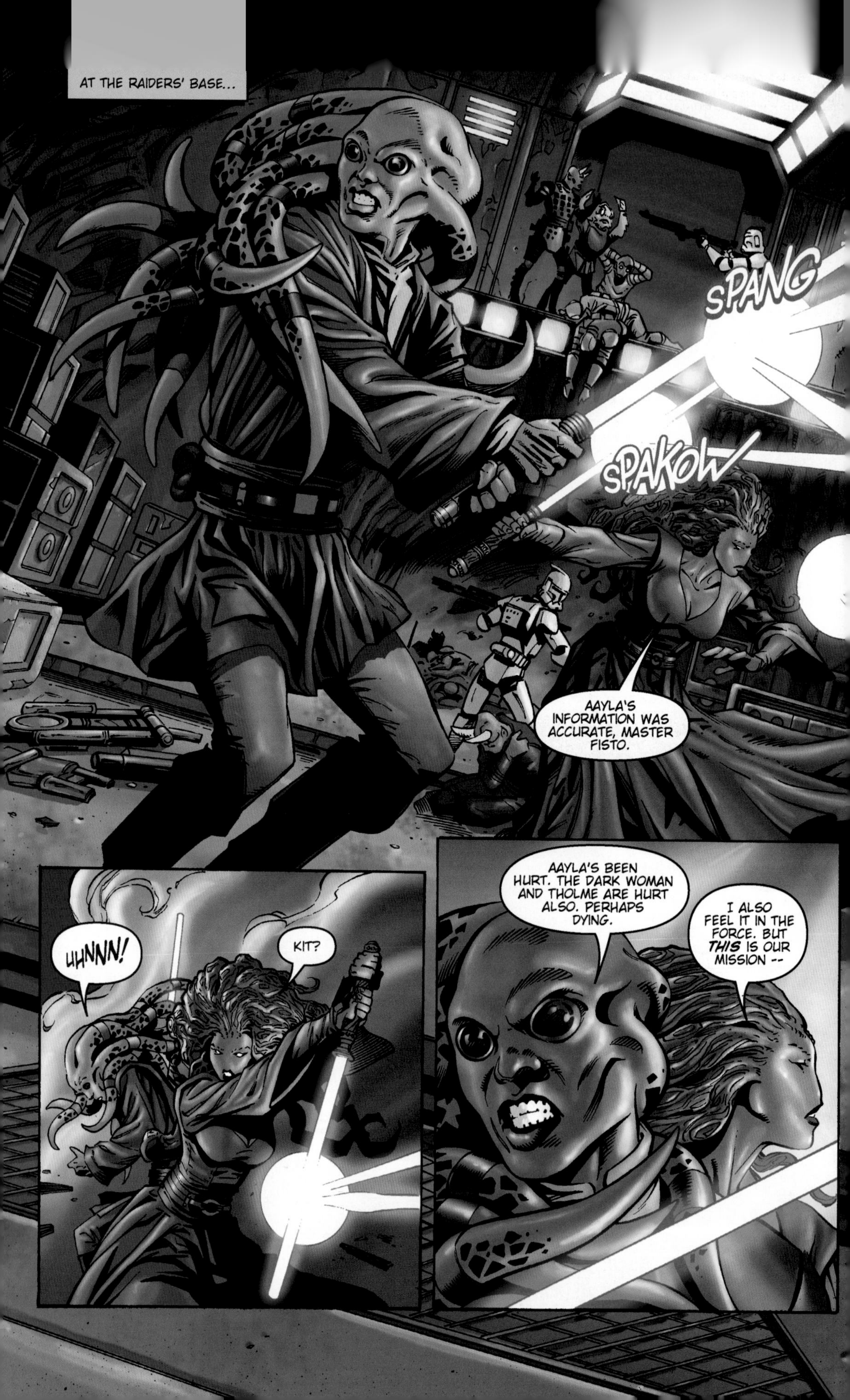
AT THE RAIDERS' BASE...
SPANG
SPAKOW
AAYLA'S INFORMATION WAS ACCURATE, MASTER FISTO.
UHNNN!
KIT?
AAYLA'S BEEN HURT. THE DARK WOMAN AND THOLME ARE HURT ALSO. PERHAPS DYING.
I ALSO FEEL IT IN THE FORCE. BUT *THIS* IS OUR MISSION --

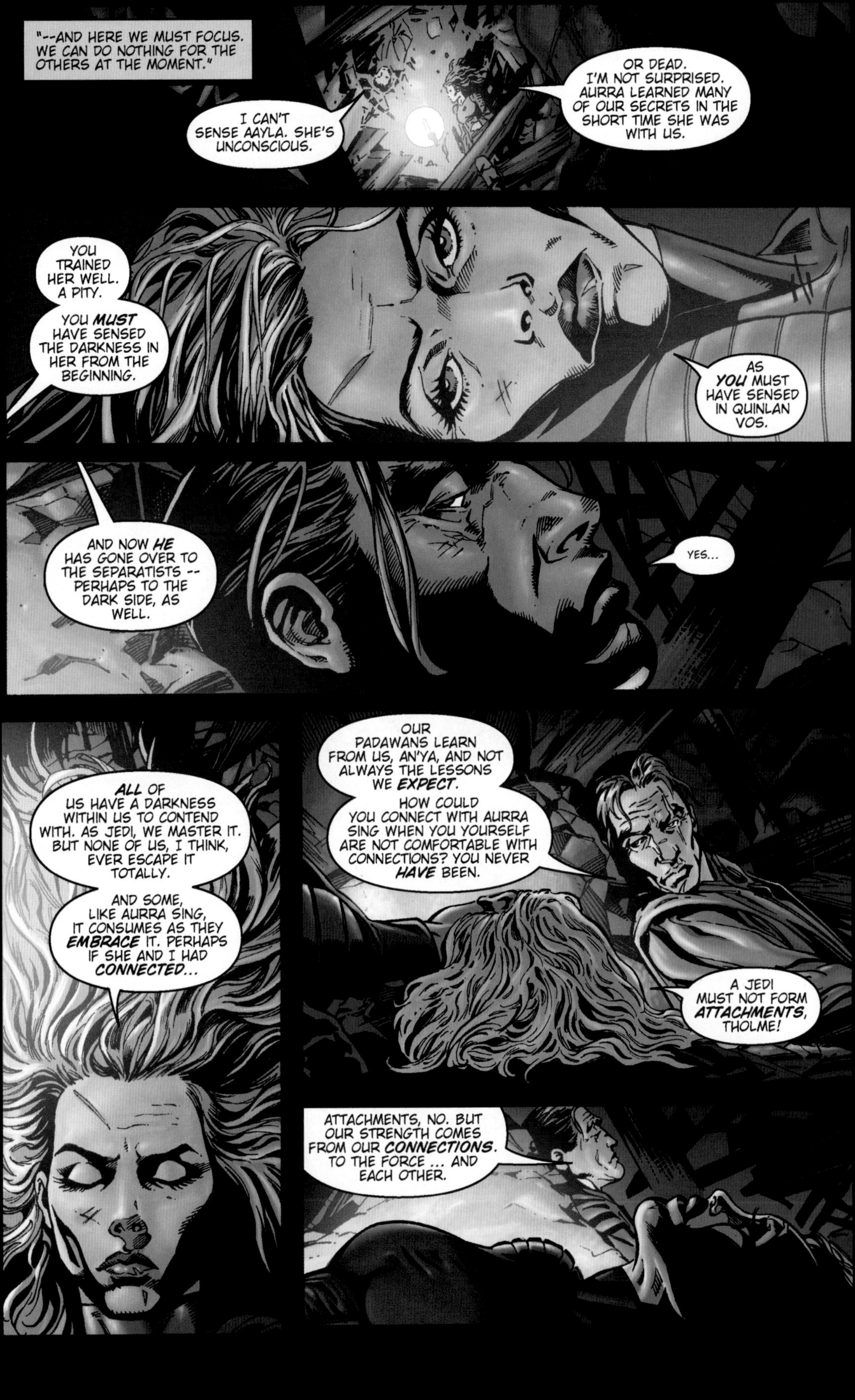
"--AND HERE WE MUST FOCUS. WE CAN DO NOTHING FOR THE OTHERS AT THE MOMENT."
I CAN'T SENSE AAYLA. SHE'S UNCONSCIOUS.
OR DEAD. I'M NOT SURPRISED. AURRA LEARNED MANY OF OUR SECRETS IN THE SHORT TIME SHE WAS WITH US.
YOU TRAINED HER WELL. A PITY.
YOU MUST HAVE SENSED THE DARKNESS IN HER FROM THE BEGINNING.
AS YOU MUST HAVE SENSED IN QUINLAN VOS.
AND NOW HE HAS GONE OVER TO THE SEPARATISTS -- PERHAPS TO THE DARK SIDE, AS WELL.
YES...
ALL OF US HAVE A DARKNESS WITHIN US TO CONTEND WITH. AS JEDI, WE MASTER IT. BUT NONE OF US, I THINK, EVER ESCAPE IT TOTALLY.
AND SOME, LIKE AURRA SING, IT CONSUMES AS THEY EMBRACE IT. PERHAPS IF SHE AND I HAD CONNECTED...
OUR PADAWANS LEARN FROM US, AN'YA, AND NOT ALWAYS THE LESSONS WE EXPECT.
HOW COULD YOU CONNECT WITH AURRA SING WHEN YOU YOURSELF ARE NOT COMFORTABLE WITH CONNECTIONS? YOU NEVER HAVE BEEN.
A JEDI MUST NOT FORM ATTACHMENTS, THOLME!
ATTACHMENTS, NO. BUT OUR STRENGTH COMES FROM OUR CONNECTIONS. TO THE FORCE ... AND EACH OTHER.

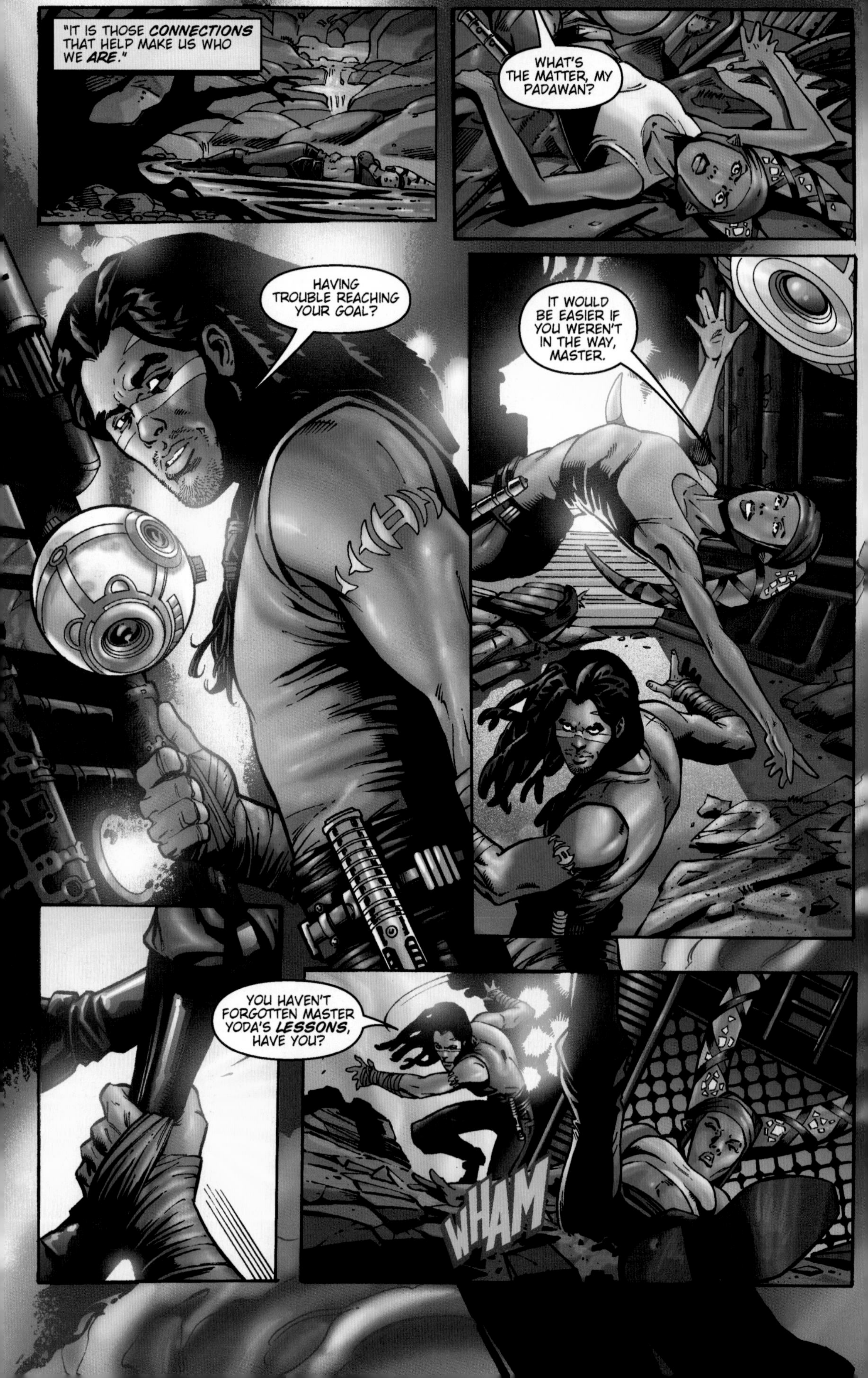
"IT IS THOSE CONNECTIONS THAT HELP MAKE US WHO WE ARE."
WHAT'S THE MATTER, MY PADAWAN?
HAVING TROUBLE REACHING YOUR GOAL?
IT WOULD BE EASIER IF YOU WEREN'T IN THE WAY, MASTER.
YOU HAVEN'T FORGOTTEN MASTER YODA'S LESSONS, HAVE YOU?
WHAM

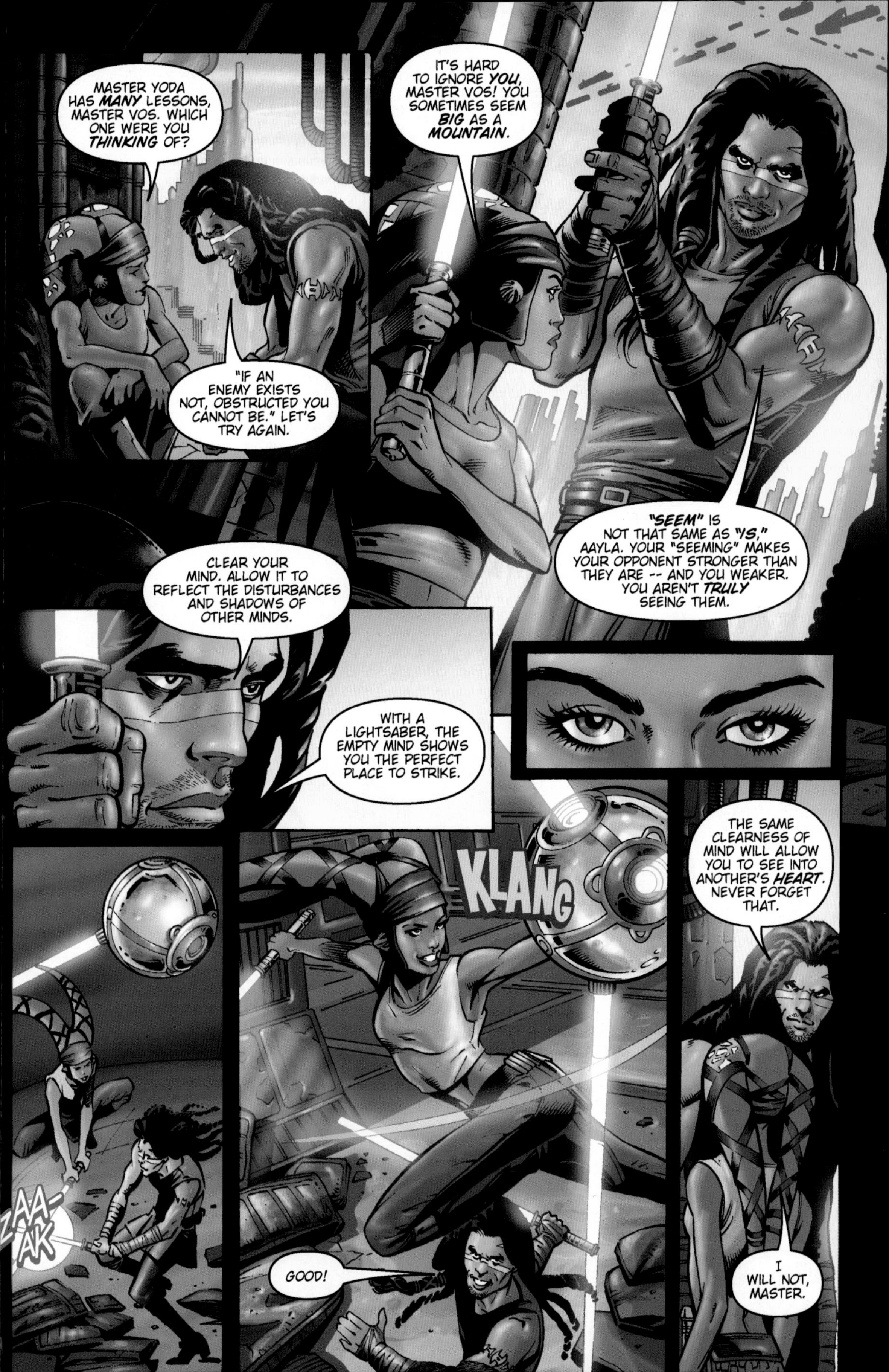
MASTER YODA HAS *MANY* LESSONS, MASTER VOS. WHICH ONE WERE YOU *THINKING* OF?
"IF AN ENEMY EXISTS NOT, OBSTRUCTED YOU CANNOT BE." LET'S TRY AGAIN.
IT'S HARD TO IGNORE *YOU*, MASTER VOS! YOU SOMETIMES SEEM *BIG* AS A *MOUNTAIN*.
"SEEM" IS NOT THAT SAME AS *"IS,"* AAYLA. YOUR "SEEMING" MAKES YOUR OPPONENT STRONGER THAN THEY ARE -- AND YOU WEAKER. YOU AREN'T *TRULY* SEEING THEM.
CLEAR YOUR MIND. ALLOW IT TO REFLECT THE DISTURBANCES AND SHADOWS OF OTHER MINDS.
WITH A LIGHTSABER, THE EMPTY MIND SHOWS YOU THE PERFECT PLACE TO STRIKE.
ZAA-AK
KLANG
GOOD!
THE SAME CLEARNESS OF MIND WILL ALLOW YOU TO SEE INTO ANOTHER'S *HEART*. NEVER FORGET THAT.
I WILL NOT, MASTER.

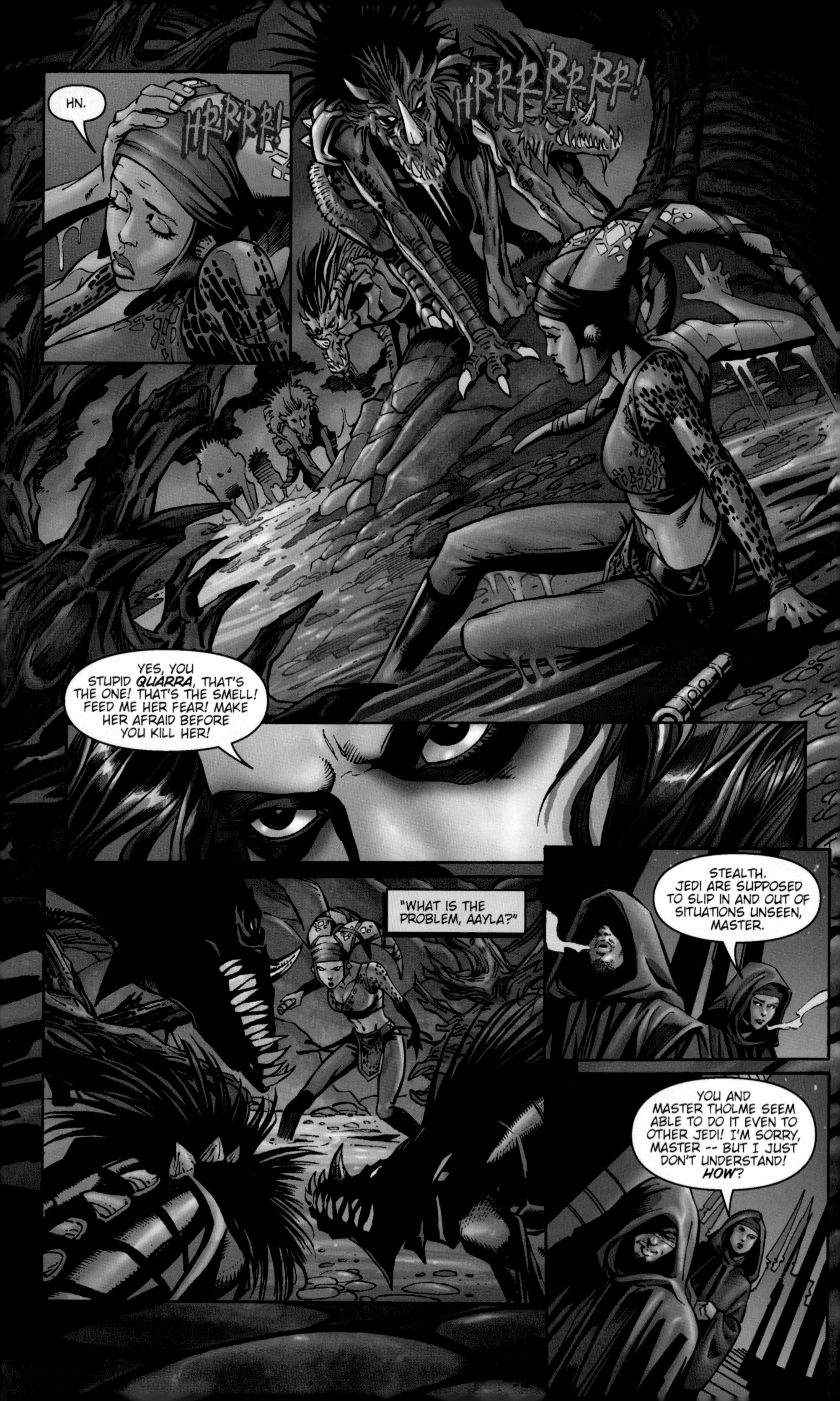
HN.
HRRRR!
HRRRRRRR!
YES, YOU STUPID QUARRA, THAT'S THE ONE! THAT'S THE SMELL! FEED ME HER FEAR! MAKE HER AFRAID BEFORE YOU KILL HER!
"WHAT IS THE PROBLEM, AAYLA?"
STEALTH. JEDI ARE SUPPOSED TO SLIP IN AND OUT OF SITUATIONS UNSEEN, MASTER.
YOU AND MASTER THOLME SEEM ABLE TO DO IT EVEN TO OTHER JEDI! I'M SORRY, MASTER -- BUT I JUST DON'T UNDERSTAND! HOW?

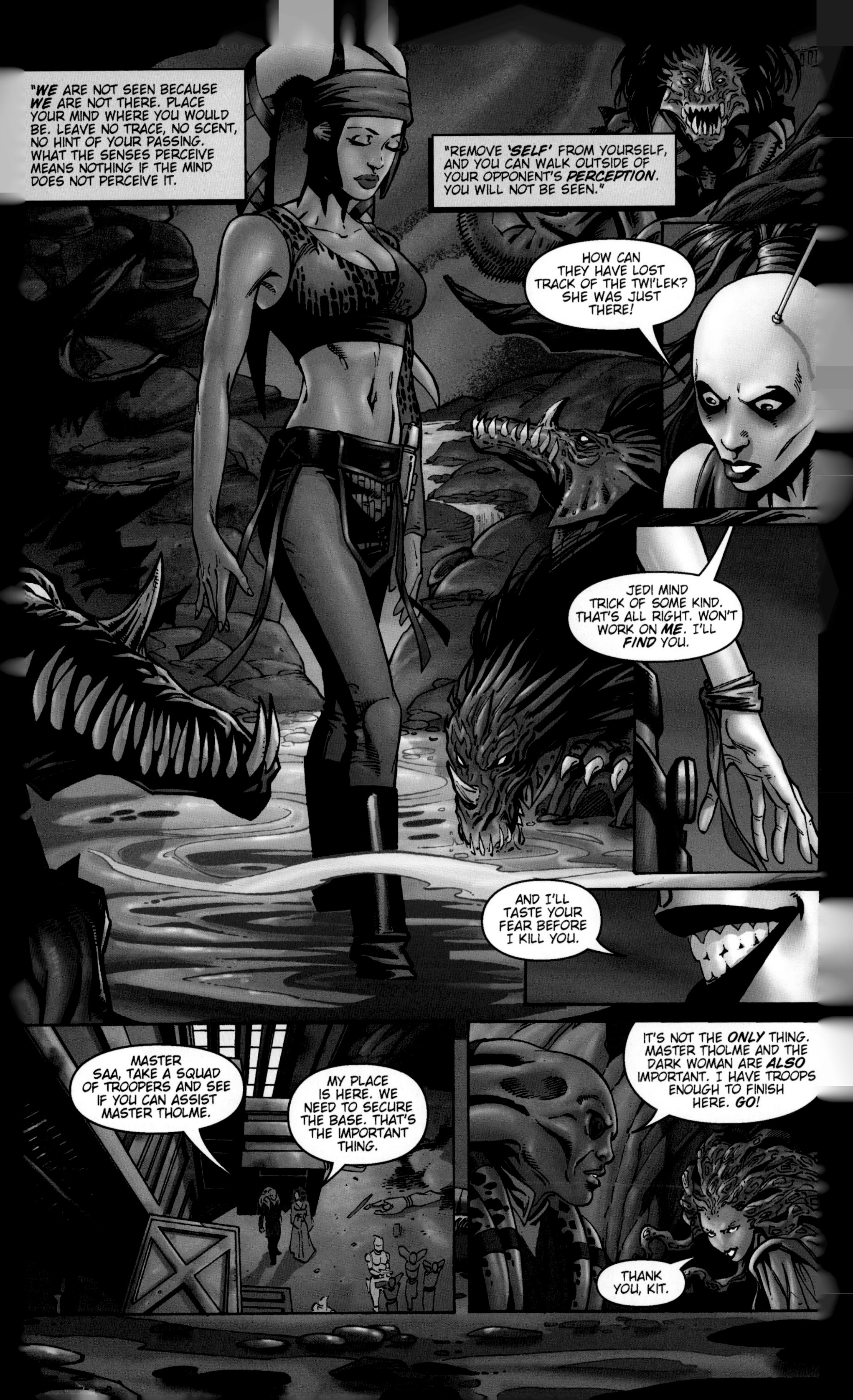
"WE ARE NOT SEEN BECAUSE WE ARE NOT THERE. PLACE YOUR MIND WHERE YOU WOULD BE. LEAVE NO TRACE, NO SCENT, NO HINT OF YOUR PASSING. WHAT THE SENSES PERCEIVE MEANS NOTHING IF THE MIND DOES NOT PERCEIVE IT.
"REMOVE 'SELF' FROM YOURSELF, AND YOU CAN WALK OUTSIDE OF YOUR OPPONENT'S PERCEPTION. YOU WILL NOT BE SEEN."
HOW CAN THEY HAVE LOST TRACK OF THE TWI'LEK? SHE WAS JUST THERE!
JEDI MIND TRICK OF SOME KIND. THAT'S ALL RIGHT. WON'T WORK ON ME. I'LL FIND YOU.
AND I'LL TASTE YOUR FEAR BEFORE I KILL YOU.
MASTER SAA, TAKE A SQUAD OF TROOPERS AND SEE IF YOU CAN ASSIST MASTER THOLME.
MY PLACE IS HERE. WE NEED TO SECURE THE BASE. THAT'S THE IMPORTANT THING.
IT'S NOT THE ONLY THING. MASTER THOLME AND THE DARK WOMAN ARE ALSO IMPORTANT. I HAVE TROOPS ENOUGH TO FINISH HERE. GO!
THANK YOU, KIT.

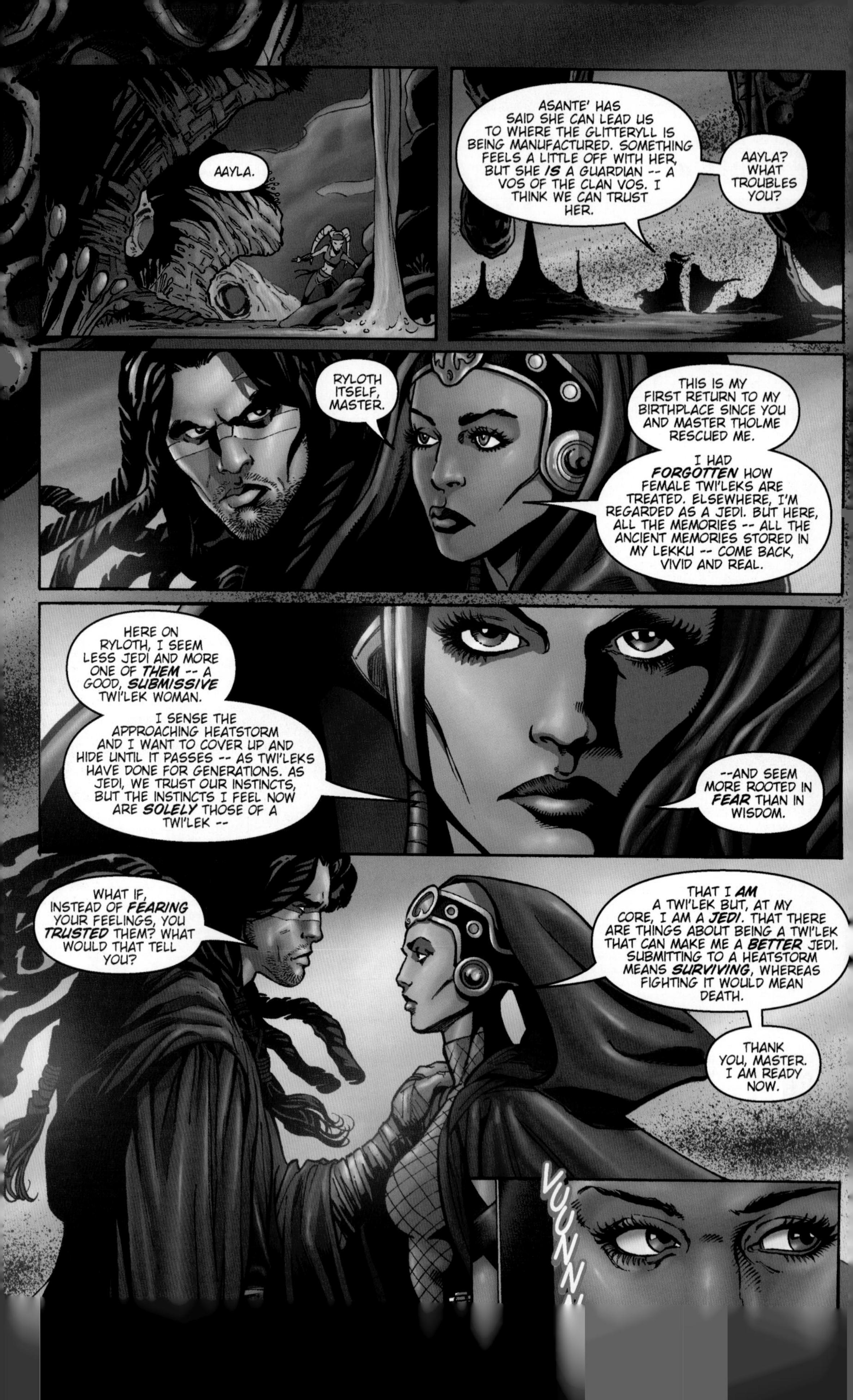
AAYLA.
ASANTE' HAS SAID SHE CAN LEAD US TO WHERE THE GLITTERYLL IS BEING MANUFACTURED. SOMETHING FEELS A LITTLE OFF WITH HER, BUT SHE *IS* A GUARDIAN -- A VOS OF THE CLAN VOS. I THINK WE CAN TRUST HER.
AAYLA? WHAT TROUBLES YOU?
RYLOTH ITSELF, MASTER.
THIS IS MY FIRST RETURN TO MY BIRTHPLACE SINCE YOU AND MASTER THOLME RESCUED ME.
I HAD ***FORGOTTEN*** HOW FEMALE TWI'LEKS ARE TREATED. ELSEWHERE, I'M REGARDED AS A JEDI. BUT HERE, ALL THE MEMORIES -- ALL THE ANCIENT MEMORIES STORED IN MY LEKKU -- COME BACK, VIVID AND REAL.
HERE ON RYLOTH, I SEEM LESS JEDI AND MORE ONE OF ***THEM*** -- A GOOD, ***SUBMISSIVE*** TWI'LEK WOMAN.
I SENSE THE APPROACHING HEATSTORM AND I WANT TO COVER UP AND HIDE UNTIL IT PASSES -- AS TWI'LEKS HAVE DONE FOR GENERATIONS. AS JEDI, WE TRUST OUR INSTINCTS, BUT THE INSTINCTS I FEEL NOW ARE ***SOLELY*** THOSE OF A TWI'LEK --
--AND SEEM MORE ROOTED IN ***FEAR*** THAN IN WISDOM.
WHAT IF, INSTEAD OF ***FEARING*** YOUR FEELINGS, YOU ***TRUSTED*** THEM? WHAT WOULD THAT TELL YOU?
THAT I ***AM*** A TWI'LEK BUT, AT MY CORE, I AM A ***JEDI***. THAT THERE ARE THINGS ABOUT BEING A TWI'LEK THAT CAN MAKE ME A ***BETTER*** JEDI. SUBMITTING TO A HEATSTORM MEANS ***SURVIVING***, WHEREAS FIGHTING IT WOULD MEAN DEATH.
THANK YOU, MASTER. I AM READY NOW.
VUUNN

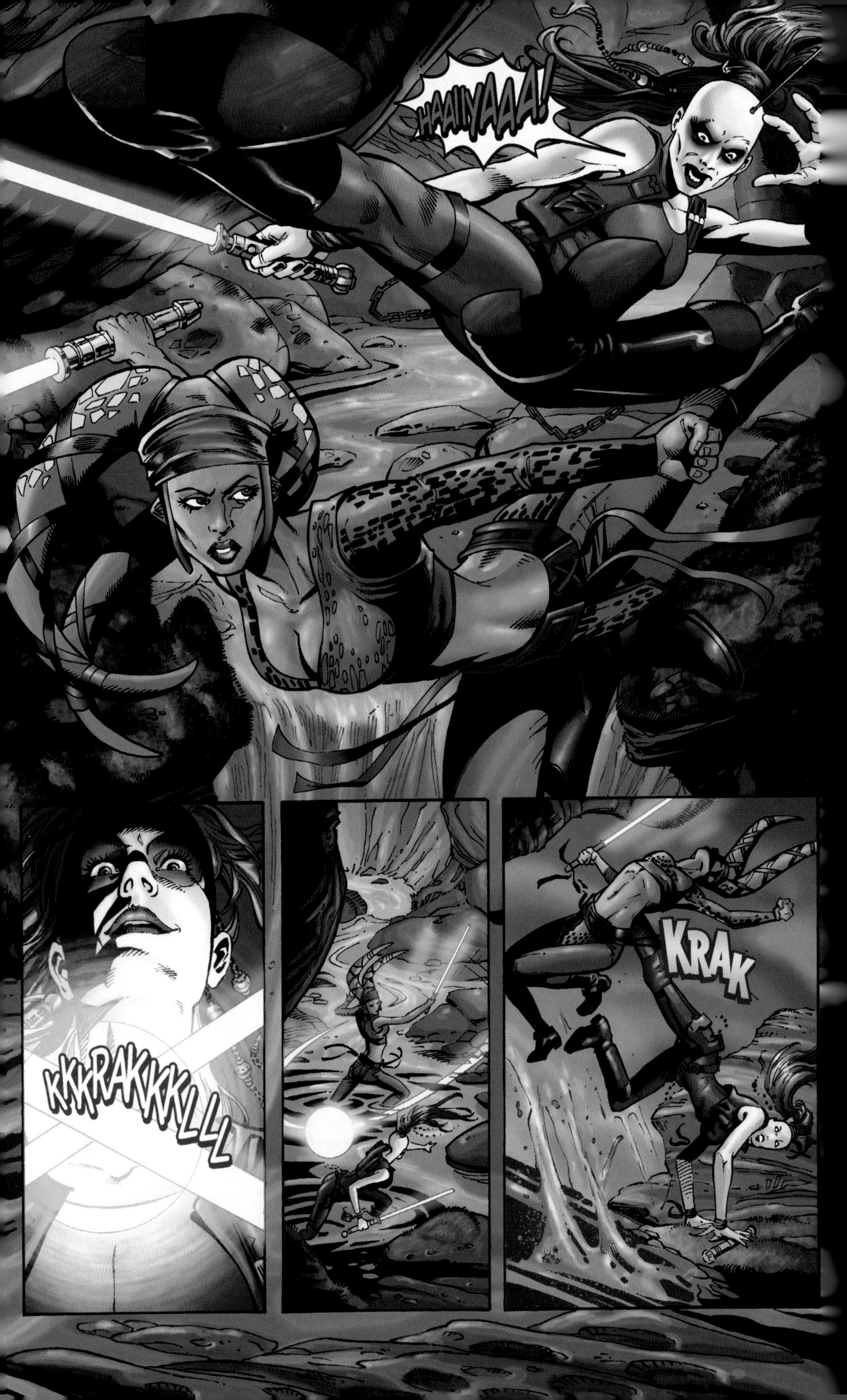
HAAIIYAAA!
KKKRAKKKKLLL
KRAK

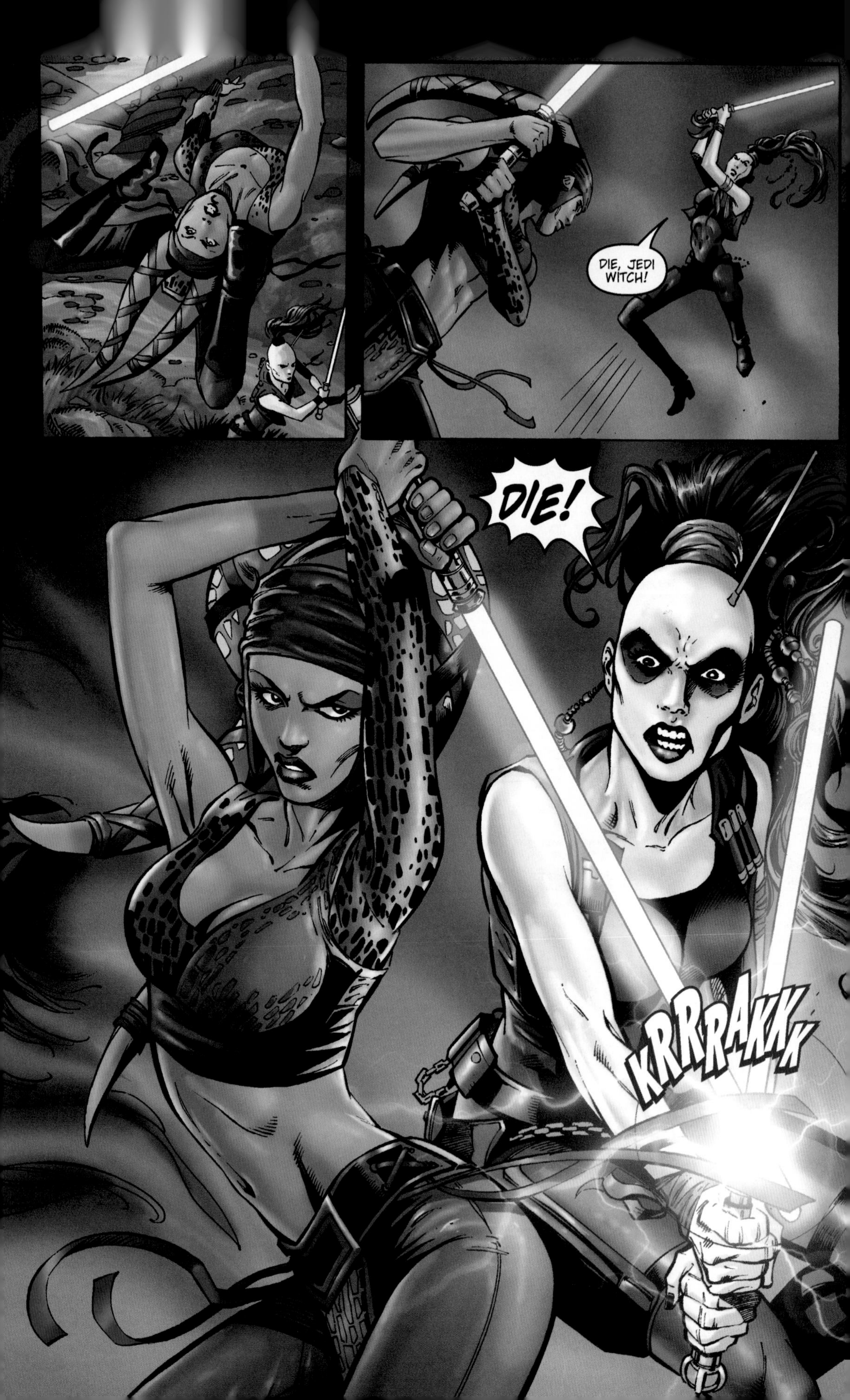
DIE, JEDI WITCH!
DIE!
KRRRAKKK

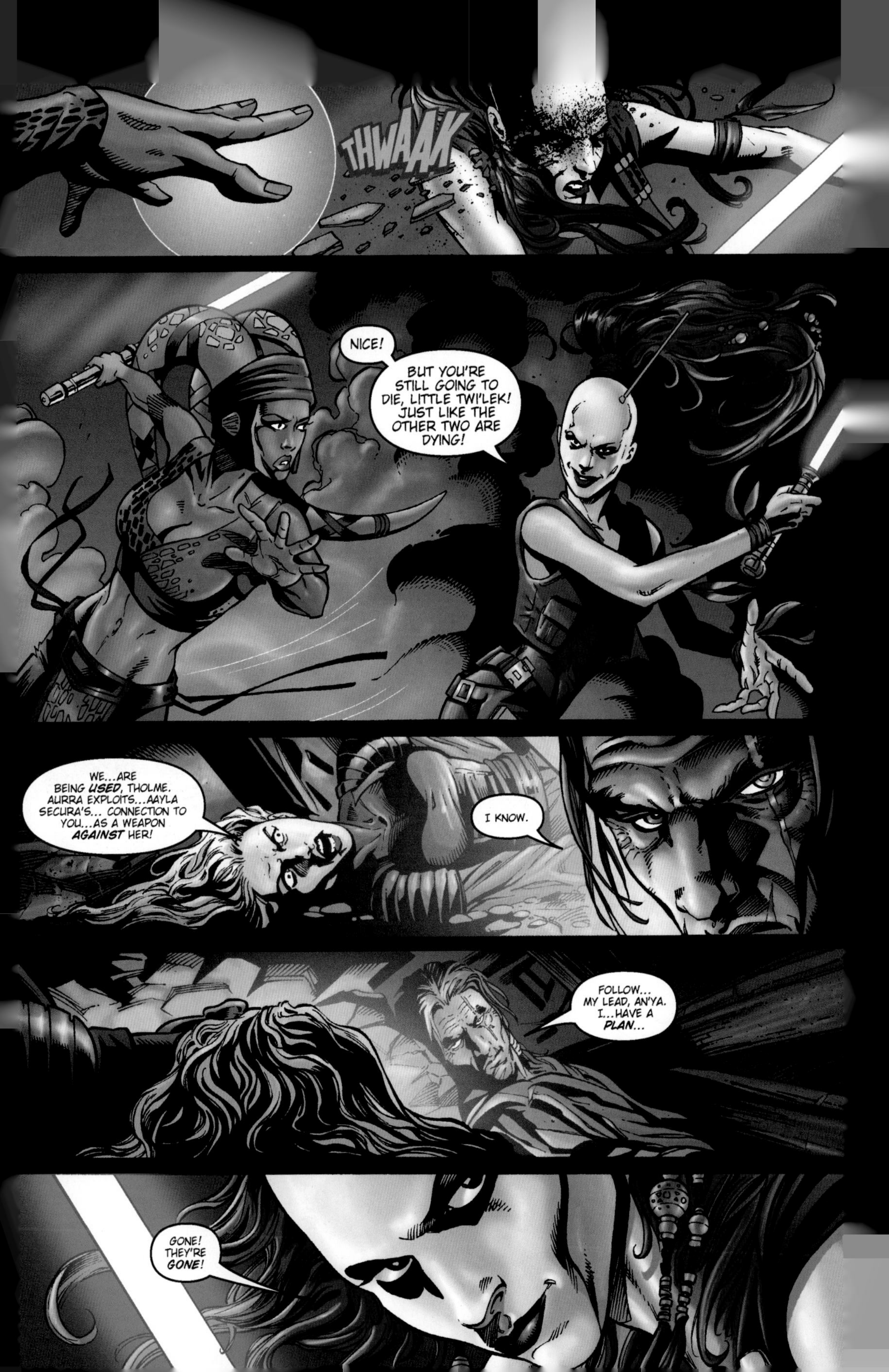
THWAAK
NICE!
BUT YOU'RE STILL GOING TO DIE, LITTLE TWI'LEK! JUST LIKE THE OTHER TWO ARE DYING!
WE...ARE BEING USED, THOLME. AURRA EXPLOITS...AAYLA SECURA'S... CONNECTION TO YOU...AS A WEAPON AGAINST HER!
I KNOW.
FOLLOW... MY LEAD, AN'YA. I...HAVE A PLAN...
GONE! THEY'RE GONE!

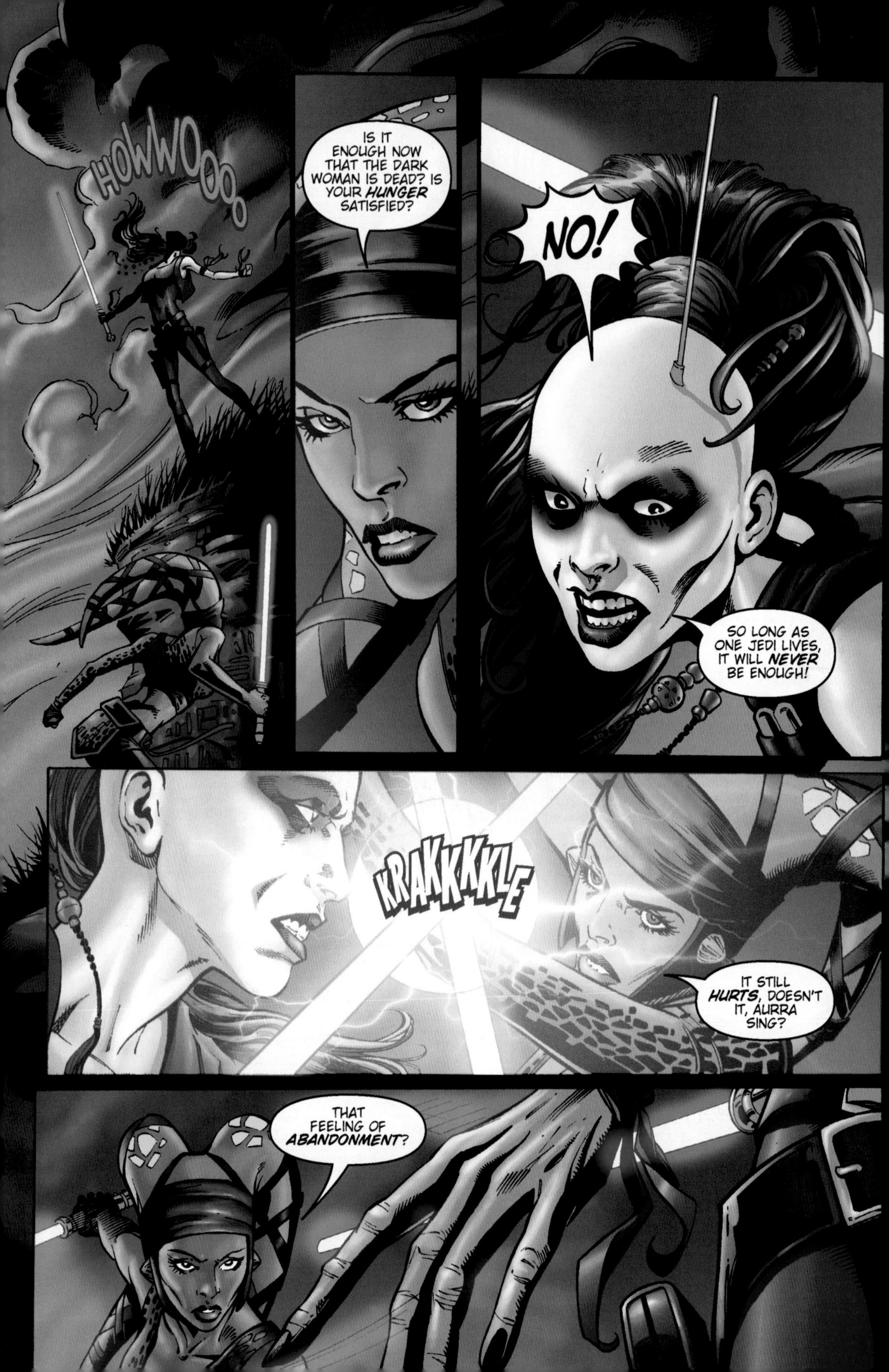
HOWWOOO
IS IT ENOUGH NOW THAT THE DARK WOMAN IS DEAD? IS YOUR HUNGER SATISFIED?
NO!
SO LONG AS ONE JEDI LIVES, IT WILL NEVER BE ENOUGH!
KRAKKKKLE
IT STILL HURTS, DOESN'T IT, AURRA SING?
THAT FEELING OF ABANDONMENT?

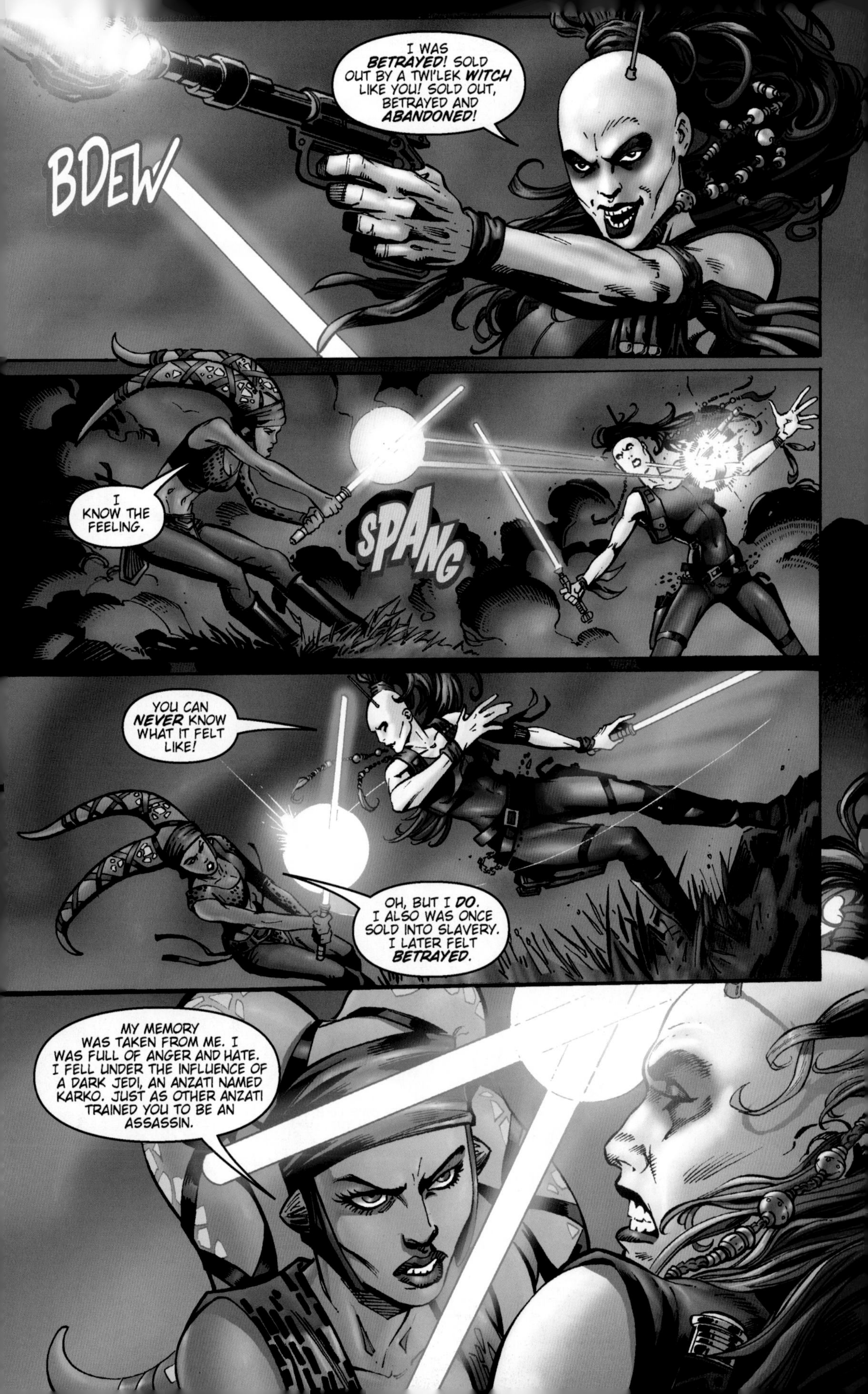
I WAS BETRAYED! SOLD OUT BY A TWI'LEK WITCH LIKE YOU! SOLD OUT, BETRAYED AND ABANDONED!
BDEW
I KNOW THE FEELING.
SPANG
YOU CAN NEVER KNOW WHAT IT FELT LIKE!
OH, BUT I DO. I ALSO WAS ONCE SOLD INTO SLAVERY. I LATER FELT BETRAYED.
MY MEMORY WAS TAKEN FROM ME. I WAS FULL OF ANGER AND HATE. I FELL UNDER THE INFLUENCE OF A DARK JEDI, AN ANZATI NAMED KARKO. JUST AS OTHER ANZATI TRAINED YOU TO BE AN ASSASSIN.

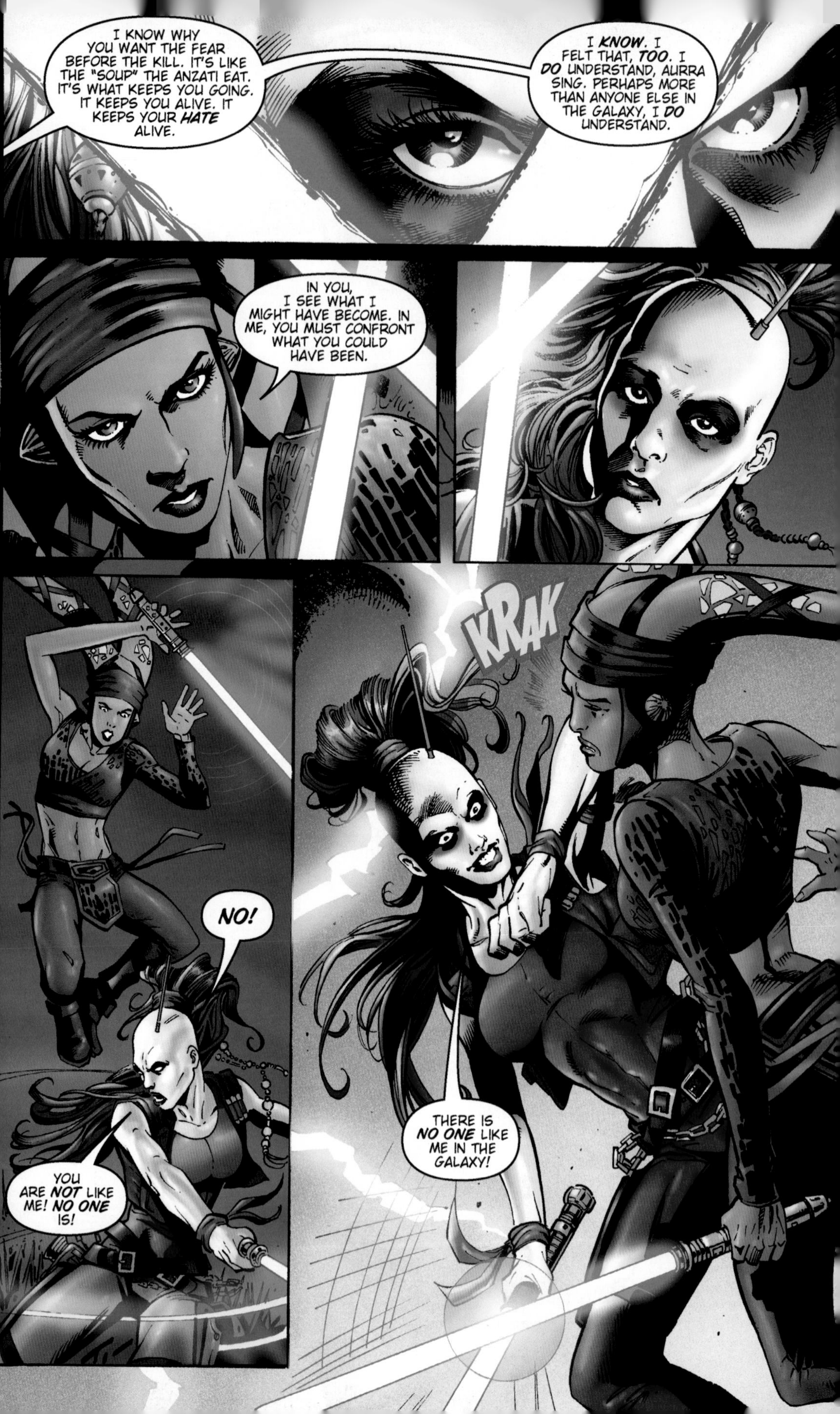
I KNOW WHY YOU WANT THE FEAR BEFORE THE KILL. IT'S LIKE THE "SOUP" THE ANZATI EAT. IT'S WHAT KEEPS YOU GOING. IT KEEPS YOU ALIVE. IT KEEPS YOUR HATE ALIVE.
I KNOW. I FELT THAT, TOO. I DO UNDERSTAND, AURRA SING. PERHAPS MORE THAN ANYONE ELSE IN THE GALAXY, I DO UNDERSTAND.
IN YOU, I SEE WHAT I MIGHT HAVE BECOME. IN ME, YOU MUST CONFRONT WHAT YOU COULD HAVE BEEN.
NO!
YOU ARE NOT LIKE ME! NO ONE IS!
KRAK
THERE IS NO ONE LIKE ME IN THE GALAXY!

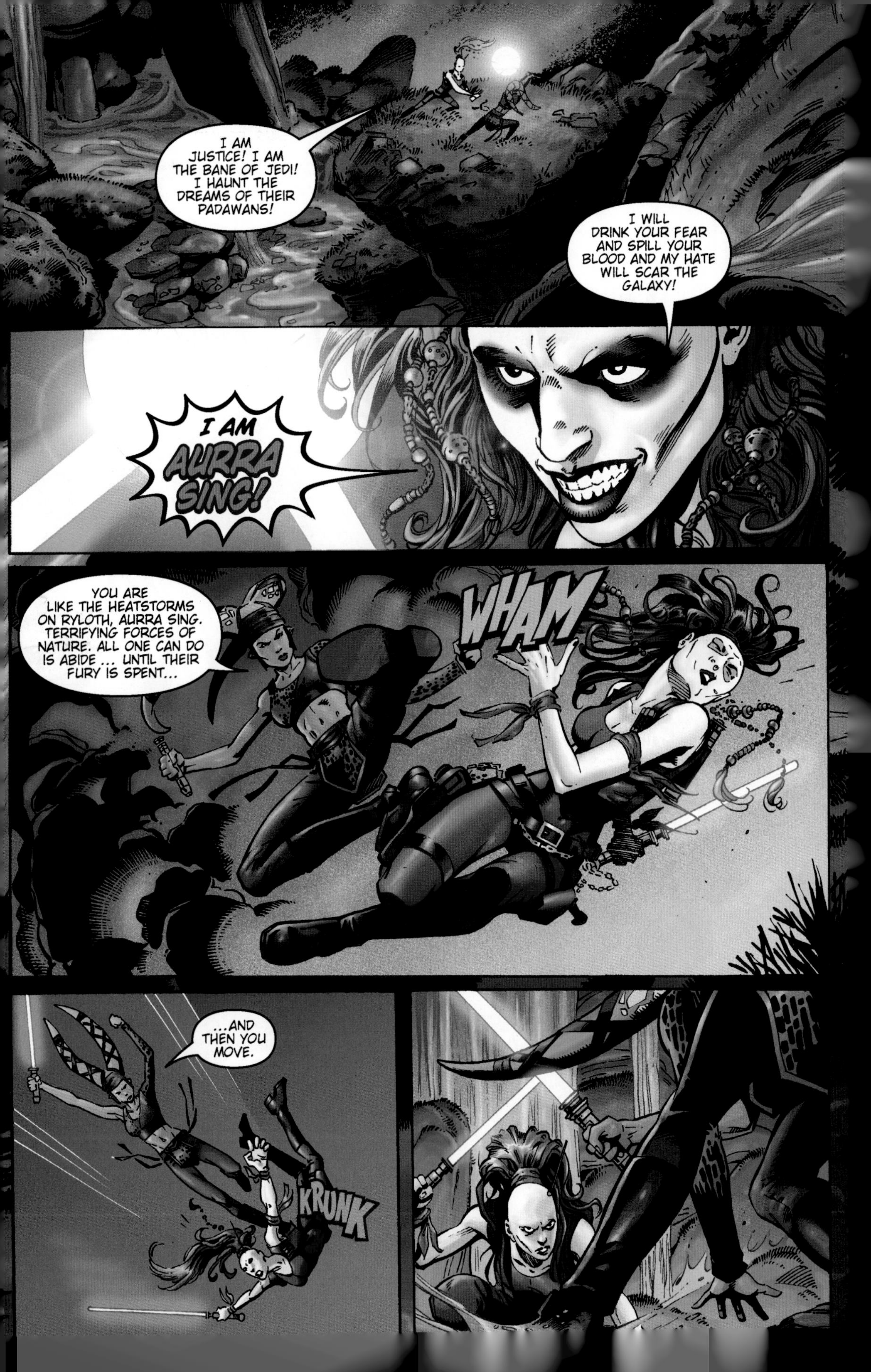
I AM JUSTICE! I AM THE BANE OF JEDI! I HAUNT THE DREAMS OF THEIR PADAWANS!
I WILL DRINK YOUR FEAR AND SPILL YOUR BLOOD AND MY HATE WILL SCAR THE GALAXY!
I AM AURRA SING!
YOU ARE LIKE THE HEATSTORMS ON RYLOTH, AURRA SING. TERRIFYING FORCES OF NATURE. ALL ONE CAN DO IS ABIDE ... UNTIL THEIR FURY IS SPENT...
WHAM
...AND THEN YOU MOVE.
KRUNK

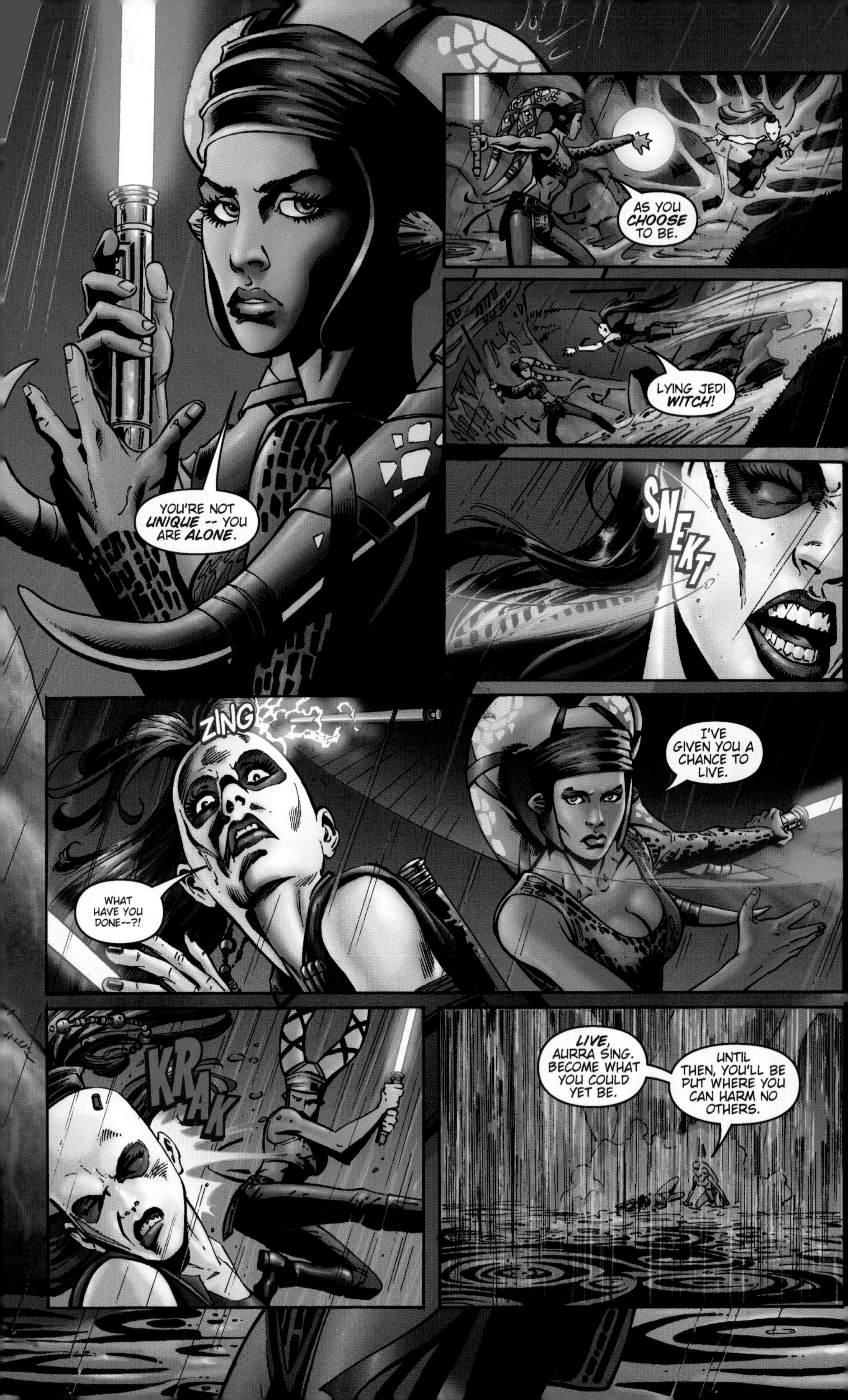
YOU'RE NOT UNIQUE -- YOU ARE ALONE.
AS YOU CHOOSE TO BE.
LYING JEDI WITCH!
SNEKT
ZING
WHAT HAVE YOU DONE--?!
I'VE GIVEN YOU A CHANCE TO LIVE.
KRAK
LIVE, AURRA SING. BECOME WHAT YOU COULD YET BE.
UNTIL THEN, YOU'LL BE PUT WHERE YOU CAN HARM NO OTHERS.

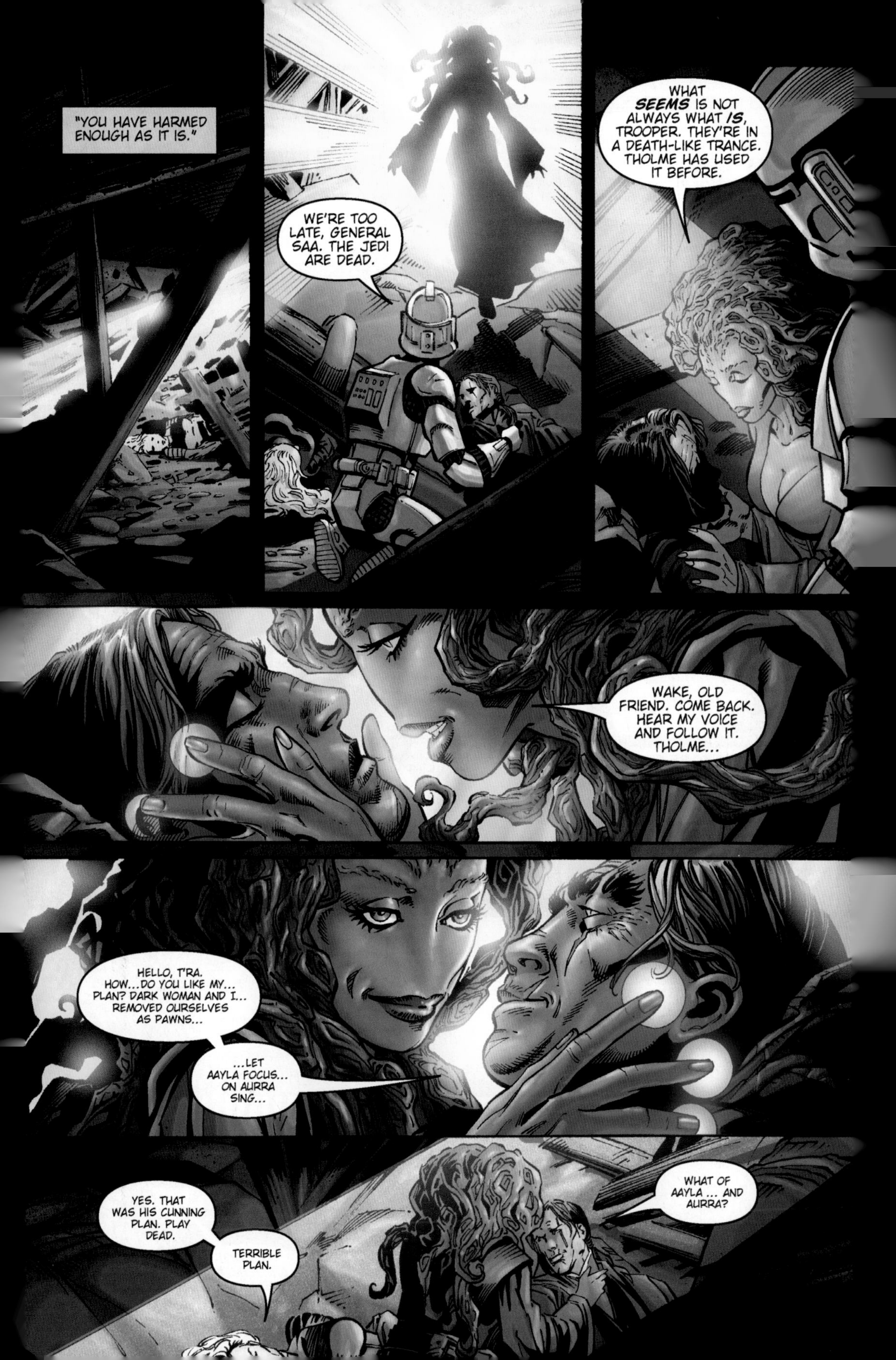
"YOU HAVE HARMED ENOUGH AS IT IS."
WE'RE TOO LATE, GENERAL SAA. THE JEDI ARE DEAD.
WHAT SEEMS IS NOT ALWAYS WHAT IS, TROOPER. THEY'RE IN A DEATH-LIKE TRANCE. THOLME HAS USED IT BEFORE.
WAKE, OLD FRIEND. COME BACK. HEAR MY VOICE AND FOLLOW IT. THOLME...
HELLO, T'RA. HOW...DO YOU LIKE MY... PLAN? DARK WOMAN AND I... REMOVED OURSELVES AS PAWNS...
...LET AAYLA FOCUS... ON AURRA SING...
YES. THAT WAS HIS CUNNING PLAN. PLAY DEAD.
TERRIBLE PLAN.
WHAT OF AAYLA ... AND AURRA?

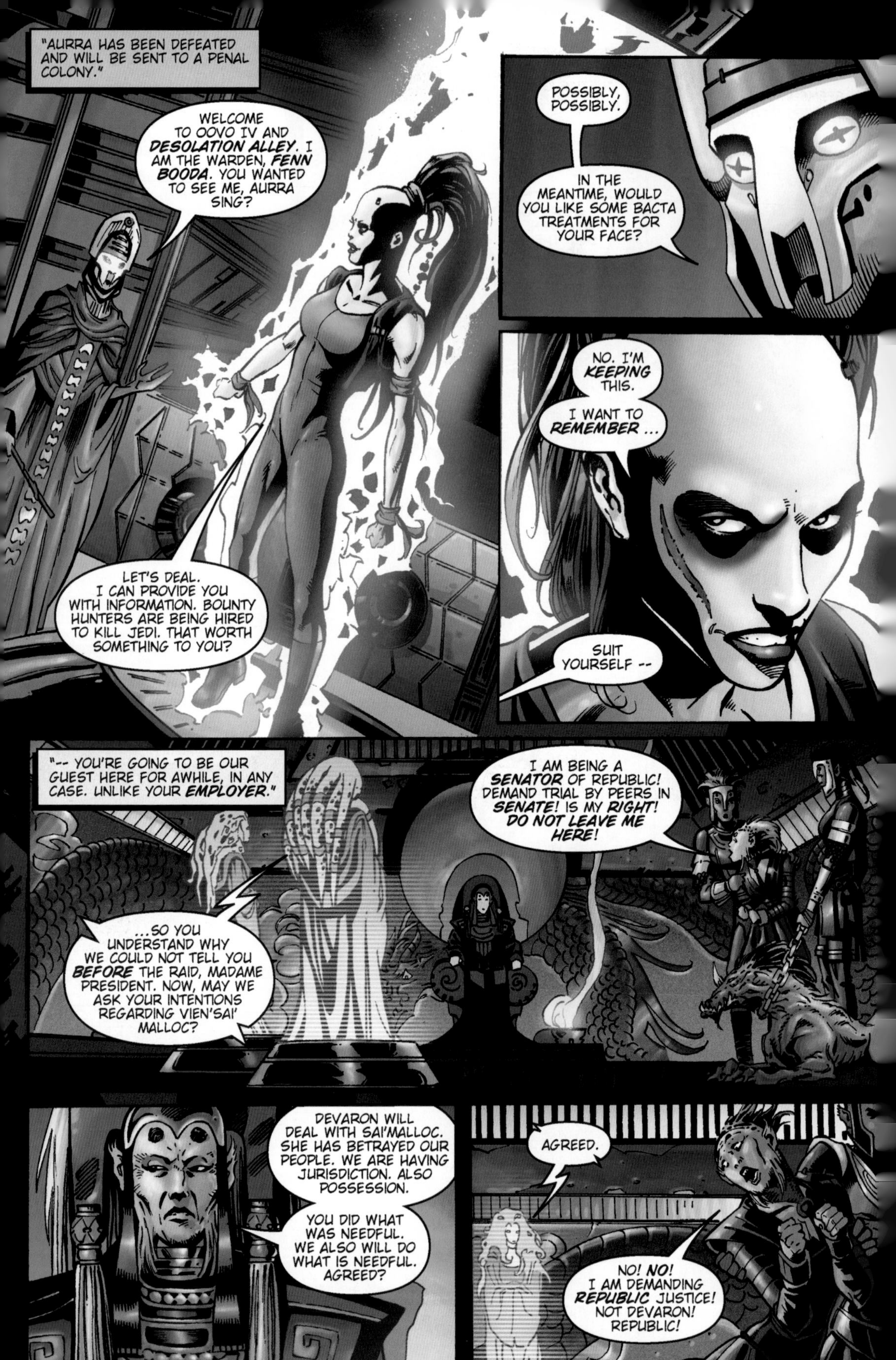
"AURRA HAS BEEN DEFEATED AND WILL BE SENT TO A PENAL COLONY."
WELCOME TO OOVO IV AND DESOLATION ALLEY. I AM THE WARDEN, FENN BOODA. YOU WANTED TO SEE ME, AURRA SING?
LET'S DEAL. I CAN PROVIDE YOU WITH INFORMATION. BOUNTY HUNTERS ARE BEING HIRED TO KILL JEDI. THAT WORTH SOMETHING TO YOU?
POSSIBLY, POSSIBLY.
IN THE MEANTIME, WOULD YOU LIKE SOME BACTA TREATMENTS FOR YOUR FACE?
NO. I'M KEEPING THIS.
I WANT TO REMEMBER ...
SUIT YOURSELF --
"-- YOU'RE GOING TO BE OUR GUEST HERE FOR AWHILE, IN ANY CASE. UNLIKE YOUR EMPLOYER."
I AM BEING A SENATOR OF REPUBLIC! DEMAND TRIAL BY PEERS IN SENATE! IS MY RIGHT! DO NOT LEAVE ME HERE!
...SO YOU UNDERSTAND WHY WE COULD NOT TELL YOU BEFORE THE RAID, MADAME PRESIDENT. NOW, MAY WE ASK YOUR INTENTIONS REGARDING VIEN'SAI' MALLOC?
DEVARON WILL DEAL WITH SAI'MALLOC. SHE HAS BETRAYED OUR PEOPLE. WE ARE HAVING JURISDICTION. ALSO POSSESSION.
YOU DID WHAT WAS NEEDFUL. WE ALSO WILL DO WHAT IS NEEDFUL. AGREED?
AGREED.
NO! NO! I AM DEMANDING REPUBLIC JUSTICE! NOT DEVARON! REPUBLIC!

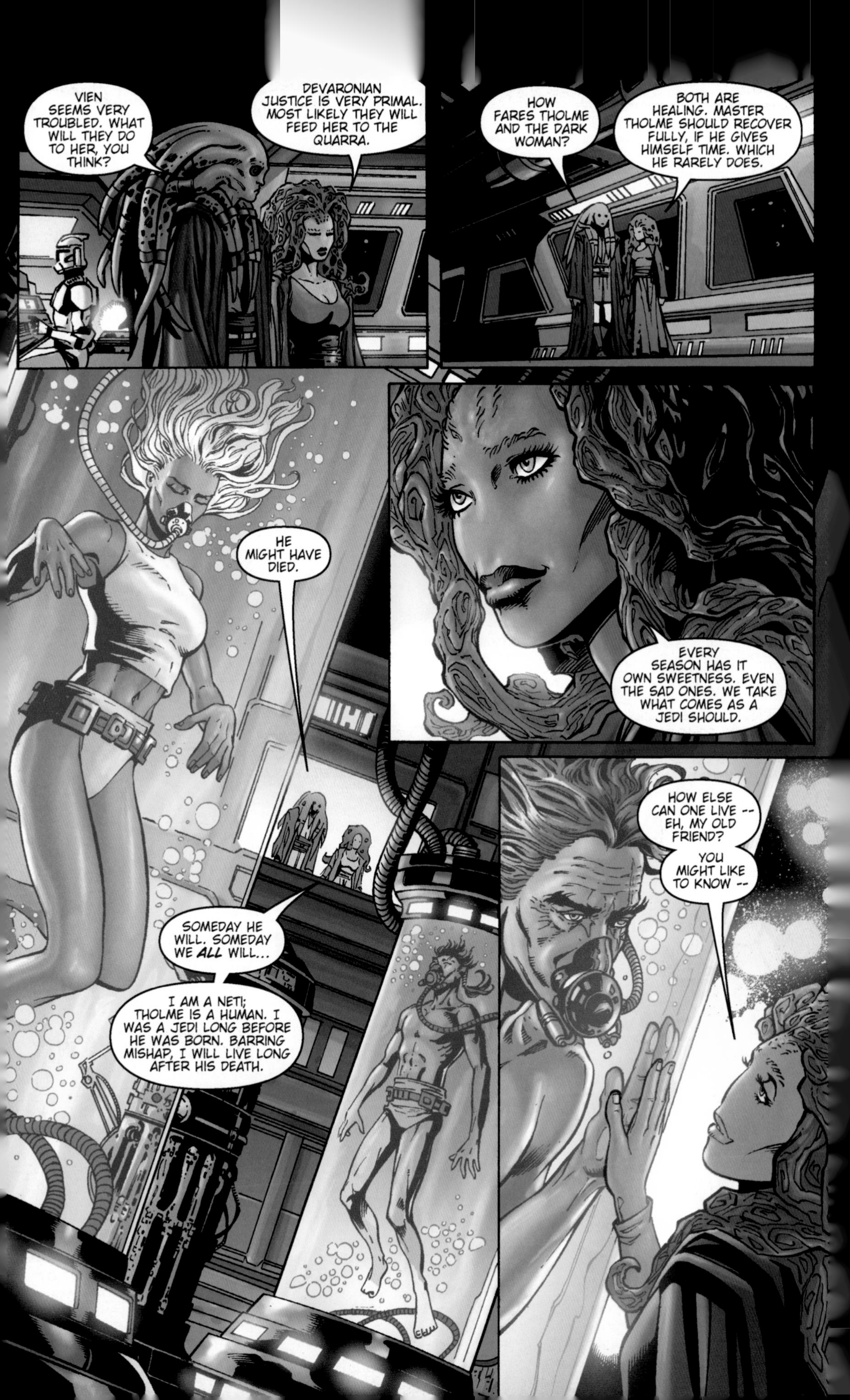
VIEN SEEMS VERY TROUBLED. WHAT WILL THEY DO TO HER, YOU THINK?
DEVARONIAN JUSTICE IS VERY PRIMAL. MOST LIKELY THEY WILL FEED HER TO THE QUARRA.
HOW FARES THOLME AND THE DARK WOMAN?
BOTH ARE HEALING. MASTER THOLME SHOULD RECOVER FULLY, IF HE GIVES HIMSELF TIME. WHICH HE RARELY DOES.
HE MIGHT HAVE DIED.
SOMEDAY HE WILL. SOMEDAY WE ALL WILL...
I AM A NETI; THOLME IS A HUMAN. I WAS A JEDI LONG BEFORE HE WAS BORN. BARRING MISHAP, I WILL LIVE LONG AFTER HIS DEATH.
EVERY SEASON HAS IT OWN SWEETNESS. EVEN THE SAD ONES. WE TAKE WHAT COMES AS A JEDI SHOULD.
HOW ELSE CAN ONE LIVE -- EH, MY OLD FRIEND?
YOU MIGHT LIKE TO KNOW --

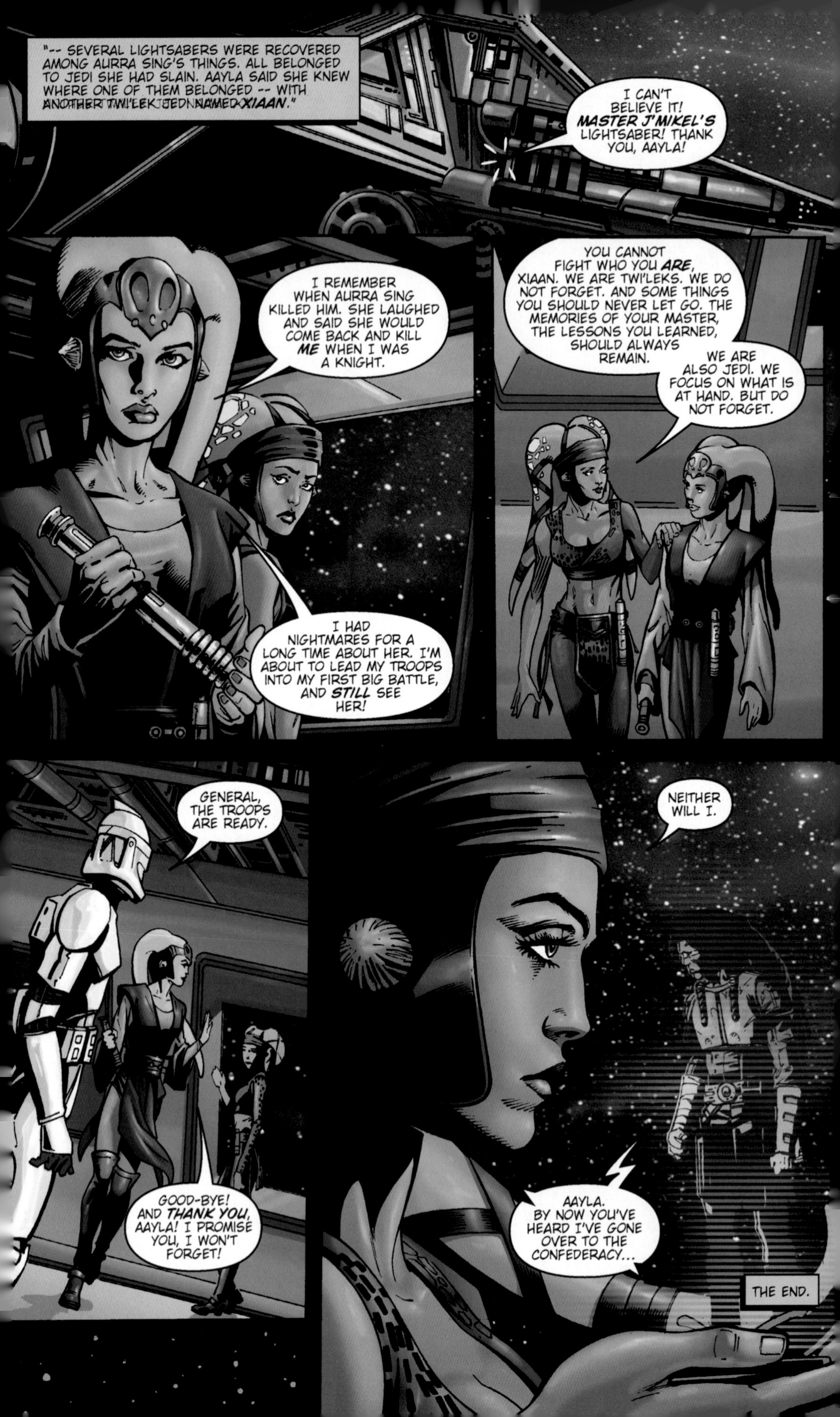
"-- SEVERAL LIGHTSABERS WERE RECOVERED AMONG AURRA SING'S THINGS. ALL BELONGED TO JEDI SHE HAD SLAIN. AAYLA SAID SHE KNEW WHERE ONE OF THEM BELONGED -- WITH ANOTHER TWI'LEK JEDI NAMED *XIAAN*."
I CAN'T BELIEVE IT! ***MASTER J'MIKEL'S*** LIGHTSABER! THANK YOU, AAYLA!
I REMEMBER WHEN AURRA SING KILLED HIM. SHE LAUGHED AND SAID SHE WOULD COME BACK AND KILL ***ME*** WHEN I WAS A KNIGHT.
I HAD NIGHTMARES FOR A LONG TIME ABOUT HER. I'M ABOUT TO LEAD MY TROOPS INTO MY FIRST BIG BATTLE, AND ***STILL*** SEE HER!
YOU CANNOT FIGHT WHO YOU ***ARE***, XIAAN. WE ARE TWI'LEKS. WE DO NOT FORGET. AND SOME THINGS YOU SHOULD NEVER LET GO. THE MEMORIES OF YOUR MASTER, THE LESSONS YOU LEARNED, SHOULD ALWAYS REMAIN.
WE ARE ALSO JEDI. WE FOCUS ON WHAT IS AT HAND. BUT DO NOT FORGET.
GENERAL, THE TROOPS ARE READY.
GOOD-BYE! AND ***THANK YOU***, AAYLA! I PROMISE YOU, I WON'T FORGET!
NEITHER WILL I.
AAYLA. BY NOW YOU'VE HEARD I'VE GONE OVER TO THE CONFEDERACY...
THE END.

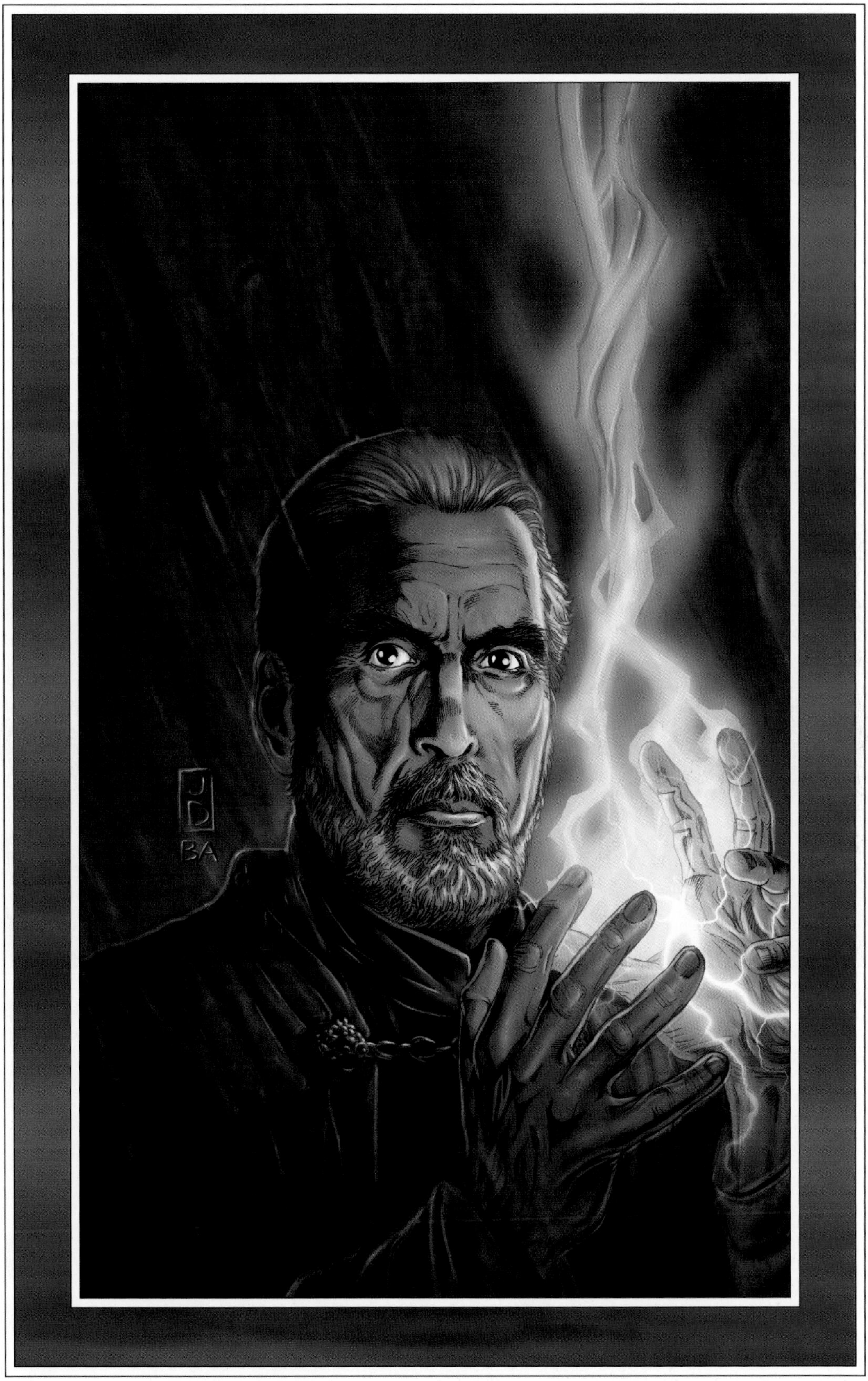

SEVEN-AND-A-HALF MONTHS AFTER THE BATTLE OF GEONOSIS...

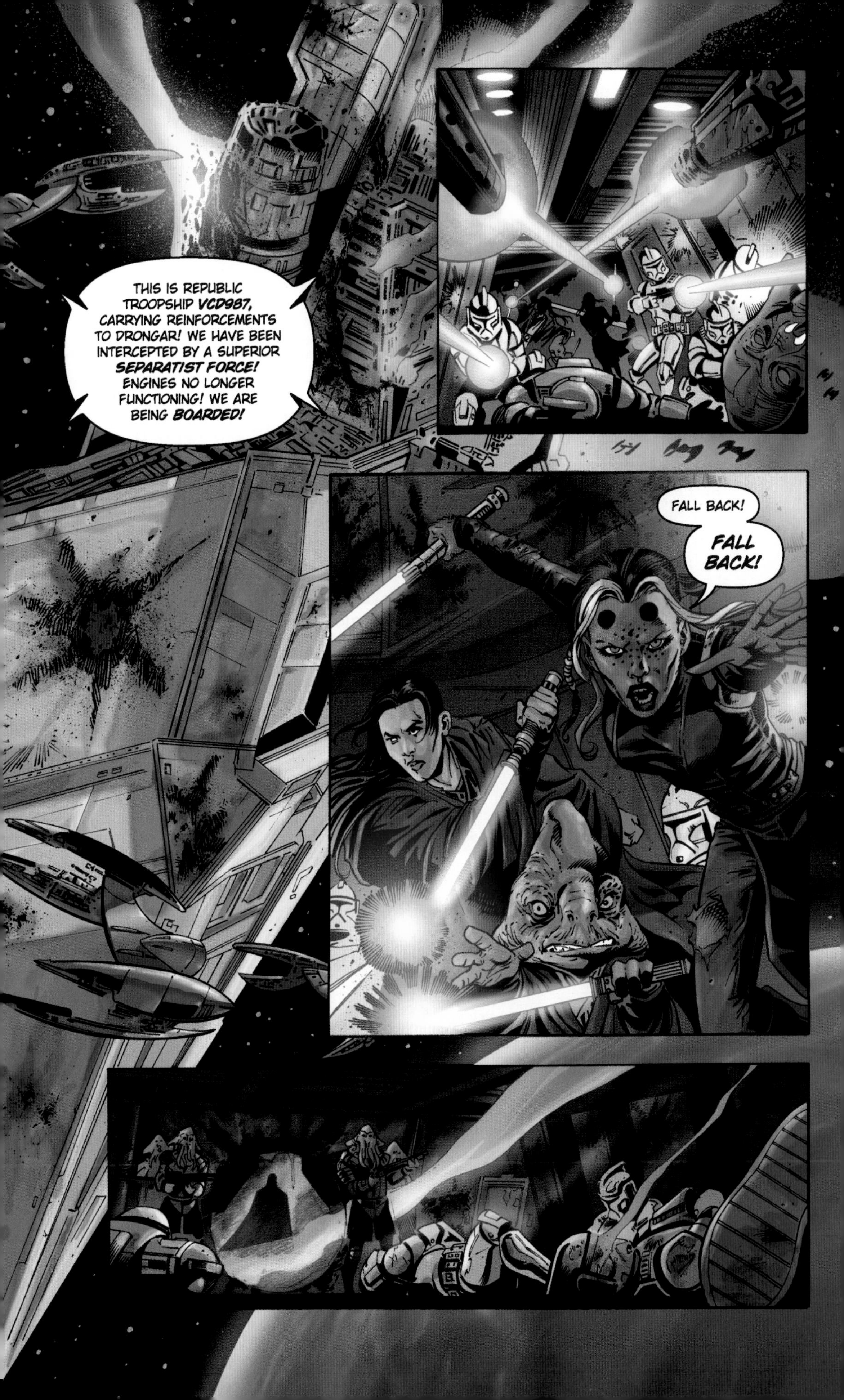
THIS IS REPUBLIC TROOPSHIP VCD987, CARRYING REINFORCEMENTS TO DRONGAR! WE HAVE BEEN INTERCEPTED BY A SUPERIOR SEPARATIST FORCE! ENGINES NO LONGER FUNCTIONING! WE ARE BEING BOARDED!
FALL BACK!
FALL BACK!

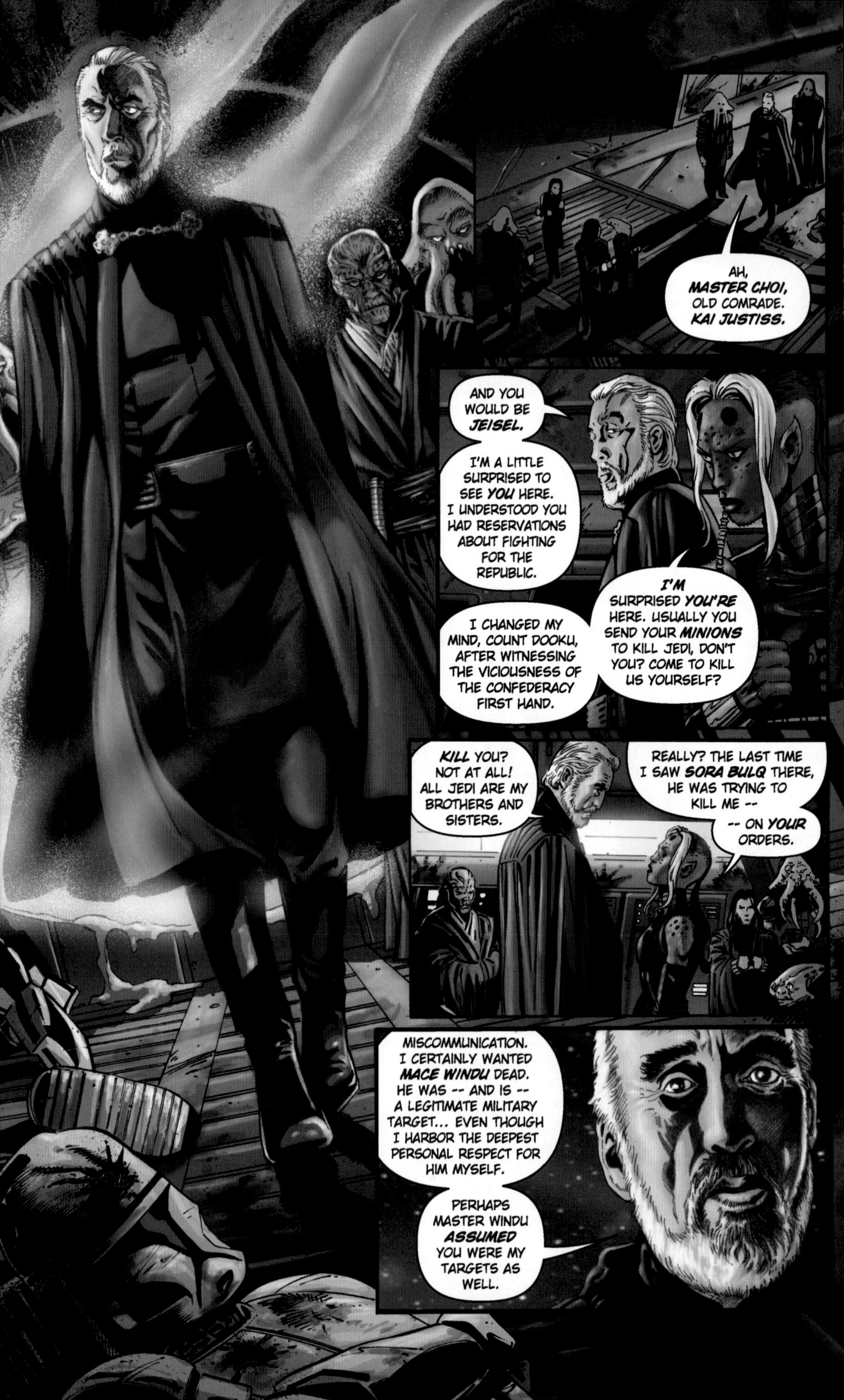

AH, MASTER CHOI, OLD COMRADE. KAI JUSTISS.
AND YOU WOULD BE JEISEL.
I'M A LITTLE SURPRISED TO SEE YOU HERE. I UNDERSTOOD YOU HAD RESERVATIONS ABOUT FIGHTING FOR THE REPUBLIC.
I CHANGED MY MIND, COUNT DOOKU, AFTER WITNESSING THE VICIOUSNESS OF THE CONFEDERACY FIRST HAND.
I'M SURPRISED YOU'RE HERE. USUALLY YOU SEND YOUR MINIONS TO KILL JEDI, DON'T YOU? COME TO KILL US YOURSELF?
KILL YOU? NOT AT ALL! ALL JEDI ARE MY BROTHERS AND SISTERS.
REALLY? THE LAST TIME I SAW SORA BULQ THERE, HE WAS TRYING TO KILL ME --
-- ON YOUR ORDERS.
MISCOMMUNICATION. I CERTAINLY WANTED MACE WINDU DEAD. HE WAS -- AND IS -- A LEGITIMATE MILITARY TARGET... EVEN THOUGH I HARBOR THE DEEPEST PERSONAL RESPECT FOR HIM MYSELF.
PERHAPS MASTER WINDU ASSUMED YOU WERE MY TARGETS AS WELL.

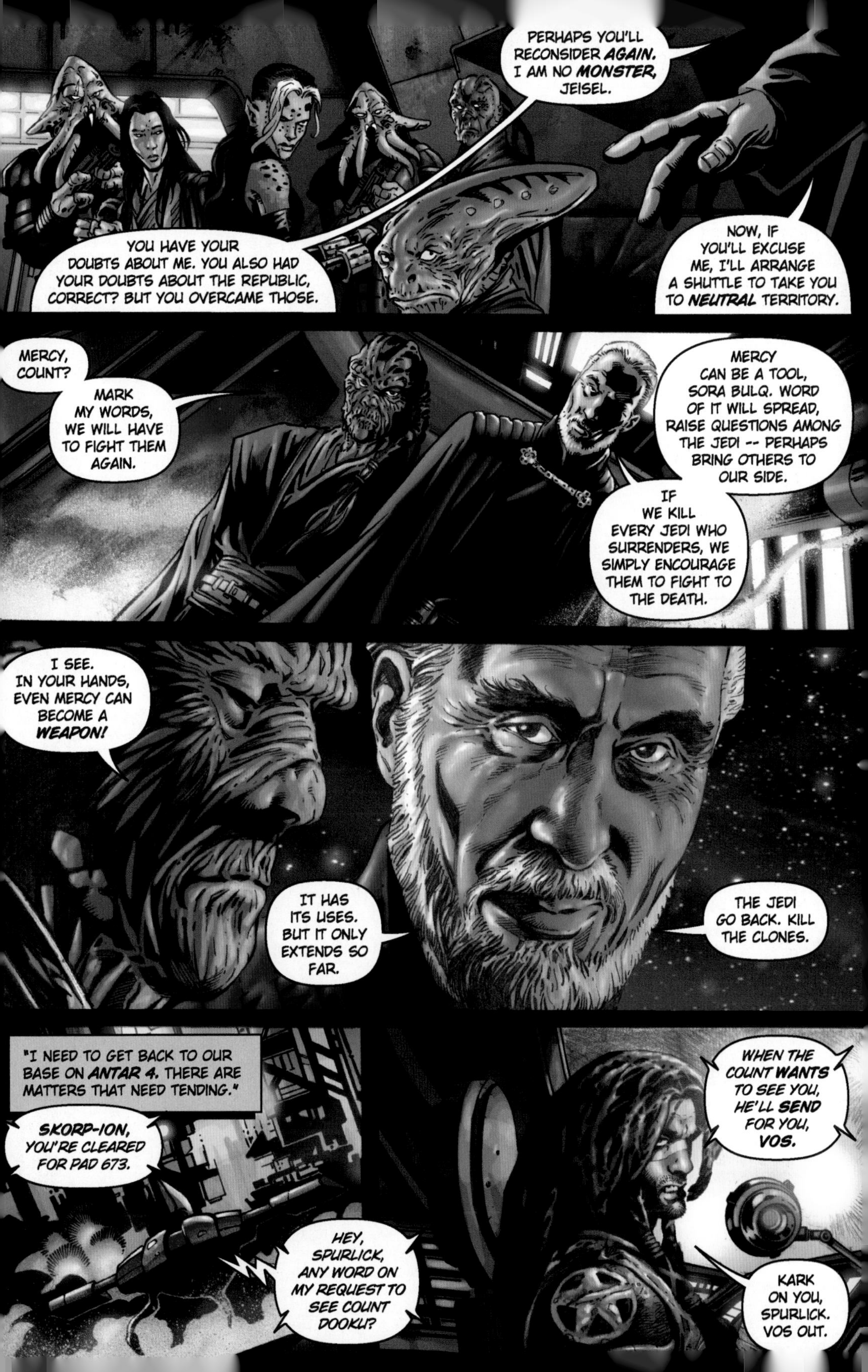
PERHAPS YOU'LL RECONSIDER AGAIN. I AM NO MONSTER, JEISEL.
YOU HAVE YOUR DOUBTS ABOUT ME. YOU ALSO HAD YOUR DOUBTS ABOUT THE REPUBLIC, CORRECT? BUT YOU OVERCAME THOSE.
NOW, IF YOU'LL EXCUSE ME, I'LL ARRANGE A SHUTTLE TO TAKE YOU TO NEUTRAL TERRITORY.
MERCY, COUNT?
MARK MY WORDS, WE WILL HAVE TO FIGHT THEM AGAIN.
MERCY CAN BE A TOOL, SORA BULQ. WORD OF IT WILL SPREAD, RAISE QUESTIONS AMONG THE JEDI -- PERHAPS BRING OTHERS TO OUR SIDE.
IF WE KILL EVERY JEDI WHO SURRENDERS, WE SIMPLY ENCOURAGE THEM TO FIGHT TO THE DEATH.
I SEE. IN YOUR HANDS, EVEN MERCY CAN BECOME A WEAPON!
IT HAS ITS USES. BUT IT ONLY EXTENDS SO FAR.
THE JEDI GO BACK. KILL THE CLONES.
"I NEED TO GET BACK TO OUR BASE ON ANTAR 4. THERE ARE MATTERS THAT NEED TENDING."
SKORP-ION, YOU'RE CLEARED FOR PAD 673.
WHEN THE COUNT WANTS TO SEE YOU, HE'LL SEND FOR YOU, VOS.
HEY, SPURLICK, ANY WORD ON MY REQUEST TO SEE COUNT DOOKU?
KARK ON YOU, SPURLICK. VOS OUT.

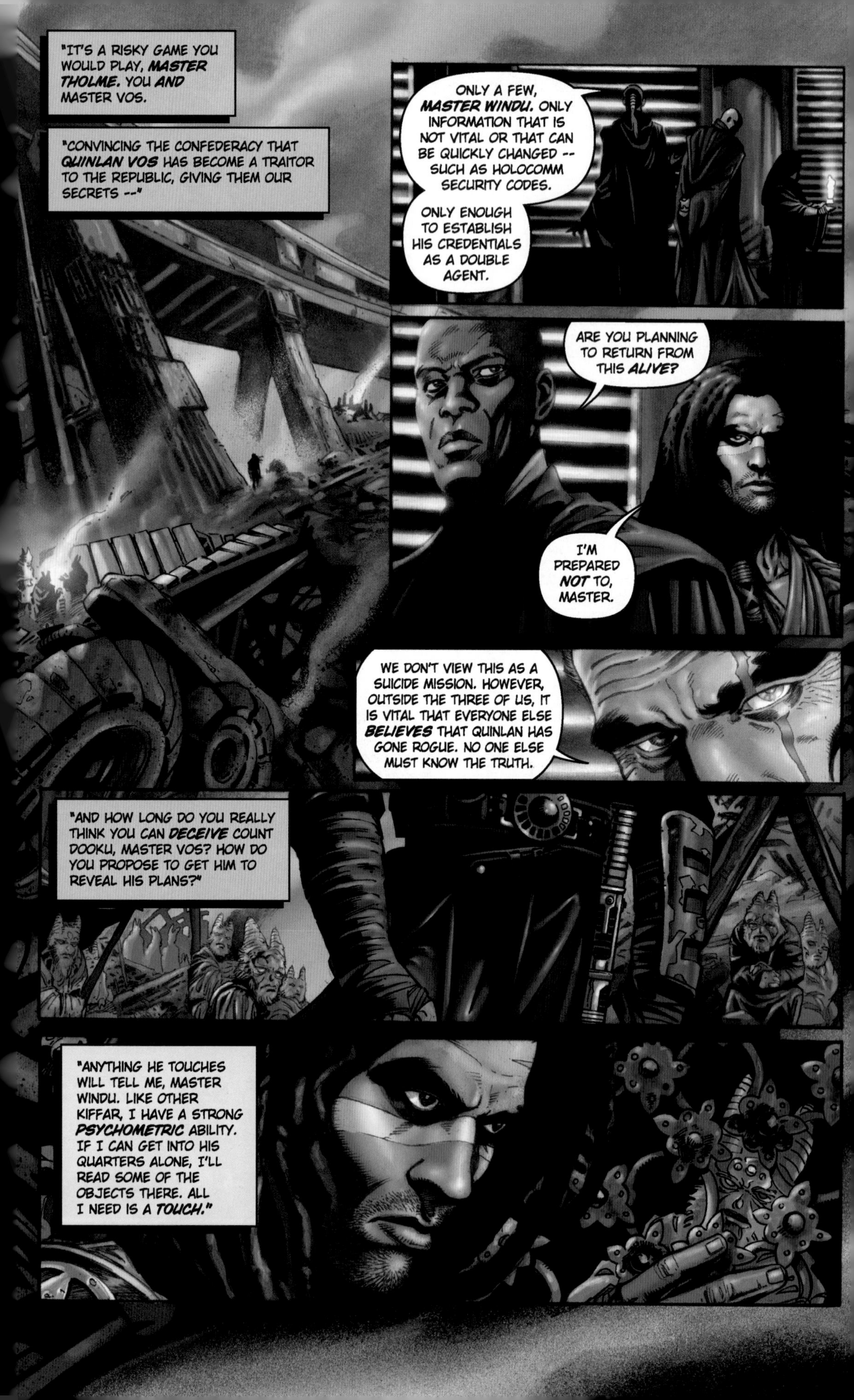
"IT'S A RISKY GAME YOU WOULD PLAY, MASTER THOLME. YOU AND MASTER VOS.
"CONVINCING THE CONFEDERACY THAT QUINLAN VOS HAS BECOME A TRAITOR TO THE REPUBLIC, GIVING THEM OUR SECRETS --"
ONLY A FEW, MASTER WINDU. ONLY INFORMATION THAT IS NOT VITAL OR THAT CAN BE QUICKLY CHANGED -- SUCH AS HOLOCOMM SECURITY CODES.
ONLY ENOUGH TO ESTABLISH HIS CREDENTIALS AS A DOUBLE AGENT.
ARE YOU PLANNING TO RETURN FROM THIS ALIVE?
I'M PREPARED NOT TO, MASTER.
WE DON'T VIEW THIS AS A SUICIDE MISSION. HOWEVER, OUTSIDE THE THREE OF US, IT IS VITAL THAT EVERYONE ELSE BELIEVES THAT QUINLAN HAS GONE ROGUE. NO ONE ELSE MUST KNOW THE TRUTH.
"AND HOW LONG DO YOU REALLY THINK YOU CAN DECEIVE COUNT DOOKU, MASTER VOS? HOW DO YOU PROPOSE TO GET HIM TO REVEAL HIS PLANS?"
"ANYTHING HE TOUCHES WILL TELL ME, MASTER WINDU. LIKE OTHER KIFFAR, I HAVE A STRONG PSYCHOMETRIC ABILITY. IF I CAN GET INTO HIS QUARTERS ALONE, I'LL READ SOME OF THE OBJECTS THERE. ALL I NEED IS A TOUCH."

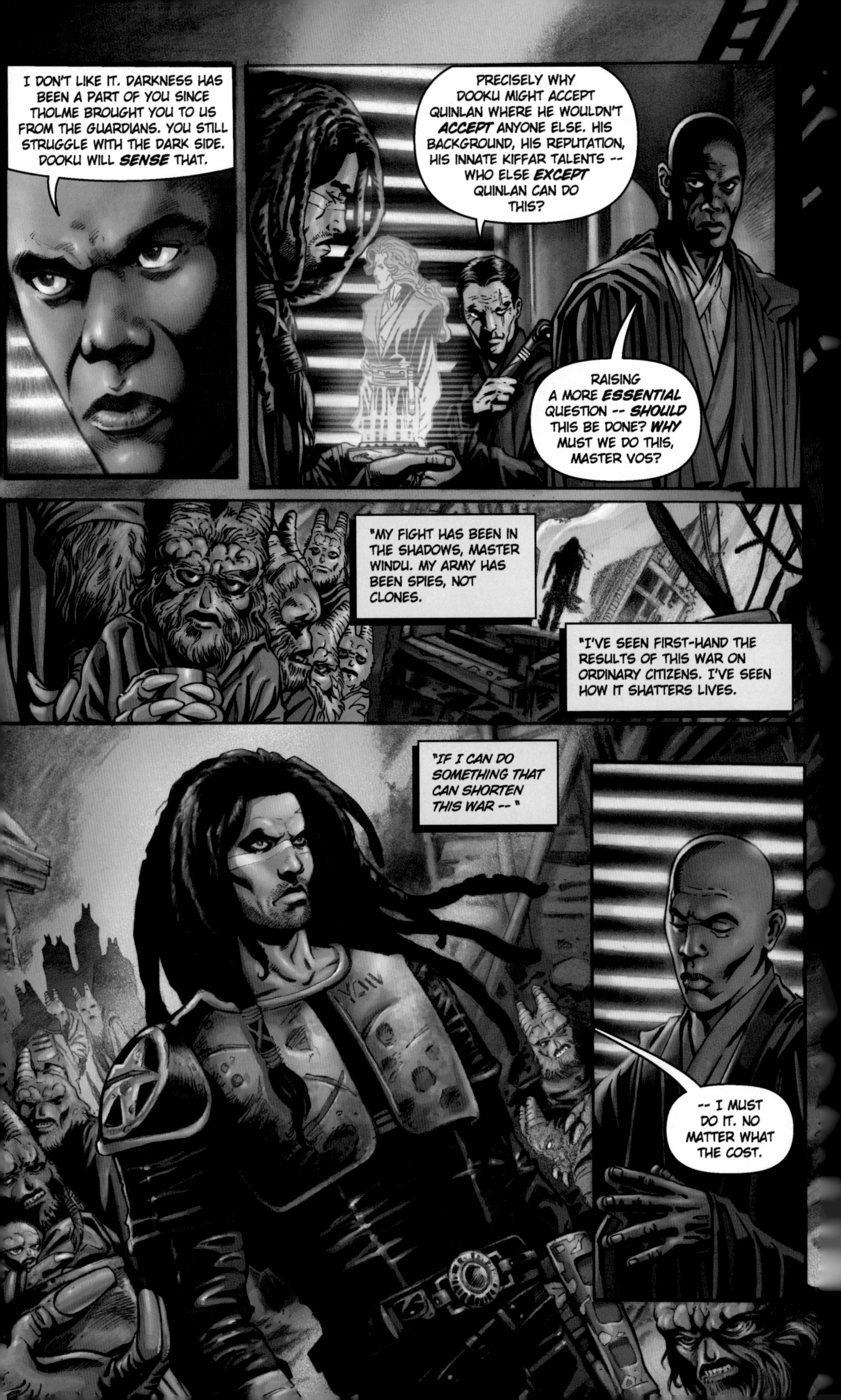
I DON'T LIKE IT. DARKNESS HAS BEEN A PART OF YOU SINCE THOLME BROUGHT YOU TO US FROM THE GUARDIANS. YOU STILL STRUGGLE WITH THE DARK SIDE. DOOKU WILL SENSE THAT.
PRECISELY WHY DOOKU MIGHT ACCEPT QUINLAN WHERE HE WOULDN'T ACCEPT ANYONE ELSE. HIS BACKGROUND, HIS REPUTATION, HIS INNATE KIFFAR TALENTS -- WHO ELSE EXCEPT QUINLAN CAN DO THIS?
RAISING A MORE ESSENTIAL QUESTION -- SHOULD THIS BE DONE? WHY MUST WE DO THIS, MASTER VOS?
"MY FIGHT HAS BEEN IN THE SHADOWS, MASTER WINDU. MY ARMY HAS BEEN SPIES, NOT CLONES.
"I'VE SEEN FIRST-HAND THE RESULTS OF THIS WAR ON ORDINARY CITIZENS. I'VE SEEN HOW IT SHATTERS LIVES.
"IF I CAN DO SOMETHING THAT CAN SHORTEN THIS WAR -- "
-- I MUST DO IT. NO MATTER WHAT THE COST.

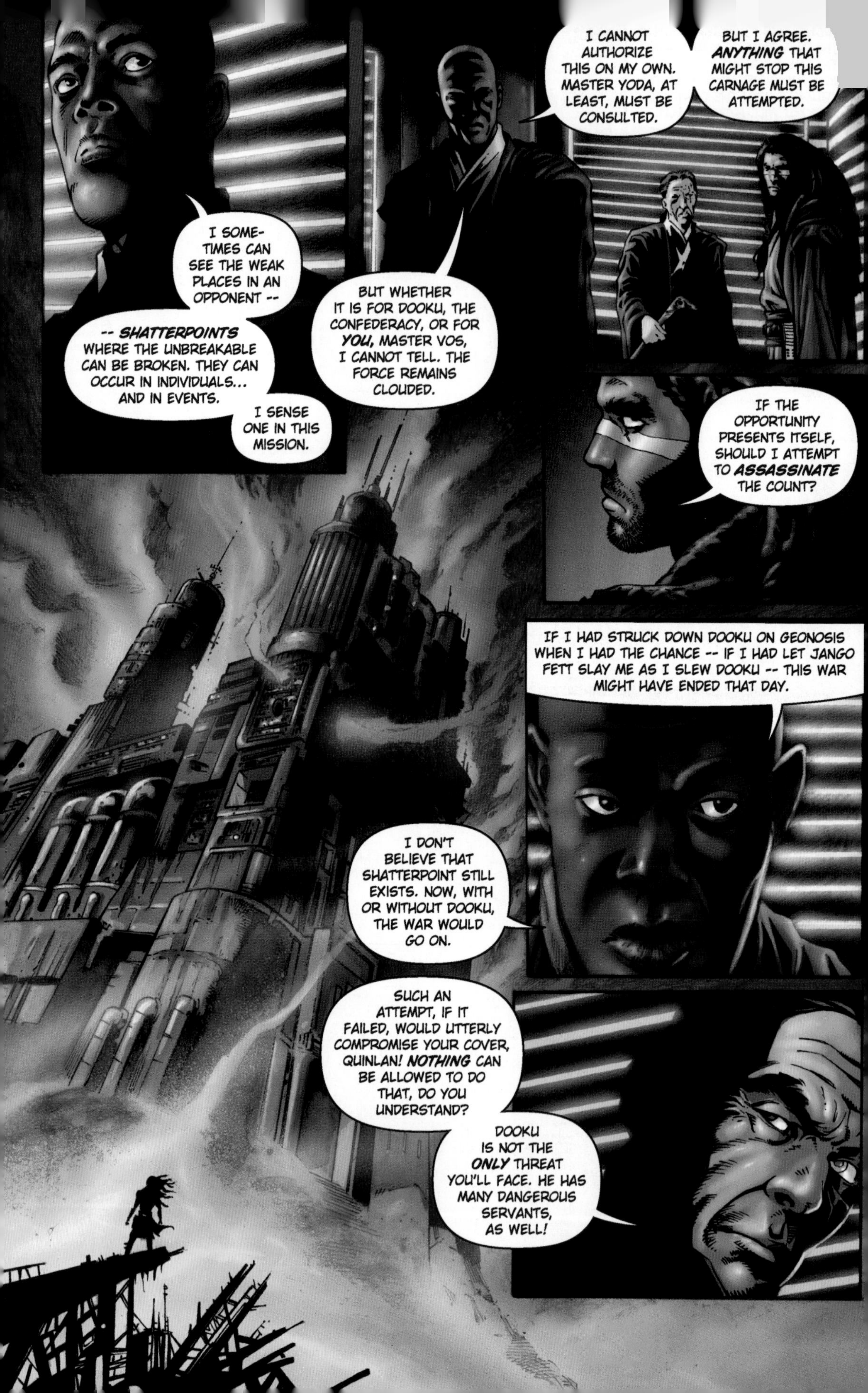
I SOME-TIMES CAN SEE THE WEAK PLACES IN AN OPPONENT --
-- SHATTERPOINTS WHERE THE UNBREAKABLE CAN BE BROKEN. THEY CAN OCCUR IN INDIVIDUALS... AND IN EVENTS.
I SENSE ONE IN THIS MISSION.
BUT WHETHER IT IS FOR DOOKU, THE CONFEDERACY, OR FOR YOU, MASTER VOS, I CANNOT TELL. THE FORCE REMAINS CLOUDED.
I CANNOT AUTHORIZE THIS ON MY OWN. MASTER YODA, AT LEAST, MUST BE CONSULTED.
BUT I AGREE. ANYTHING THAT MIGHT STOP THIS CARNAGE MUST BE ATTEMPTED.
IF THE OPPORTUNITY PRESENTS ITSELF, SHOULD I ATTEMPT TO ASSASSINATE THE COUNT?
IF I HAD STRUCK DOWN DOOKU ON GEONOSIS WHEN I HAD THE CHANCE -- IF I HAD LET JANGO FETT SLAY ME AS I SLEW DOOKU -- THIS WAR MIGHT HAVE ENDED THAT DAY.
I DON'T BELIEVE THAT SHATTERPOINT STILL EXISTS. NOW, WITH OR WITHOUT DOOKU, THE WAR WOULD GO ON.
SUCH AN ATTEMPT, IF IT FAILED, WOULD UTTERLY COMPROMISE YOUR COVER, QUINLAN! NOTHING CAN BE ALLOWED TO DO THAT, DO YOU UNDERSTAND?
DOOKU IS NOT THE ONLY THREAT YOU'LL FACE. HE HAS MANY DANGEROUS SERVANTS, AS WELL!

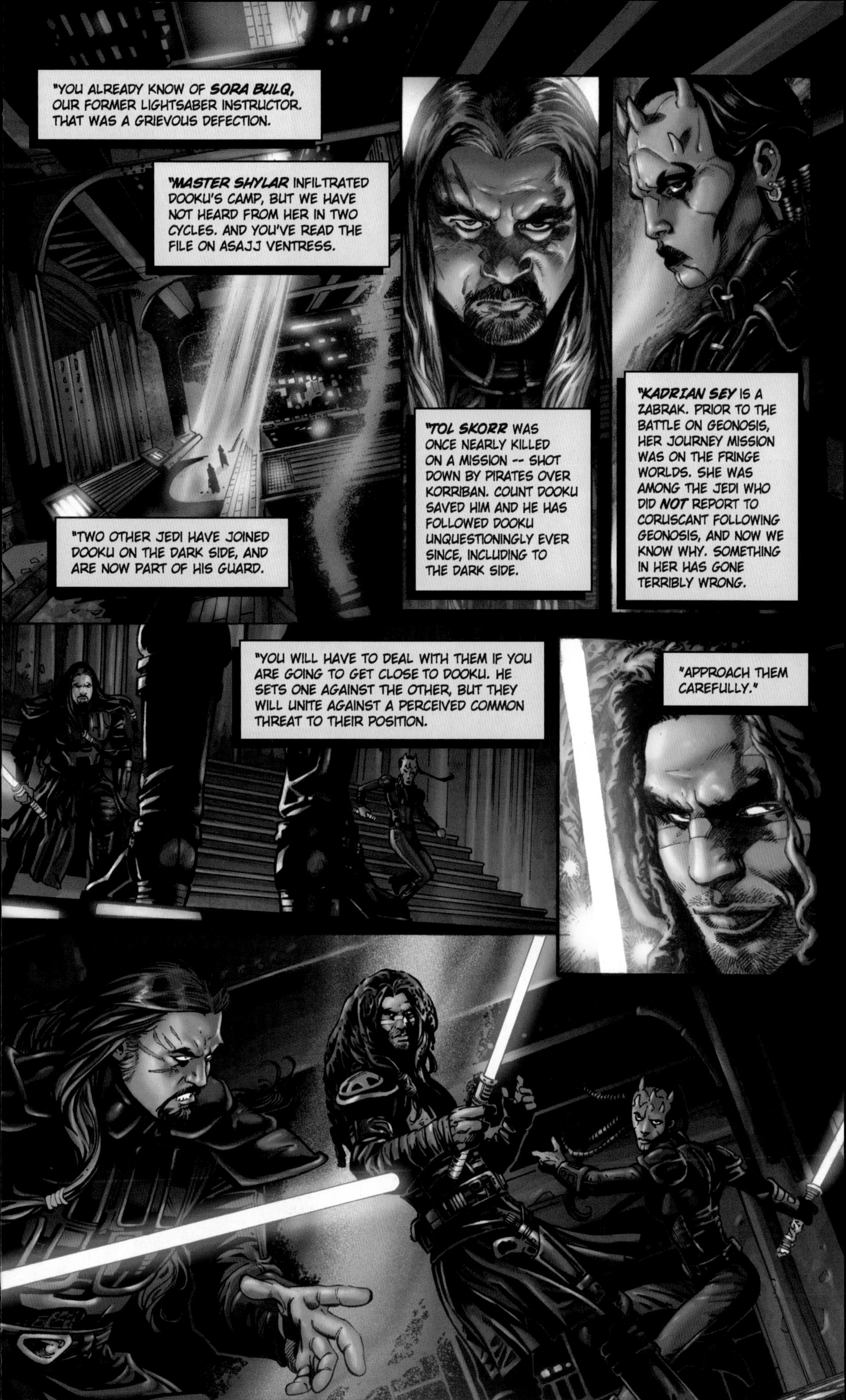
"YOU ALREADY KNOW OF SORA BULQ, OUR FORMER LIGHTSABER INSTRUCTOR. THAT WAS A GRIEVOUS DEFECTION.
"MASTER SHYLAR INFILTRATED DOOKU'S CAMP, BUT WE HAVE NOT HEARD FROM HER IN TWO CYCLES. AND YOU'VE READ THE FILE ON ASAJJ VENTRESS.
"TWO OTHER JEDI HAVE JOINED DOOKU ON THE DARK SIDE, AND ARE NOW PART OF HIS GUARD.
"TOL SKORR WAS ONCE NEARLY KILLED ON A MISSION -- SHOT DOWN BY PIRATES OVER KORRIBAN. COUNT DOOKU SAVED HIM AND HE HAS FOLLOWED DOOKU UNQUESTIONINGLY EVER SINCE, INCLUDING TO THE DARK SIDE.
"KADRIAN SEY IS A ZABRAK. PRIOR TO THE BATTLE ON GEONOSIS, HER JOURNEY MISSION WAS ON THE FRINGE WORLDS. SHE WAS AMONG THE JEDI WHO DID NOT REPORT TO CORUSCANT FOLLOWING GEONOSIS, AND NOW WE KNOW WHY. SOMETHING IN HER HAS GONE TERRIBLY WRONG.
"YOU WILL HAVE TO DEAL WITH THEM IF YOU ARE GOING TO GET CLOSE TO DOOKU. HE SETS ONE AGAINST THE OTHER, BUT THEY WILL UNITE AGAINST A PERCEIVED COMMON THREAT TO THEIR POSITION.
"APPROACH THEM CAREFULLY."

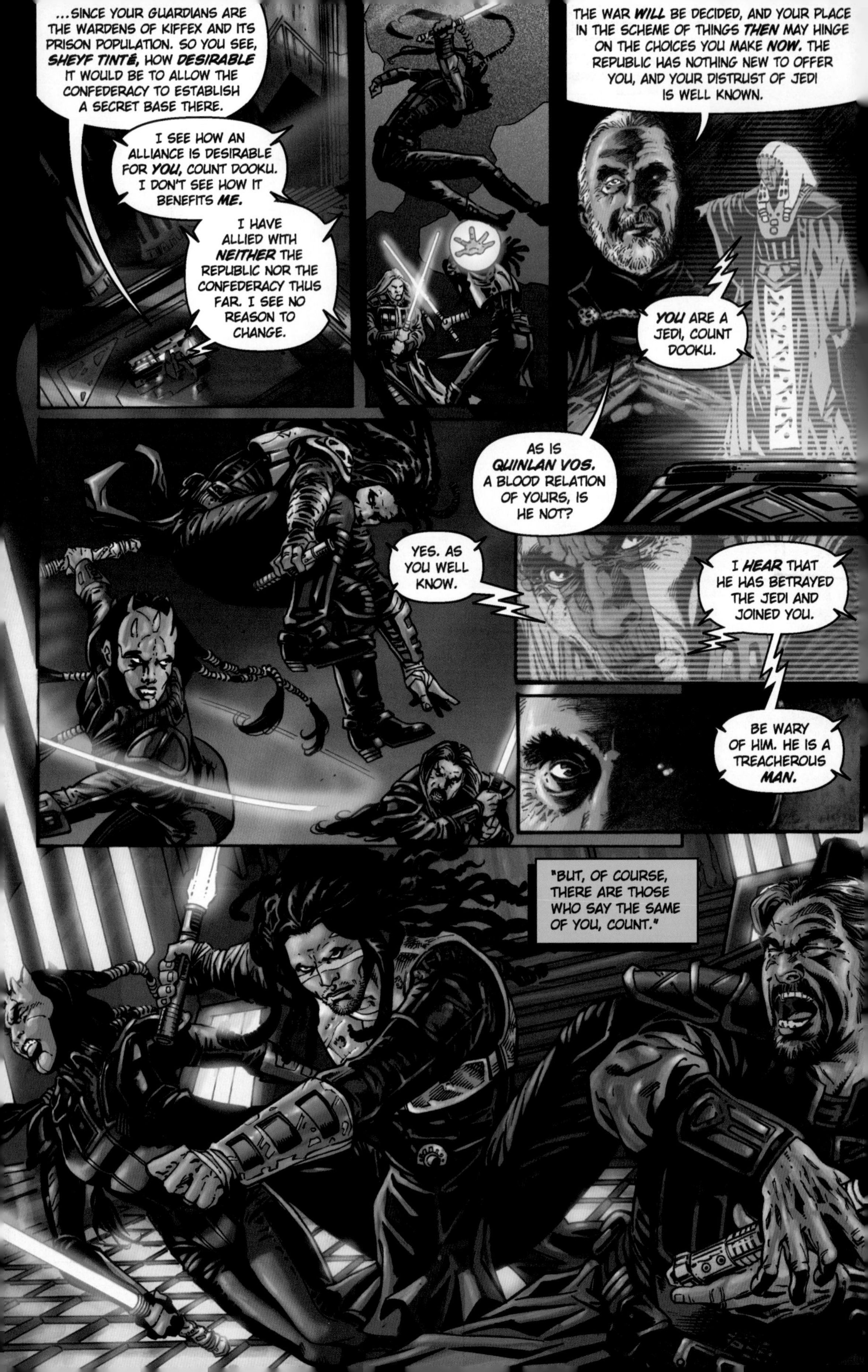
...SINCE YOUR GUARDIANS ARE THE WARDENS OF KIFFEX AND ITS PRISON POPULATION. SO YOU SEE, *SHEYF TINTÉ*, HOW *DESIRABLE* IT WOULD BE TO ALLOW THE CONFEDERACY TO ESTABLISH A SECRET BASE THERE.
I SEE HOW AN ALLIANCE IS DESIRABLE FOR *YOU*, COUNT DOOKU. I DON'T SEE HOW IT BENEFITS *ME.*
I HAVE ALLIED WITH *NEITHER* THE REPUBLIC NOR THE CONFEDERACY THUS FAR. I SEE NO REASON TO CHANGE.
THE WAR *WILL* BE DECIDED, AND YOUR PLACE IN THE SCHEME OF THINGS *THEN* MAY HINGE ON THE CHOICES YOU MAKE *NOW.* THE REPUBLIC HAS NOTHING NEW TO OFFER YOU, AND YOUR DISTRUST OF JEDI IS WELL KNOWN.
YOU ARE A JEDI, COUNT DOOKU.
AS IS *QUINLAN VOS.* A BLOOD RELATION OF YOURS, IS HE NOT?
YES. AS YOU WELL KNOW.
I *HEAR* THAT HE HAS BETRAYED THE JEDI AND JOINED YOU.
BE WARY OF HIM. HE IS A TREACHEROUS *MAN.*
"BUT, OF COURSE, THERE ARE THOSE WHO SAY THE SAME OF YOU, COUNT."

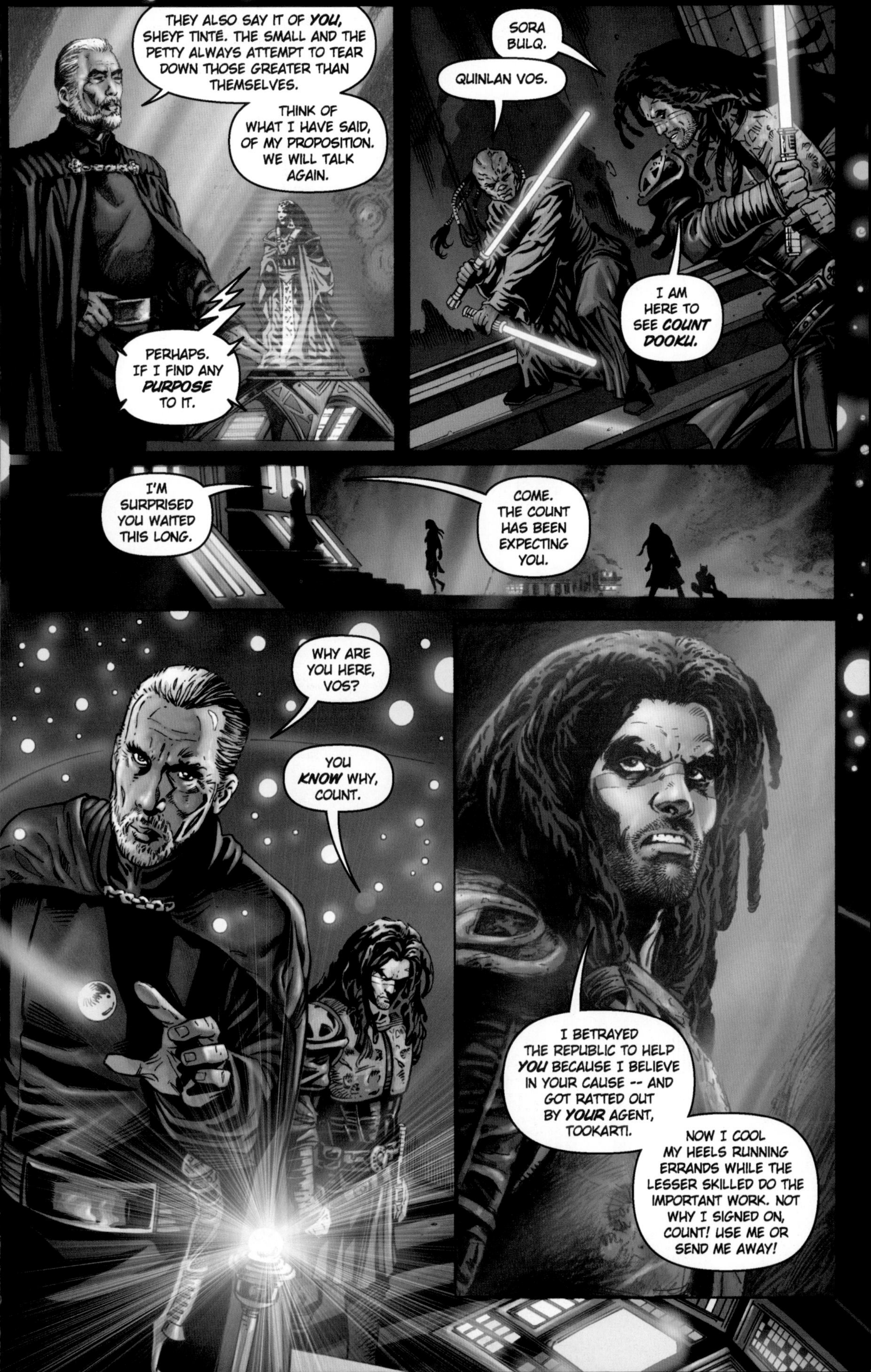
THEY ALSO SAY IT OF YOU, SHEYF TINTÉ. THE SMALL AND THE PETTY ALWAYS ATTEMPT TO TEAR DOWN THOSE GREATER THAN THEMSELVES.
THINK OF WHAT I HAVE SAID, OF MY PROPOSITION. WE WILL TALK AGAIN.
PERHAPS. IF I FIND ANY PURPOSE TO IT.
SORA BULQ.
QUINLAN VOS.
I AM HERE TO SEE COUNT DOOKU.
I'M SURPRISED YOU WAITED THIS LONG.
COME. THE COUNT HAS BEEN EXPECTING YOU.
WHY ARE YOU HERE, VOS?
YOU KNOW WHY, COUNT.
I BETRAYED THE REPUBLIC TO HELP YOU BECAUSE I BELIEVE IN YOUR CAUSE -- AND GOT RATTED OUT BY YOUR AGENT, TOOKARTI.
NOW I COOL MY HEELS RUNNING ERRANDS WHILE THE LESSER SKILLED DO THE IMPORTANT WORK. NOT WHY I SIGNED ON, COUNT! USE ME OR SEND ME AWAY!

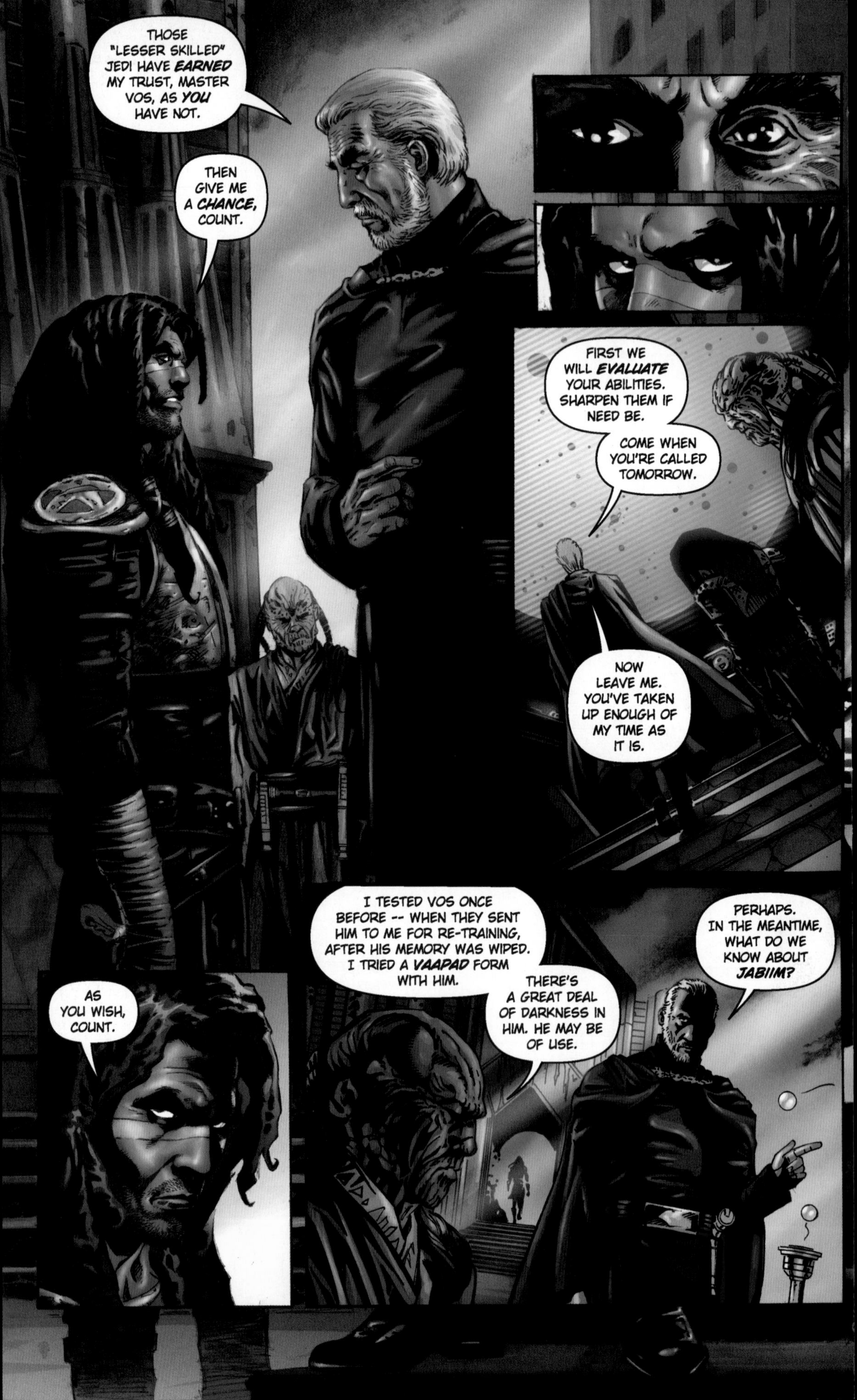
THOSE "LESSER SKILLED" JEDI HAVE EARNED MY TRUST, MASTER VOS, AS YOU HAVE NOT.
THEN GIVE ME A CHANCE, COUNT.
FIRST WE WILL EVALUATE YOUR ABILITIES. SHARPEN THEM IF NEED BE.
COME WHEN YOU'RE CALLED TOMORROW.
NOW LEAVE ME. YOU'VE TAKEN UP ENOUGH OF MY TIME AS IT IS.
AS YOU WISH, COUNT.
I TESTED VOS ONCE BEFORE -- WHEN THEY SENT HIM TO ME FOR RE-TRAINING, AFTER HIS MEMORY WAS WIPED. I TRIED A VAAPAD FORM WITH HIM.
THERE'S A GREAT DEAL OF DARKNESS IN HIM. HE MAY BE OF USE.
PERHAPS. IN THE MEANTIME, WHAT DO WE KNOW ABOUT JABIIM?

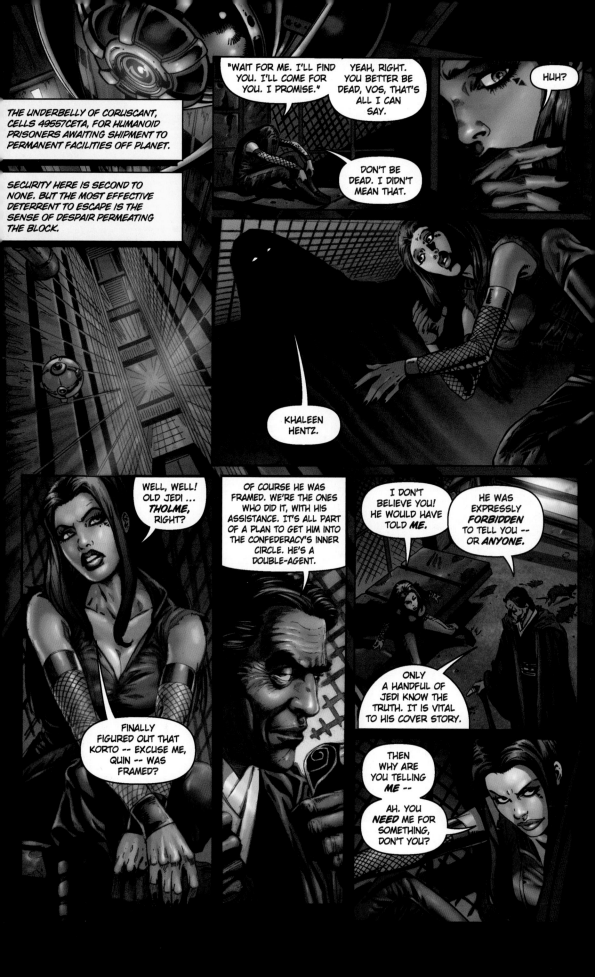

THE UNDERBELLY OF CORUSCANT, CELLS 49557CETA, FOR HUMANOID PRISONERS AWAITING SHIPMENT TO PERMANENT FACILITIES OFF PLANET.

SECURITY HERE IS SECOND TO NONE. BUT THE MOST EFFECTIVE DETERRENT TO ESCAPE IS THE SENSE OF DESPAIR PERMEATING THE BLOCK.

"WAIT FOR ME. I'LL FIND YOU. I'LL COME FOR YOU. I PROMISE."

YEAH, RIGHT. YOU BETTER BE DEAD, VOS, THAT'S ALL I CAN SAY.

DON'T BE DEAD. I DIDN'T MEAN THAT.

HUH?

KHALEEN HENTZ.

WELL, WELL! OLD JEDI ... *THOLME*, RIGHT?

FINALLY FIGURED OUT THAT KORTO -- EXCUSE ME, QUIN -- WAS FRAMED?

OF COURSE HE WAS FRAMED. WE'RE THE ONES WHO DID IT, WITH HIS ASSISTANCE. IT'S ALL PART OF A PLAN TO GET HIM INTO THE CONFEDERACY'S INNER CIRCLE. HE'S A DOUBLE-AGENT.

I DON'T BELIEVE YOU! HE WOULD HAVE TOLD *ME*.

HE WAS EXPRESSLY *FORBIDDEN* TO TELL YOU -- OR *ANYONE*.

ONLY A HANDFUL OF JEDI KNOW THE TRUTH. IT IS VITAL TO HIS COVER STORY.

THEN WHY ARE YOU TELLING *ME* --

AH. YOU *NEED* ME FOR SOMETHING, DON'T YOU?

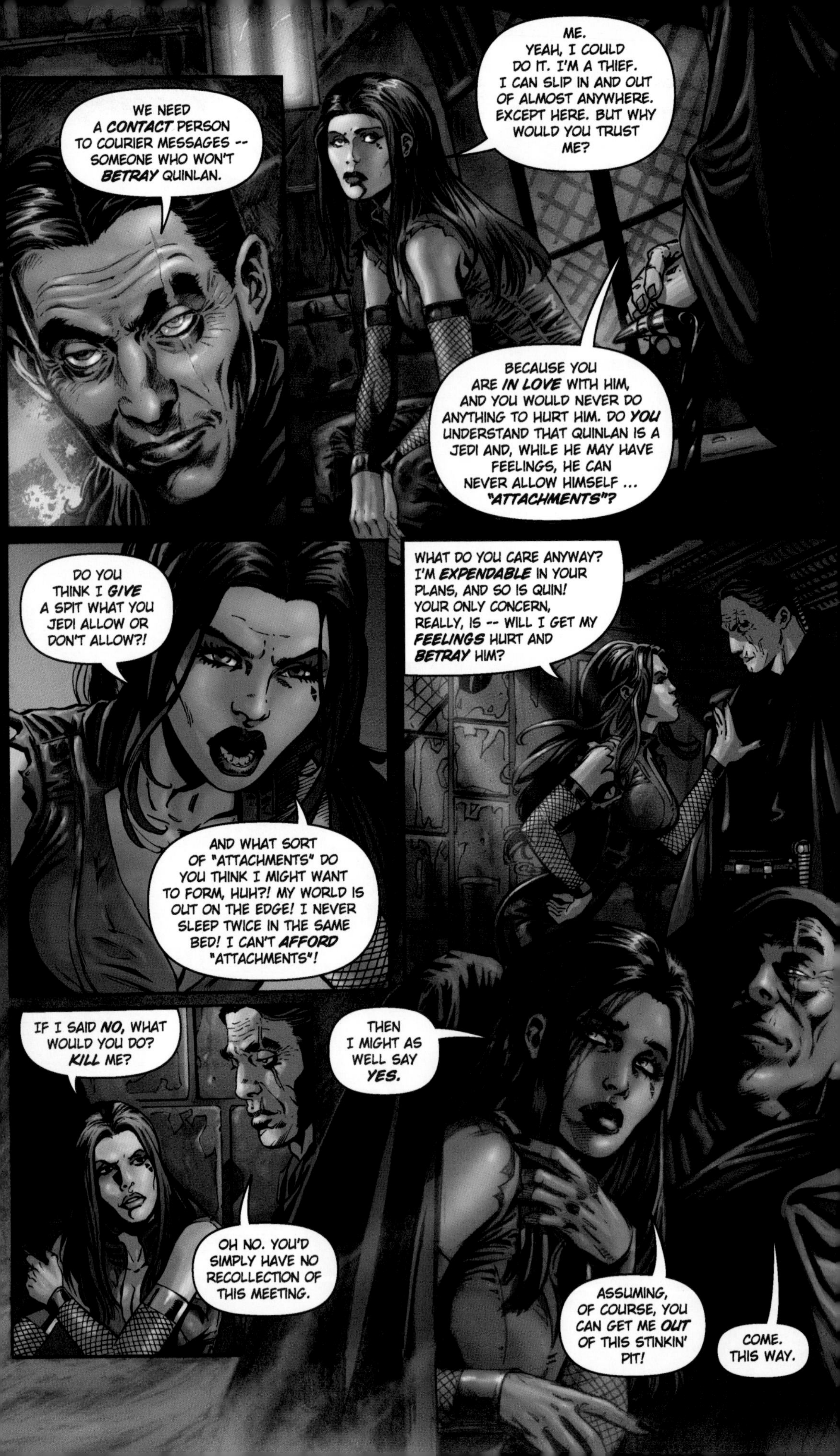
WE NEED A CONTACT PERSON TO COURIER MESSAGES -- SOMEONE WHO WON'T BETRAY QUINLAN.
ME. YEAH, I COULD DO IT. I'M A THIEF. I CAN SLIP IN AND OUT OF ALMOST ANYWHERE. EXCEPT HERE. BUT WHY WOULD YOU TRUST ME?
BECAUSE YOU ARE IN LOVE WITH HIM, AND YOU WOULD NEVER DO ANYTHING TO HURT HIM. DO YOU UNDERSTAND THAT QUINLAN IS A JEDI AND, WHILE HE MAY HAVE FEELINGS, HE CAN NEVER ALLOW HIMSELF ... "ATTACHMENTS"?
DO YOU THINK I GIVE A SPIT WHAT YOU JEDI ALLOW OR DON'T ALLOW?!
AND WHAT SORT OF "ATTACHMENTS" DO YOU THINK I MIGHT WANT TO FORM, HUH?! MY WORLD IS OUT ON THE EDGE! I NEVER SLEEP TWICE IN THE SAME BED! I CAN'T AFFORD "ATTACHMENTS"!
WHAT DO YOU CARE ANYWAY? I'M EXPENDABLE IN YOUR PLANS, AND SO IS QUIN! YOUR ONLY CONCERN, REALLY, IS -- WILL I GET MY FEELINGS HURT AND BETRAY HIM?
IF I SAID NO, WHAT WOULD YOU DO? KILL ME?
OH NO. YOU'D SIMPLY HAVE NO RECOLLECTION OF THIS MEETING.
THEN I MIGHT AS WELL SAY YES.
ASSUMING, OF COURSE, YOU CAN GET ME OUT OF THIS STINKIN' PIT!
COME. THIS WAY.

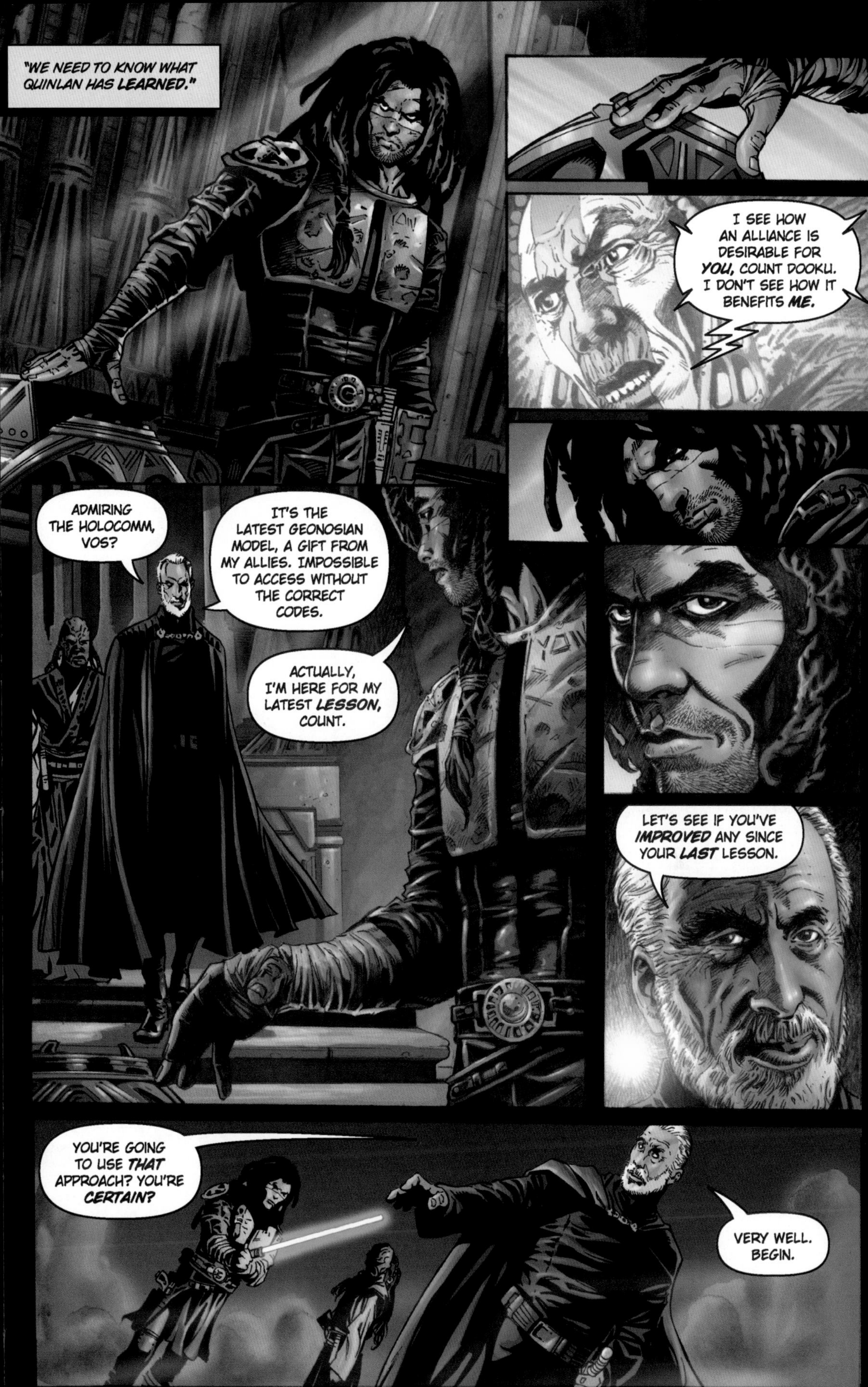
"WE NEED TO KNOW WHAT QUINLAN HAS LEARNED."
I SEE HOW AN ALLIANCE IS DESIRABLE FOR YOU, COUNT DOOKU. I DON'T SEE HOW IT BENEFITS ME.
ADMIRING THE HOLOCOMM, VOS?
IT'S THE LATEST GEONOSIAN MODEL, A GIFT FROM MY ALLIES. IMPOSSIBLE TO ACCESS WITHOUT THE CORRECT CODES.
ACTUALLY, I'M HERE FOR MY LATEST LESSON, COUNT.
LET'S SEE IF YOU'VE IMPROVED ANY SINCE YOUR LAST LESSON.
YOU'RE GOING TO USE THAT APPROACH? YOU'RE CERTAIN?
VERY WELL. BEGIN.

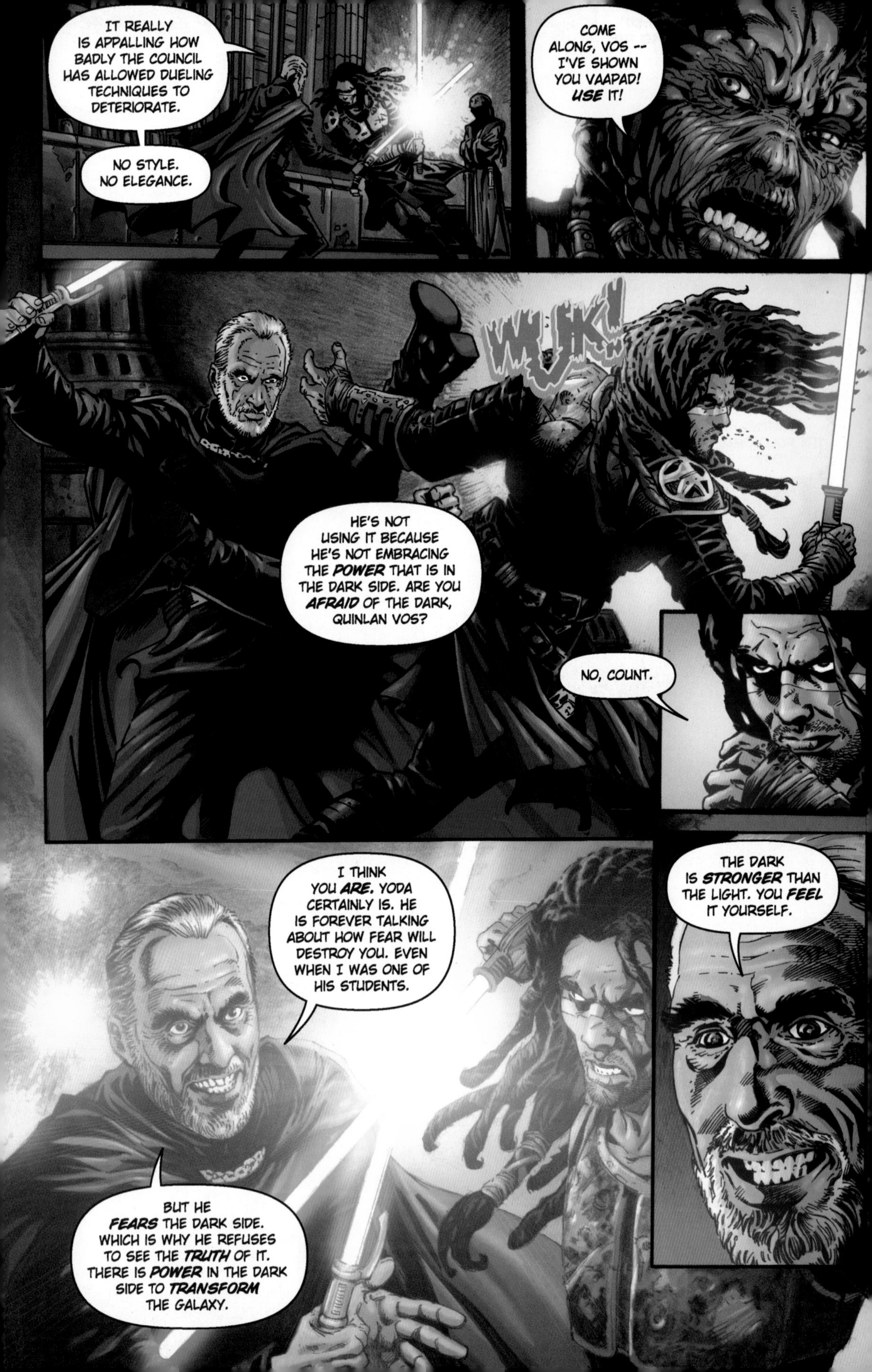

IT REALLY IS APPALLING HOW BADLY THE COUNCIL HAS ALLOWED DUELING TECHNIQUES TO DETERIORATE.
NO STYLE. NO ELEGANCE.
COME ALONG, VOS -- I'VE SHOWN YOU VAAPAD! USE IT!
WUK!!
HE'S NOT USING IT BECAUSE HE'S NOT EMBRACING THE POWER THAT IS IN THE DARK SIDE. ARE YOU AFRAID OF THE DARK, QUINLAN VOS?
NO, COUNT.
I THINK YOU ARE. YODA CERTAINLY IS. HE IS FOREVER TALKING ABOUT HOW FEAR WILL DESTROY YOU. EVEN WHEN I WAS ONE OF HIS STUDENTS.
BUT HE FEARS THE DARK SIDE. WHICH IS WHY HE REFUSES TO SEE THE TRUTH OF IT. THERE IS POWER IN THE DARK SIDE TO TRANSFORM THE GALAXY.
THE DARK IS STRONGER THAN THE LIGHT. YOU FEEL IT YOURSELF.

YOU, QUINLAN VOS, HAVE TRAVELED THE GALAXY RECENTLY AS YODA HAS *NOT.* YOU HAVE SEEN THE *SHAM* THE REPUBLIC HAS BECOME.

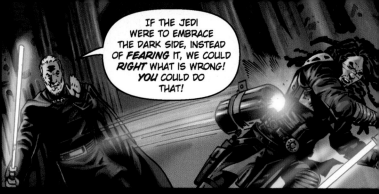

IF THE JEDI WERE TO EMBRACE THE DARK SIDE, INSTEAD OF *FEARING* IT, WE COULD *RIGHT* WHAT IS WRONG! *YOU* COULD DO THAT!

QUI-GON JINN WAS MY PADAWAN. HE *OFTEN* DEFIED THE COUNCIL, AND *PAID* FOR IT! IF HE HAD LIVED, HE WOULD BE AT MY SIDE *NOW!*

BUT THE COUNCIL CAUSED HIS DEATH BY INVOLVING HIM IN THE WEB OF *POLITICS* STRANGLING THE REPUBLIC.

YOU *KNOW* THIS TO BE TRUE, QUINLAN VOS! WHY WON'T YOU *DO* SOMETHING *ABOUT* IT?!

YAAAH!

BETTER.

VERY WELL, MASTER VOS, PREPARE YOUR SHIP. I WANT YOU TO JOIN ME.

WHAM!

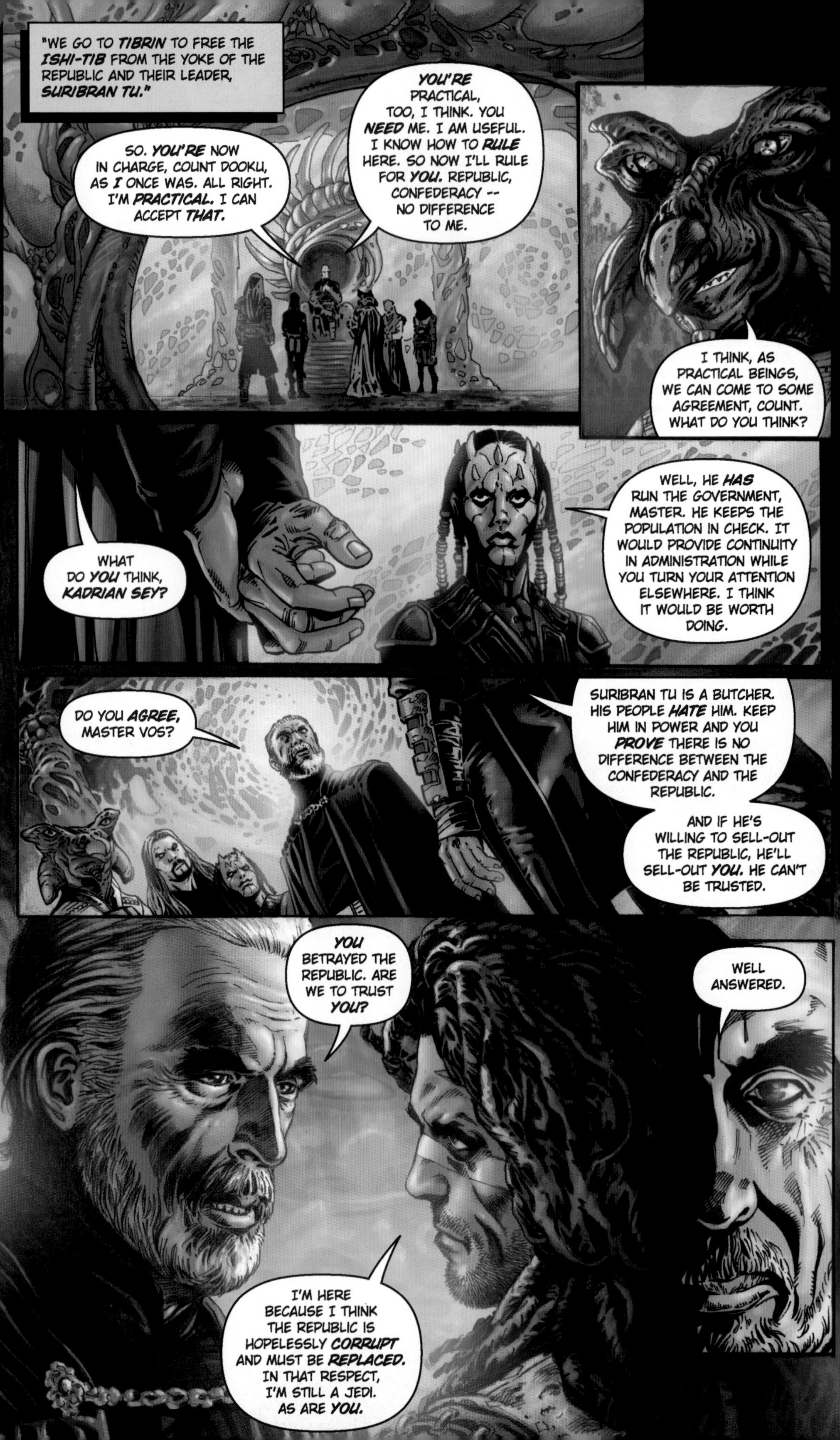
"WE GO TO TIBRIN TO FREE THE ISHI-TIB FROM THE YOKE OF THE REPUBLIC AND THEIR LEADER, SURIBRAN TU."
SO. YOU'RE NOW IN CHARGE, COUNT DOOKU, AS I ONCE WAS. ALL RIGHT. I'M PRACTICAL. I CAN ACCEPT THAT.
YOU'RE PRACTICAL, TOO, I THINK. YOU NEED ME. I AM USEFUL. I KNOW HOW TO RULE HERE. SO NOW I'LL RULE FOR YOU. REPUBLIC, CONFEDERACY -- NO DIFFERENCE TO ME.
I THINK, AS PRACTICAL BEINGS, WE CAN COME TO SOME AGREEMENT, COUNT. WHAT DO YOU THINK?
WHAT DO YOU THINK, KADRIAN SEY?
WELL, HE HAS RUN THE GOVERNMENT, MASTER. HE KEEPS THE POPULATION IN CHECK. IT WOULD PROVIDE CONTINUITY IN ADMINISTRATION WHILE YOU TURN YOUR ATTENTION ELSEWHERE. I THINK IT WOULD BE WORTH DOING.
DO YOU AGREE, MASTER VOS?
SURIBRAN TU IS A BUTCHER. HIS PEOPLE HATE HIM. KEEP HIM IN POWER AND YOU PROVE THERE IS NO DIFFERENCE BETWEEN THE CONFEDERACY AND THE REPUBLIC.
AND IF HE'S WILLING TO SELL-OUT THE REPUBLIC, HE'LL SELL-OUT YOU. HE CAN'T BE TRUSTED.
YOU BETRAYED THE REPUBLIC. ARE WE TO TRUST YOU?
I'M HERE BECAUSE I THINK THE REPUBLIC IS HOPELESSLY CORRUPT AND MUST BE REPLACED. IN THAT RESPECT, I'M STILL A JEDI. AS ARE YOU.
WELL ANSWERED.

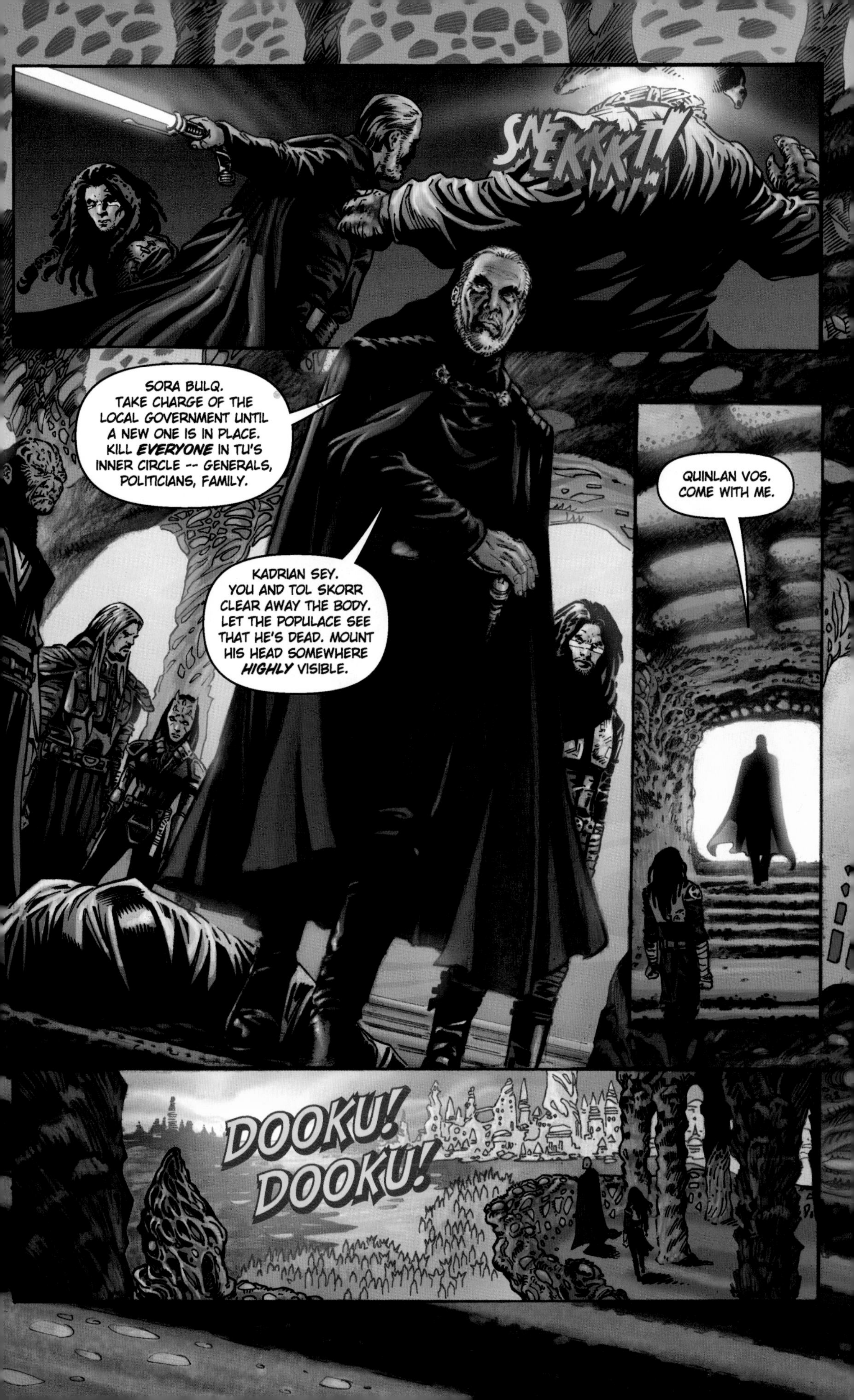
SNEKKKT!
SORA BULQ. TAKE CHARGE OF THE LOCAL GOVERNMENT UNTIL A NEW ONE IS IN PLACE. KILL EVERYONE IN TU'S INNER CIRCLE -- GENERALS, POLITICIANS, FAMILY.
KADRIAN SEY. YOU AND TOL SKORR CLEAR AWAY THE BODY. LET THE POPULACE SEE THAT HE'S DEAD. MOUNT HIS HEAD SOMEWHERE HIGHLY VISIBLE.
QUINLAN VOS. COME WITH ME.
DOOKU! DOOKU!

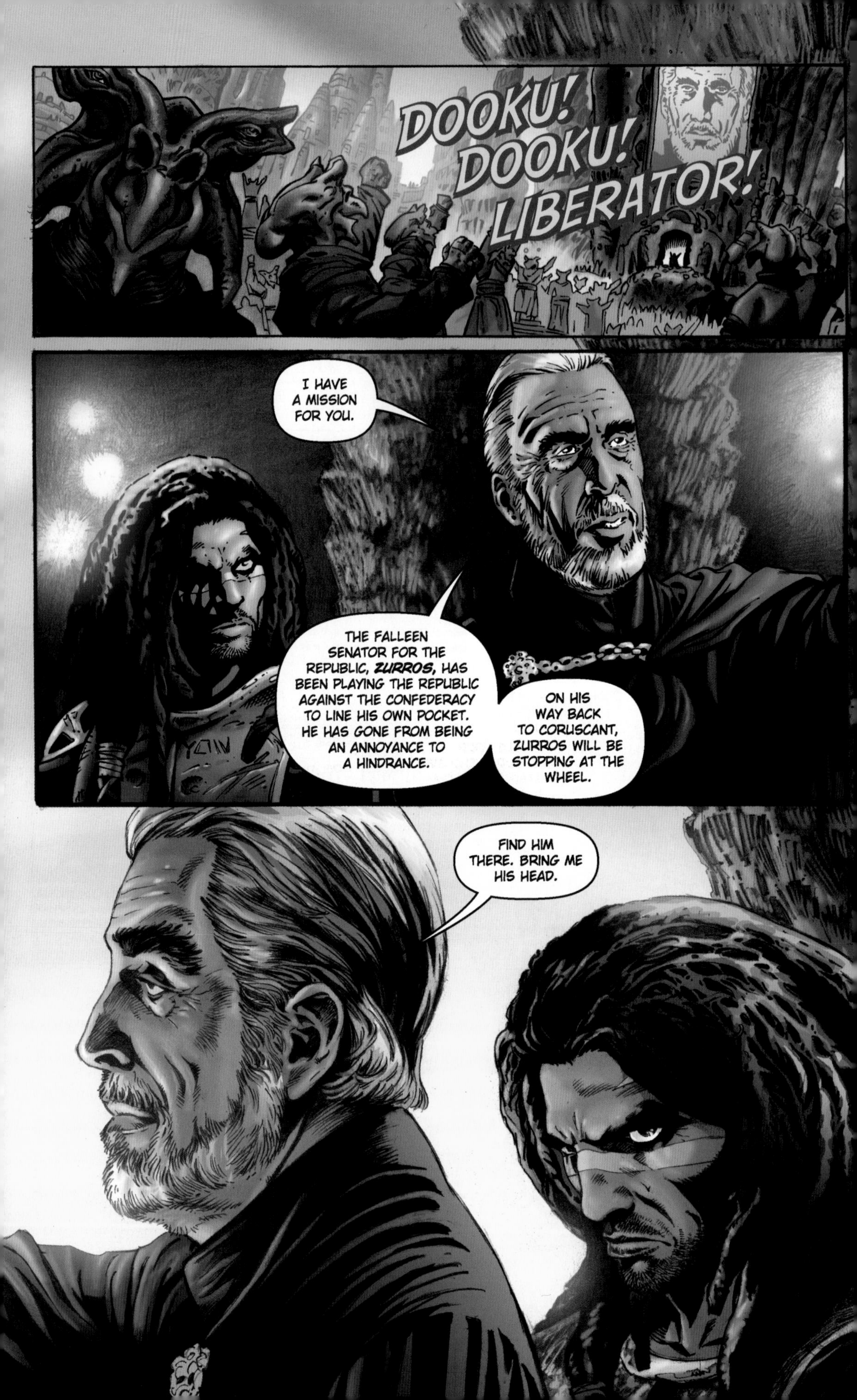
DOOKU! DOOKU! LIBERATOR!
I HAVE A MISSION FOR YOU.
THE FALLEEN SENATOR FOR THE REPUBLIC, ZURROS, HAS BEEN PLAYING THE REPUBLIC AGAINST THE CONFEDERACY TO LINE HIS OWN POCKET. HE HAS GONE FROM BEING AN ANNOYANCE TO A HINDRANCE.
ON HIS WAY BACK TO CORUSCANT, ZURROS WILL BE STOPPING AT THE WHEEL.
FIND HIM THERE. BRING ME HIS HEAD.

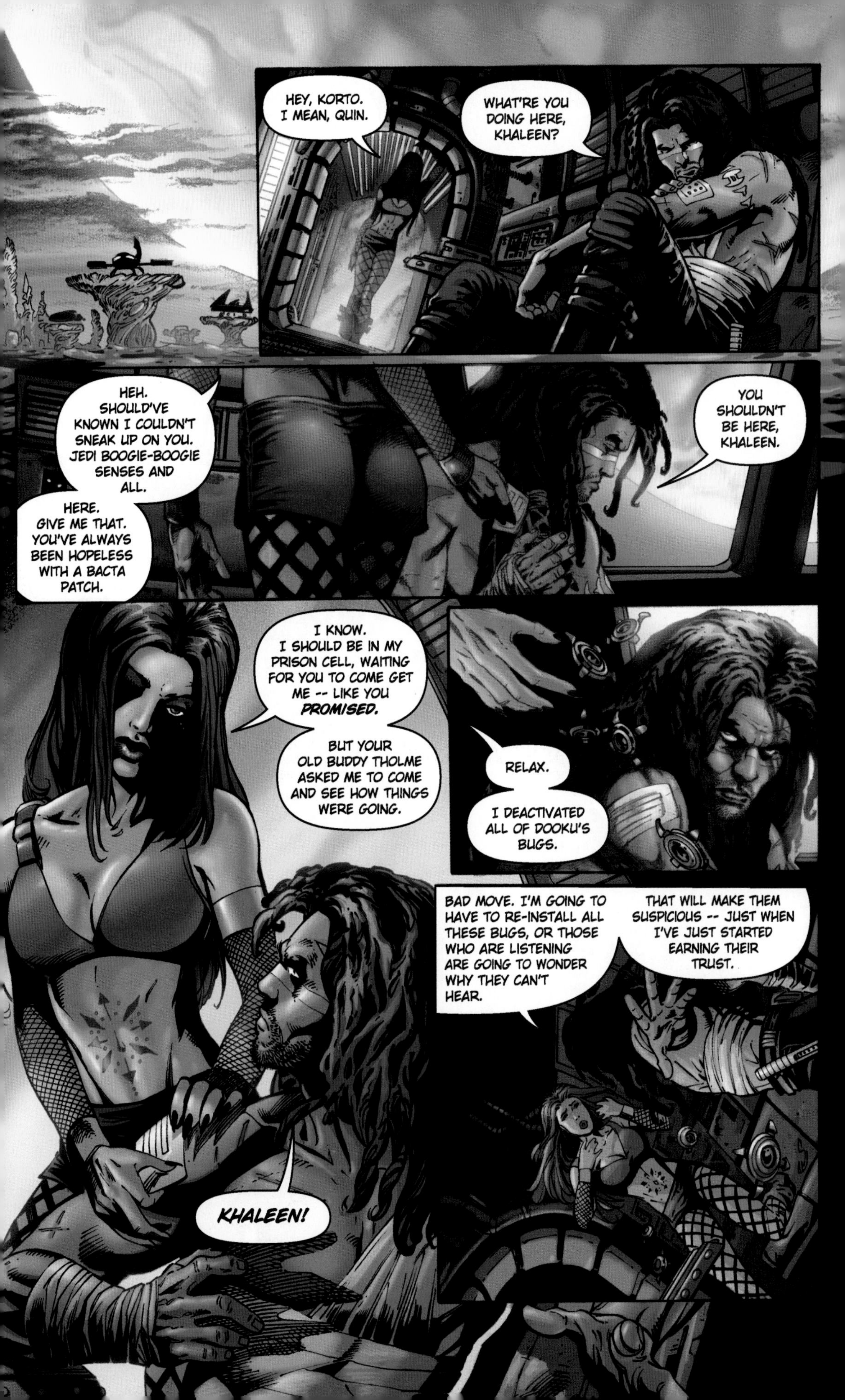
HEY, KORTO. I MEAN, QUIN.
WHAT'RE YOU DOING HERE, KHALEEN?
HEH. SHOULD'VE KNOWN I COULDN'T SNEAK UP ON YOU. JEDI BOOGIE-BOOGIE SENSES AND ALL.
HERE. GIVE ME THAT. YOU'VE ALWAYS BEEN HOPELESS WITH A BACTA PATCH.
YOU SHOULDN'T BE HERE, KHALEEN.
I KNOW. I SHOULD BE IN MY PRISON CELL, WAITING FOR YOU TO COME GET ME -- LIKE YOU PROMISED.
BUT YOUR OLD BUDDY THOLME ASKED ME TO COME AND SEE HOW THINGS WERE GOING.
RELAX.
I DEACTIVATED ALL OF DOOKU'S BUGS.
BAD MOVE. I'M GOING TO HAVE TO RE-INSTALL ALL THESE BUGS, OR THOSE WHO ARE LISTENING ARE GOING TO WONDER WHY THEY CAN'T HEAR.
THAT WILL MAKE THEM SUSPICIOUS -- JUST WHEN I'VE JUST STARTED EARNING THEIR TRUST.
KHALEEN!

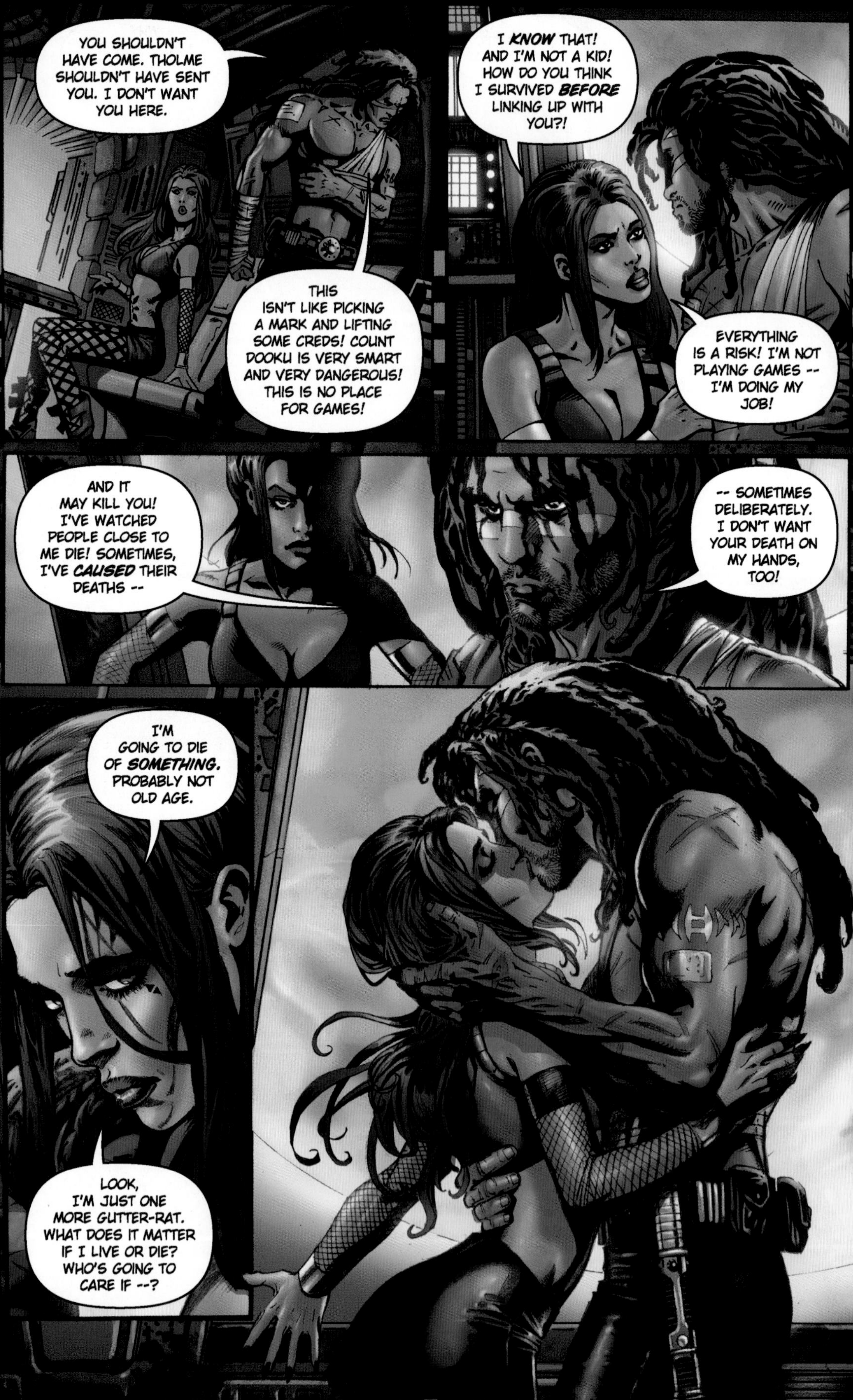
YOU SHOULDN'T HAVE COME. THOLME SHOULDN'T HAVE SENT YOU. I DON'T WANT YOU HERE.
THIS ISN'T LIKE PICKING A MARK AND LIFTING SOME CREDS! COUNT DOOKU IS VERY SMART AND VERY DANGEROUS! THIS IS NO PLACE FOR GAMES!
I KNOW THAT! AND I'M NOT A KID! HOW DO YOU THINK I SURVIVED BEFORE LINKING UP WITH YOU?!
EVERYTHING IS A RISK! I'M NOT PLAYING GAMES -- I'M DOING MY JOB!
AND IT MAY KILL YOU! I'VE WATCHED PEOPLE CLOSE TO ME DIE! SOMETIMES, I'VE CAUSED THEIR DEATHS --
-- SOMETIMES DELIBERATELY. I DON'T WANT YOUR DEATH ON MY HANDS, TOO!
I'M GOING TO DIE OF SOMETHING. PROBABLY NOT OLD AGE.
LOOK, I'M JUST ONE MORE GUTTER-RAT. WHAT DOES IT MATTER IF I LIVE OR DIE? WHO'S GOING TO CARE IF --?

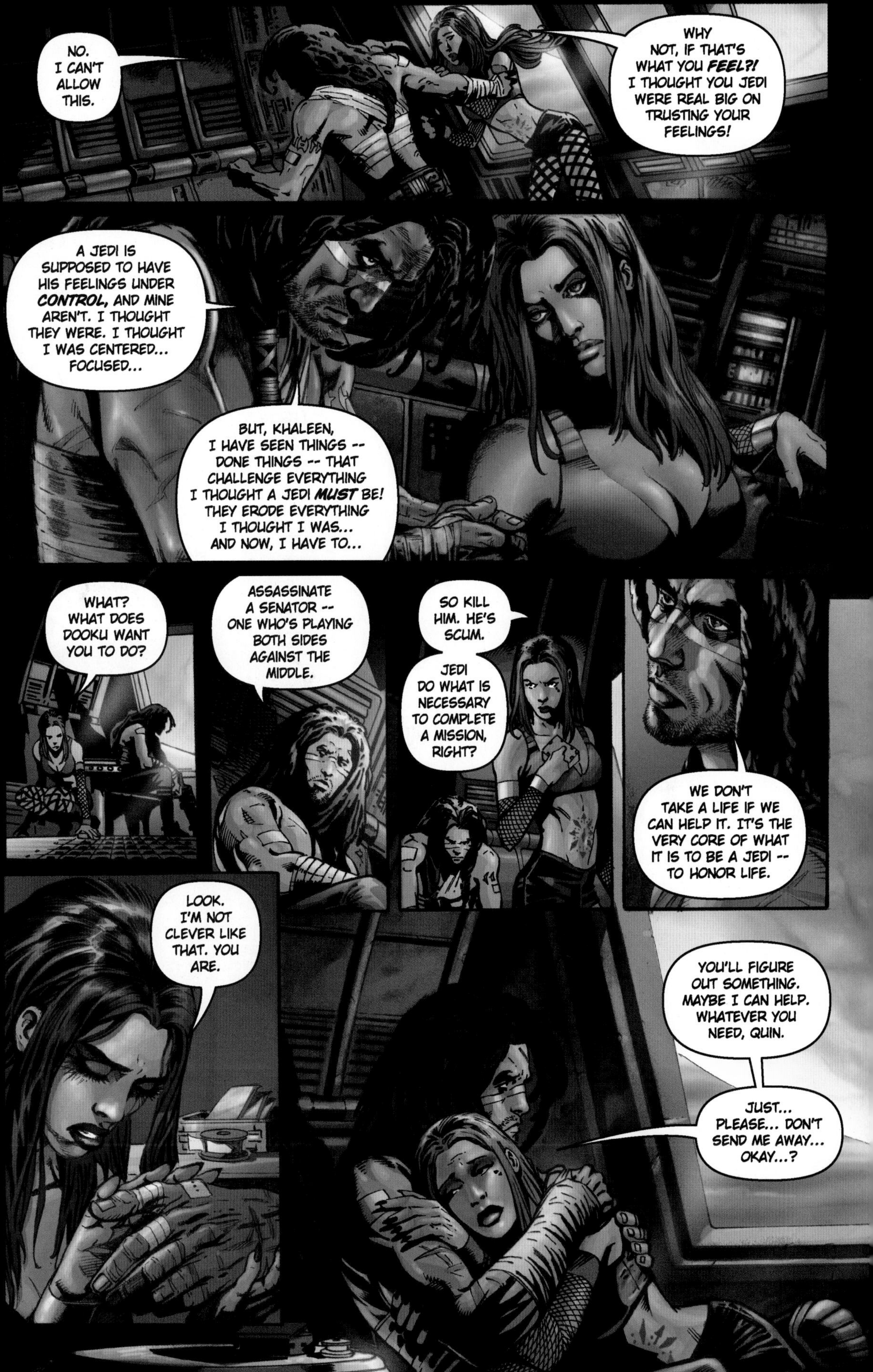
NO. I CAN'T ALLOW THIS.
WHY NOT, IF THAT'S WHAT YOU *FEEL?!* I THOUGHT YOU JEDI WERE REAL BIG ON TRUSTING YOUR FEELINGS!
A JEDI IS SUPPOSED TO HAVE HIS FEELINGS UNDER *CONTROL,* AND MINE AREN'T. I THOUGHT THEY WERE. I THOUGHT I WAS CENTERED... FOCUSED...
BUT, KHALEEN, I HAVE SEEN THINGS -- DONE THINGS -- THAT CHALLENGE EVERYTHING I THOUGHT A JEDI *MUST* BE! THEY ERODE EVERYTHING I THOUGHT I WAS... AND NOW, I HAVE TO...
WHAT? WHAT DOES DOOKU WANT YOU TO DO?
ASSASSINATE A SENATOR -- ONE WHO'S PLAYING BOTH SIDES AGAINST THE MIDDLE.
SO KILL HIM. HE'S SCUM.
JEDI DO WHAT IS NECESSARY TO COMPLETE A MISSION, RIGHT?
WE DON'T TAKE A LIFE IF WE CAN HELP IT. IT'S THE VERY CORE OF WHAT IT IS TO BE A JEDI -- TO HONOR LIFE.
LOOK. I'M NOT CLEVER LIKE THAT. YOU ARE.
YOU'LL FIGURE OUT SOMETHING. MAYBE I CAN HELP. WHATEVER YOU NEED, QUIN.
JUST... PLEASE... DON'T SEND ME AWAY... OKAY...?

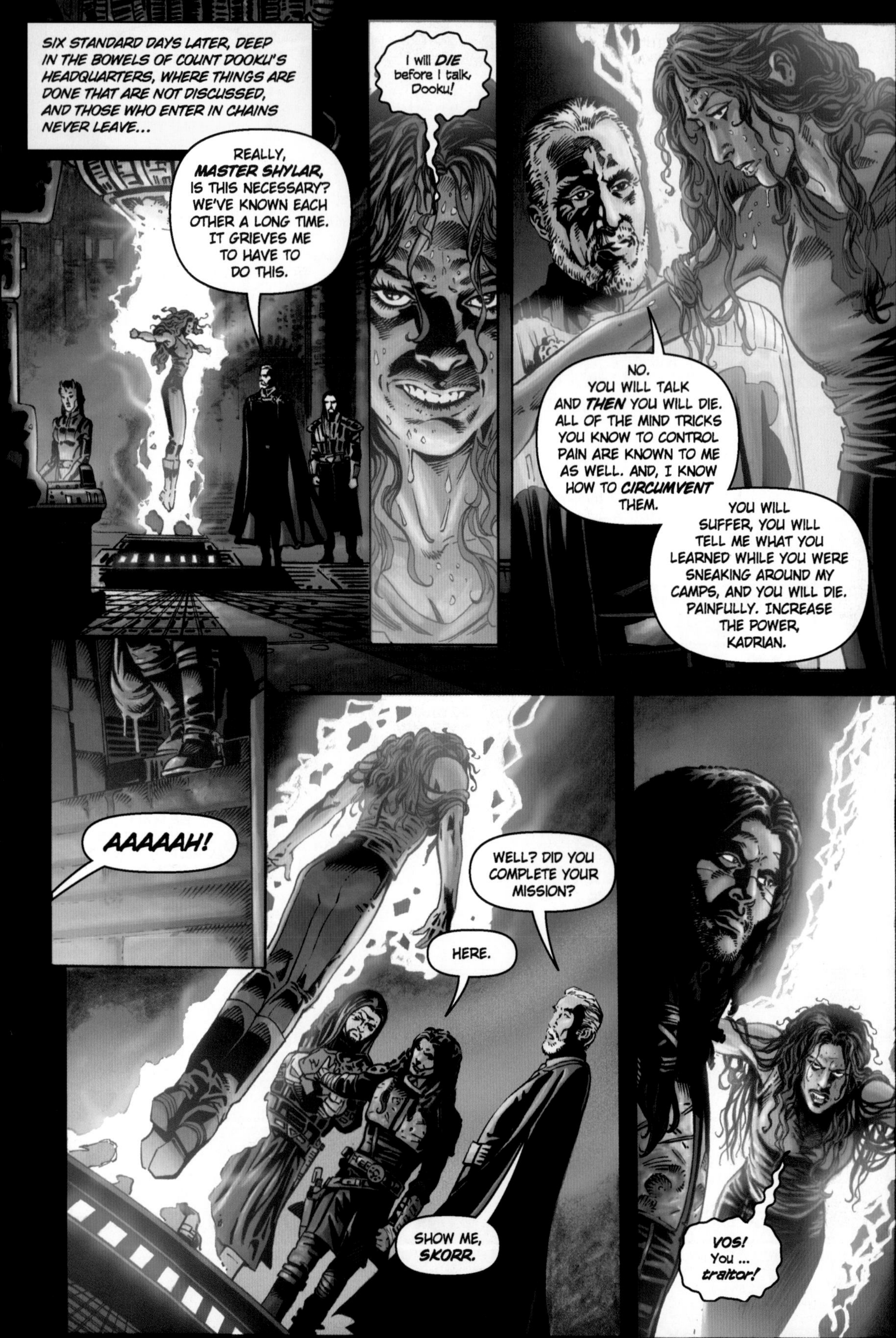
SIX STANDARD DAYS LATER, DEEP IN THE BOWELS OF COUNT DOOKU'S HEADQUARTERS, WHERE THINGS ARE DONE THAT ARE NOT DISCUSSED, AND THOSE WHO ENTER IN CHAINS NEVER LEAVE...
REALLY, MASTER SHYLAR, IS THIS NECESSARY? WE'VE KNOWN EACH OTHER A LONG TIME. IT GRIEVES ME TO HAVE TO DO THIS.
I will DIE before I talk, Dooku!
NO. YOU WILL TALK AND THEN YOU WILL DIE. ALL OF THE MIND TRICKS YOU KNOW TO CONTROL PAIN ARE KNOWN TO ME AS WELL. AND, I KNOW HOW TO CIRCUMVENT THEM.
YOU WILL SUFFER, YOU WILL TELL ME WHAT YOU LEARNED WHILE YOU WERE SNEAKING AROUND MY CAMPS, AND YOU WILL DIE. PAINFULLY. INCREASE THE POWER, KADRIAN.
AAAAAH!
WELL? DID YOU COMPLETE YOUR MISSION?
HERE.
SHOW ME, SKORR.
VOS! You ... traitor!

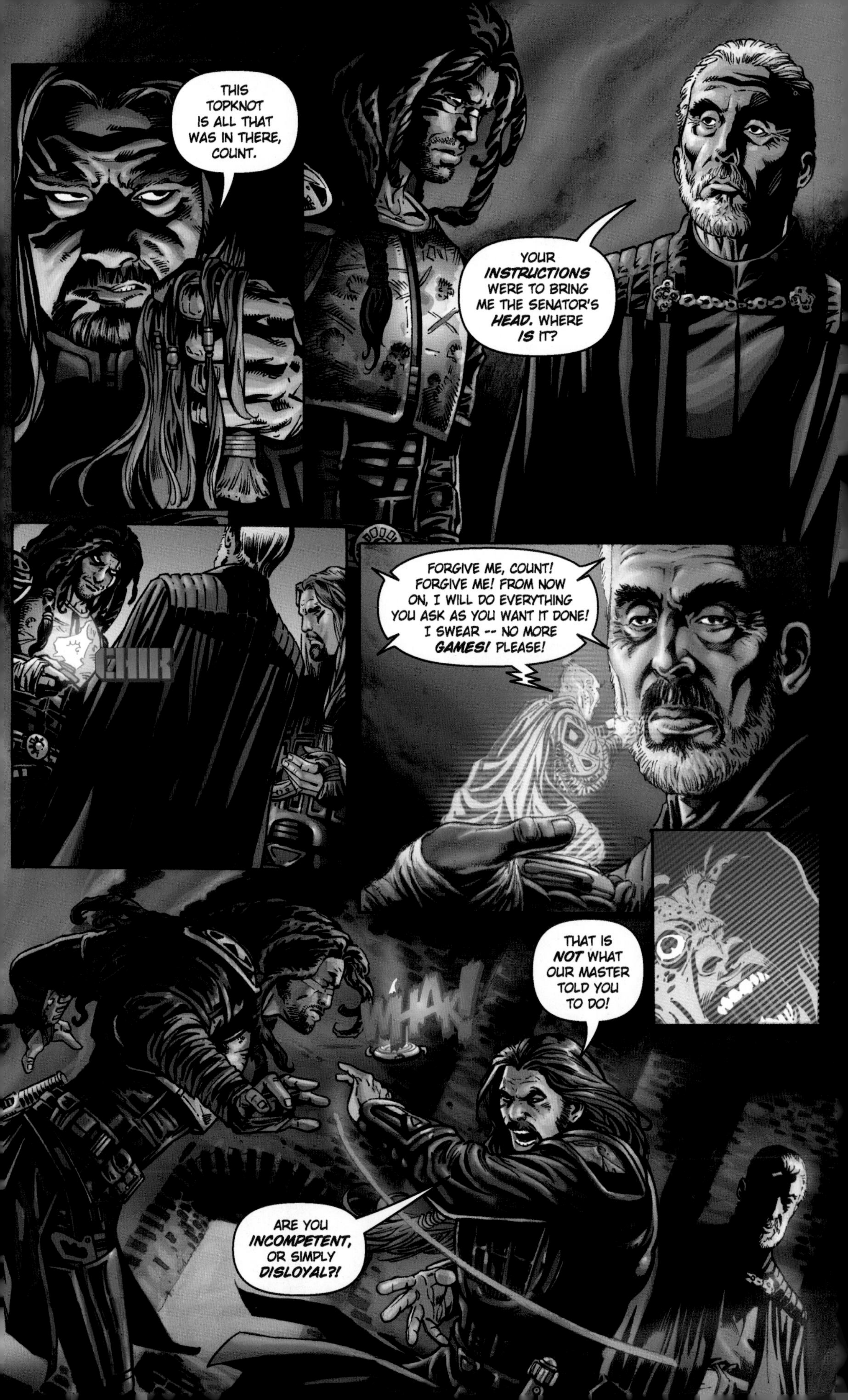
THIS TOPKNOT IS ALL THAT WAS IN THERE, COUNT.
YOUR INSTRUCTIONS WERE TO BRING ME THE SENATOR'S HEAD. WHERE IS IT?
CHIK
FORGIVE ME, COUNT! FORGIVE ME! FROM NOW ON, I WILL DO EVERYTHING YOU ASK AS YOU WANT IT DONE! I SWEAR -- NO MORE GAMES! PLEASE!
THAT IS NOT WHAT OUR MASTER TOLD YOU TO DO!
WHAK!
ARE YOU INCOMPETENT, OR SIMPLY DISLOYAL?!

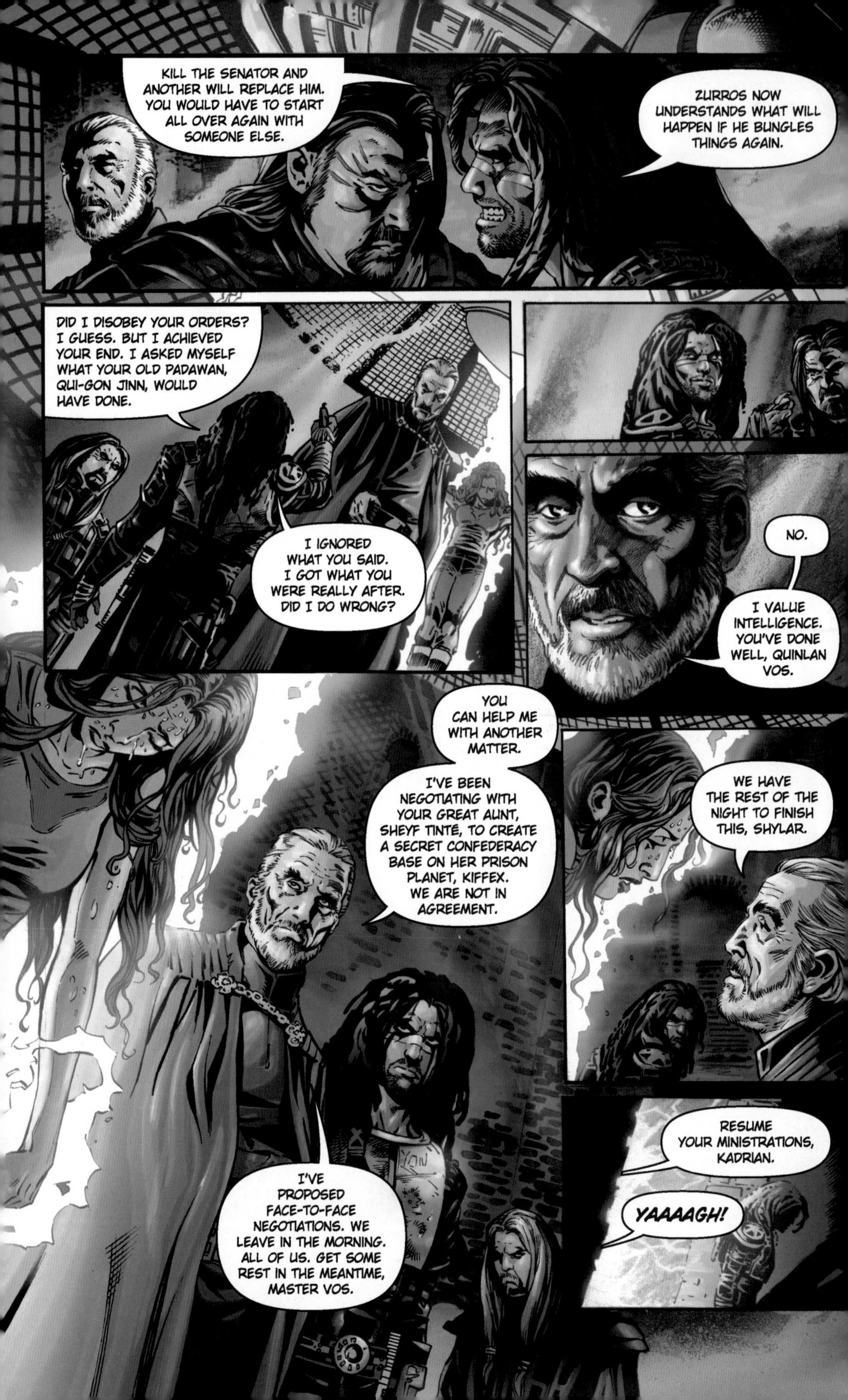
KILL THE SENATOR AND ANOTHER WILL REPLACE HIM. YOU WOULD HAVE TO START ALL OVER AGAIN WITH SOMEONE ELSE.
ZURROS NOW UNDERSTANDS WHAT WILL HAPPEN IF HE BUNGLES THINGS AGAIN.
DID I DISOBEY YOUR ORDERS? I GUESS. BUT I ACHIEVED YOUR END. I ASKED MYSELF WHAT YOUR OLD PADAWAN, QUI-GON JINN, WOULD HAVE DONE.
I IGNORED WHAT YOU SAID. I GOT WHAT YOU WERE REALLY AFTER. DID I DO WRONG?
NO.
I VALUE INTELLIGENCE. YOU'VE DONE WELL, QUINLAN VOS.
YOU CAN HELP ME WITH ANOTHER MATTER.
I'VE BEEN NEGOTIATING WITH YOUR GREAT AUNT, SHEYF TINTÉ, TO CREATE A SECRET CONFEDERACY BASE ON HER PRISON PLANET, KIFFEX. WE ARE NOT IN AGREEMENT.
I'VE PROPOSED FACE-TO-FACE NEGOTIATIONS. WE LEAVE IN THE MORNING. ALL OF US. GET SOME REST IN THE MEANTIME, MASTER VOS.
WE HAVE THE REST OF THE NIGHT TO FINISH THIS, SHYLAR.
RESUME YOUR MINISTRATIONS, KADRIAN.
YAAAAGH!

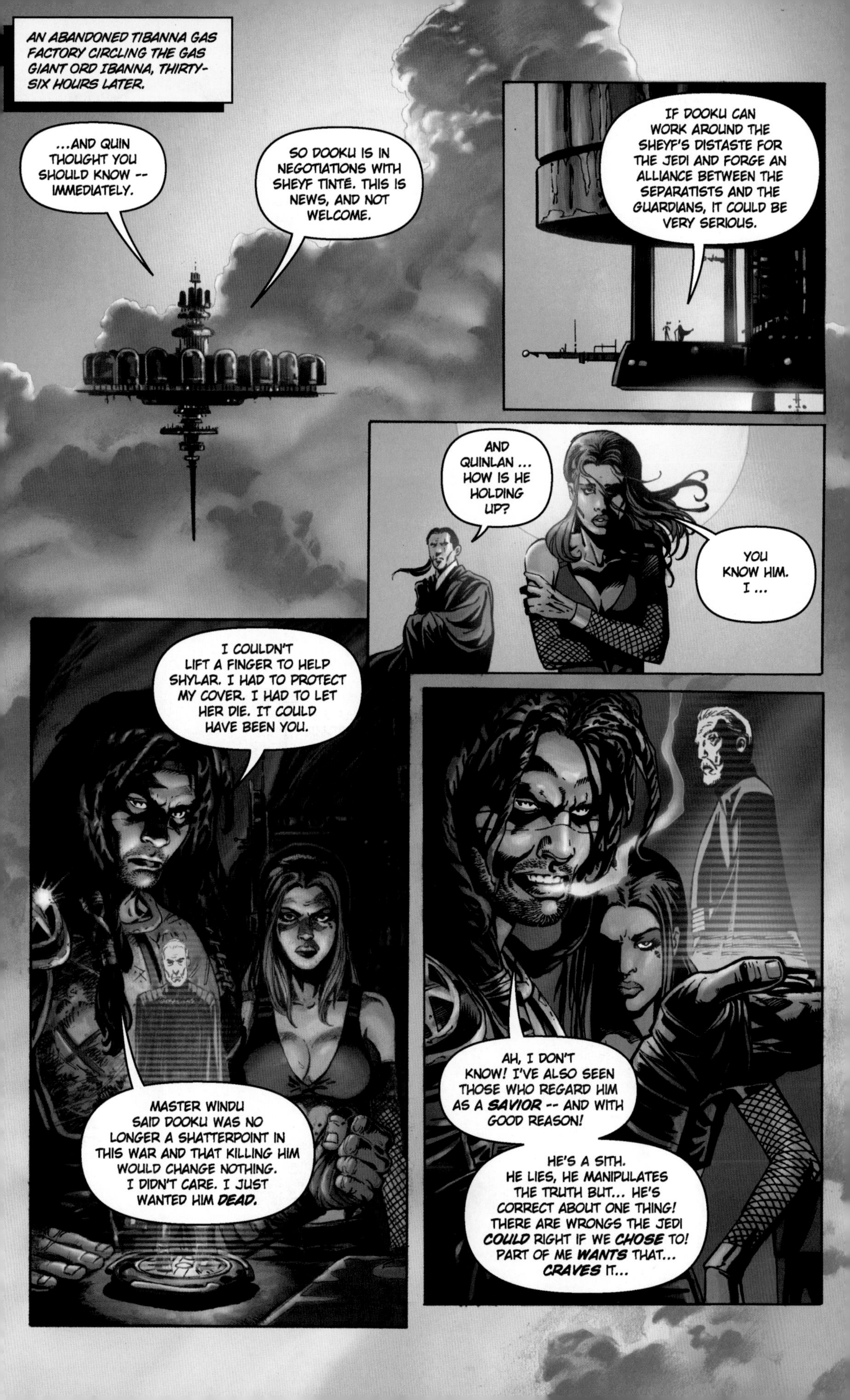
AN ABANDONED TIBANNA GAS FACTORY CIRCLING THE GAS GIANT ORD IBANNA, THIRTY-SIX HOURS LATER.
...AND QUIN THOUGHT YOU SHOULD KNOW -- IMMEDIATELY.
SO DOOKU IS IN NEGOTIATIONS WITH SHEYF TINTE. THIS IS NEWS, AND NOT WELCOME.
IF DOOKU CAN WORK AROUND THE SHEYF'S DISTASTE FOR THE JEDI AND FORGE AN ALLIANCE BETWEEN THE SEPARATISTS AND THE GUARDIANS, IT COULD BE VERY SERIOUS.
AND QUINLAN ... HOW IS HE HOLDING UP?
YOU KNOW HIM. I ...
I COULDN'T LIFT A FINGER TO HELP SHYLAR. I HAD TO PROTECT MY COVER. I HAD TO LET HER DIE. IT COULD HAVE BEEN YOU.
MASTER WINDU SAID DOOKU WAS NO LONGER A SHATTERPOINT IN THIS WAR AND THAT KILLING HIM WOULD CHANGE NOTHING. I DIDN'T CARE. I JUST WANTED HIM DEAD.
AH, I DON'T KNOW! I'VE ALSO SEEN THOSE WHO REGARD HIM AS A SAVIOR -- AND WITH GOOD REASON!
HE'S A SITH. HE LIES, HE MANIPULATES THE TRUTH BUT... HE'S CORRECT ABOUT ONE THING! THERE ARE WRONGS THE JEDI COULD RIGHT IF WE CHOSE TO! PART OF ME WANTS THAT... CRAVES IT...

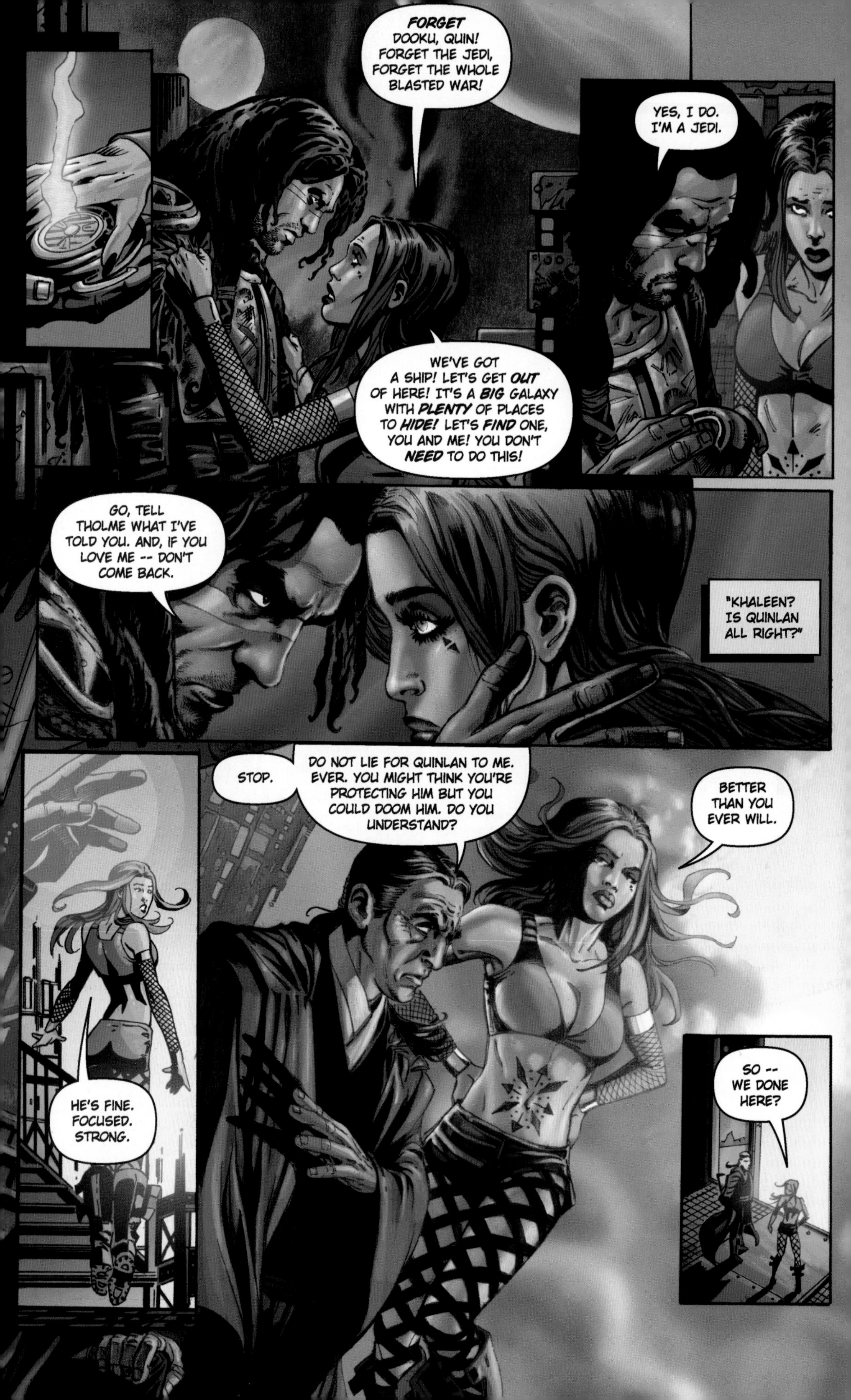
FORGET DOOKU, QUIN! FORGET THE JEDI, FORGET THE WHOLE BLASTED WAR!
WE'VE GOT A SHIP! LET'S GET OUT OF HERE! IT'S A BIG GALAXY WITH PLENTY OF PLACES TO HIDE! LET'S FIND ONE, YOU AND ME! YOU DON'T NEED TO DO THIS!
YES, I DO. I'M A JEDI.
GO, TELL THOLME WHAT I'VE TOLD YOU. AND, IF YOU LOVE ME -- DON'T COME BACK.
"KHALEEN? IS QUINLAN ALL RIGHT?"
HE'S FINE. FOCUSED. STRONG.
STOP.
DO NOT LIE FOR QUINLAN TO ME. EVER. YOU MIGHT THINK YOU'RE PROTECTING HIM BUT YOU COULD DOOM HIM. DO YOU UNDERSTAND?
BETTER THAN YOU EVER WILL.
SO -- WE DONE HERE?

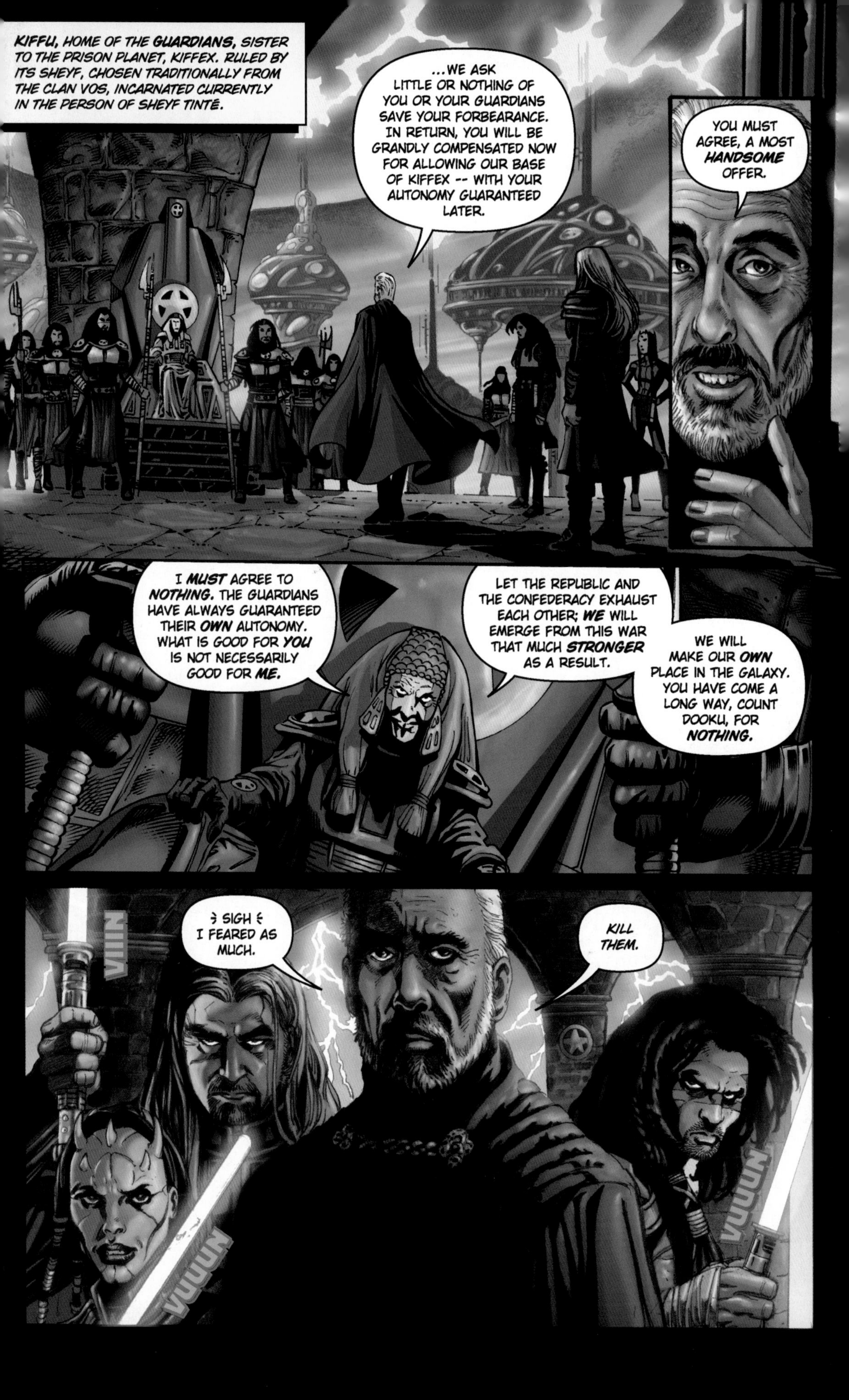
KIFFU, HOME OF THE GUARDIANS, SISTER TO THE PRISON PLANET, KIFFEX. RULED BY ITS SHEYF, CHOSEN TRADITIONALLY FROM THE CLAN VOS, INCARNATED CURRENTLY IN THE PERSON OF SHEYF TINTÉ.
...WE ASK LITTLE OR NOTHING OF YOU OR YOUR GUARDIANS SAVE YOUR FORBEARANCE. IN RETURN, YOU WILL BE GRANDLY COMPENSATED NOW FOR ALLOWING OUR BASE OF KIFFEX -- WITH YOUR AUTONOMY GUARANTEED LATER.
YOU MUST AGREE, A MOST HANDSOME OFFER.
I MUST AGREE TO NOTHING. THE GUARDIANS HAVE ALWAYS GUARANTEED THEIR OWN AUTONOMY. WHAT IS GOOD FOR YOU IS NOT NECESSARILY GOOD FOR ME.
LET THE REPUBLIC AND THE CONFEDERACY EXHAUST EACH OTHER; WE WILL EMERGE FROM THIS WAR THAT MUCH STRONGER AS A RESULT.
WE WILL MAKE OUR OWN PLACE IN THE GALAXY. YOU HAVE COME A LONG WAY, COUNT DOOKU, FOR NOTHING.
VIIIN
SIGH
I FEARED AS MUCH.
KILL THEM.
VUUUN
VUUUN

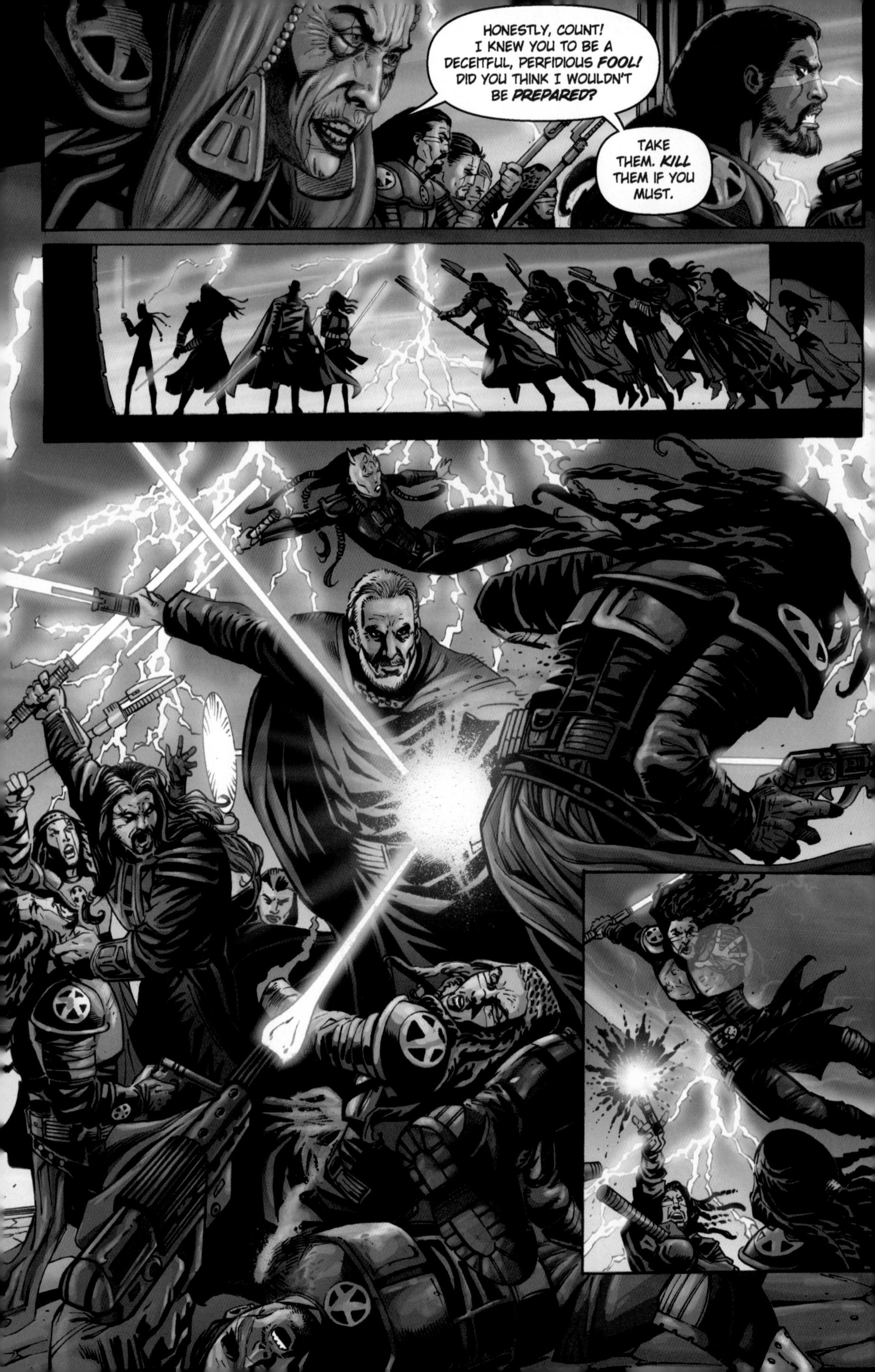
HONESTLY, COUNT! I KNEW YOU TO BE A DECEITFUL, PERFIDIOUS FOOL! DID YOU THINK I WOULDN'T BE PREPARED?
TAKE THEM. KILL THEM IF YOU MUST.

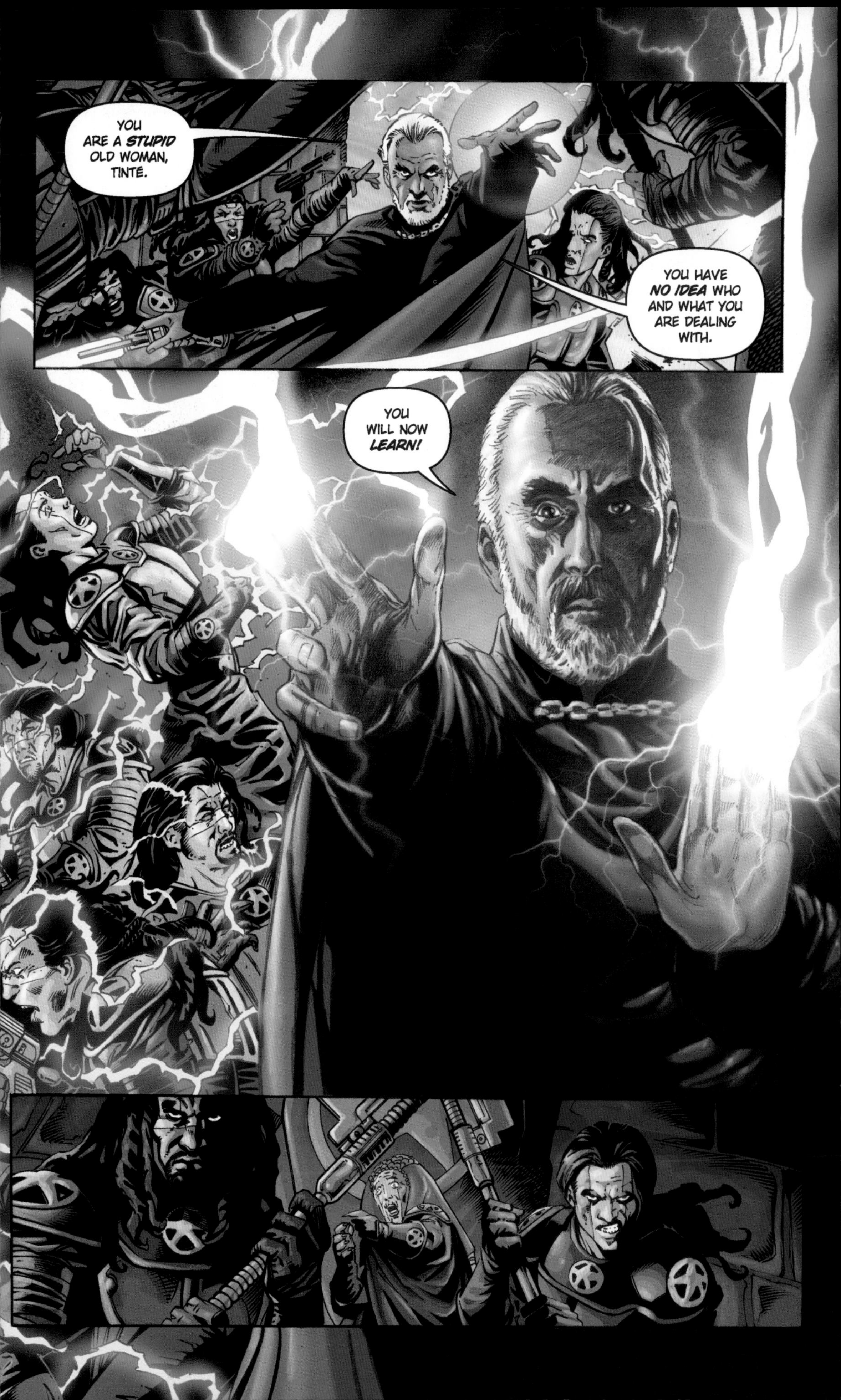
YOU ARE A STUPID OLD WOMAN, TINTÉ.
YOU HAVE NO IDEA WHO AND WHAT YOU ARE DEALING WITH.
YOU WILL NOW LEARN!

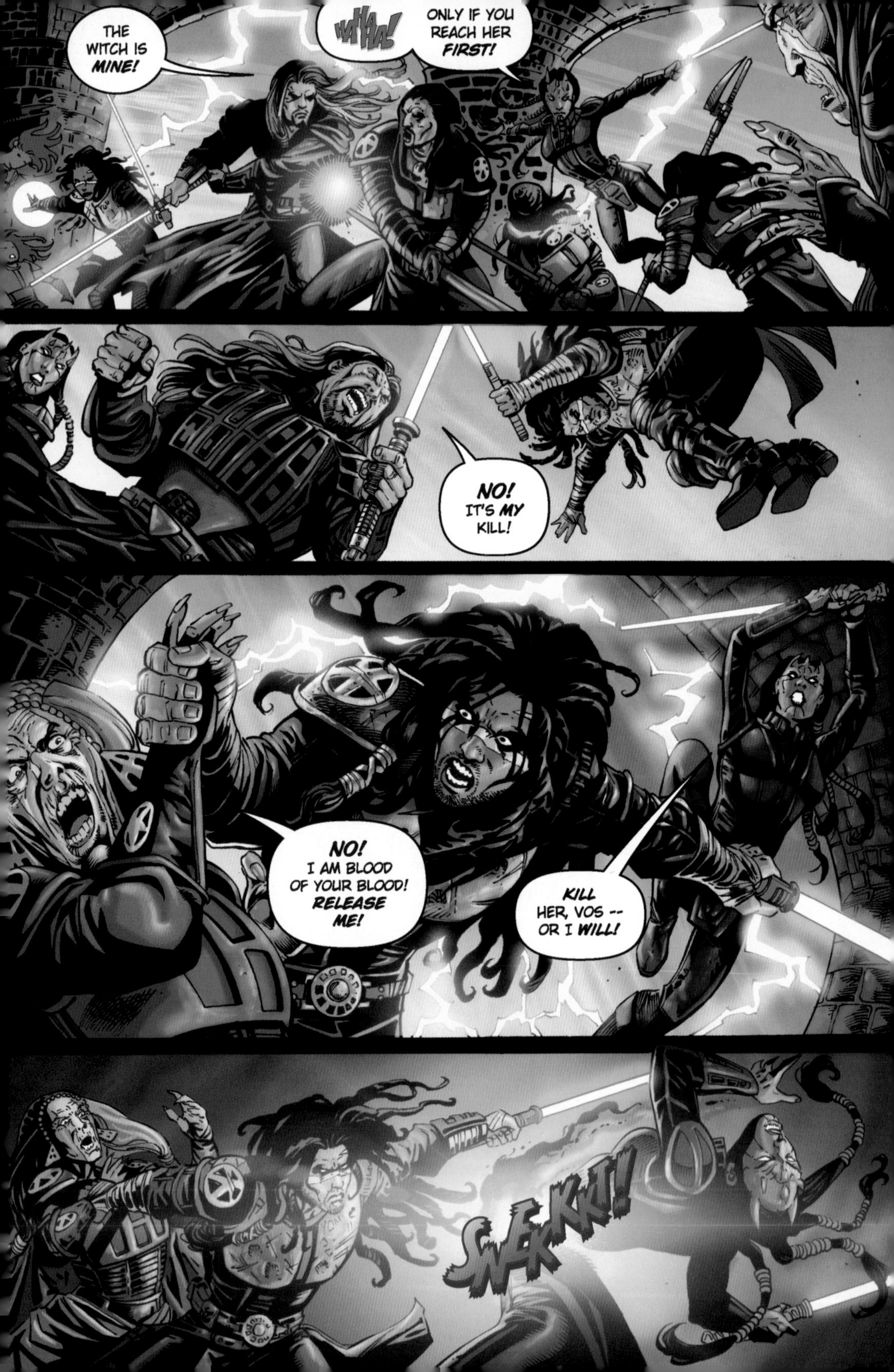

THE WITCH IS MINE!
HAHAHA!
ONLY IF YOU REACH HER FIRST!
NO! IT'S MY KILL!
NO! I AM BLOOD OF YOUR BLOOD! RELEASE ME!
KILL HER, VOS -- OR I WILL!
SNEKKT!

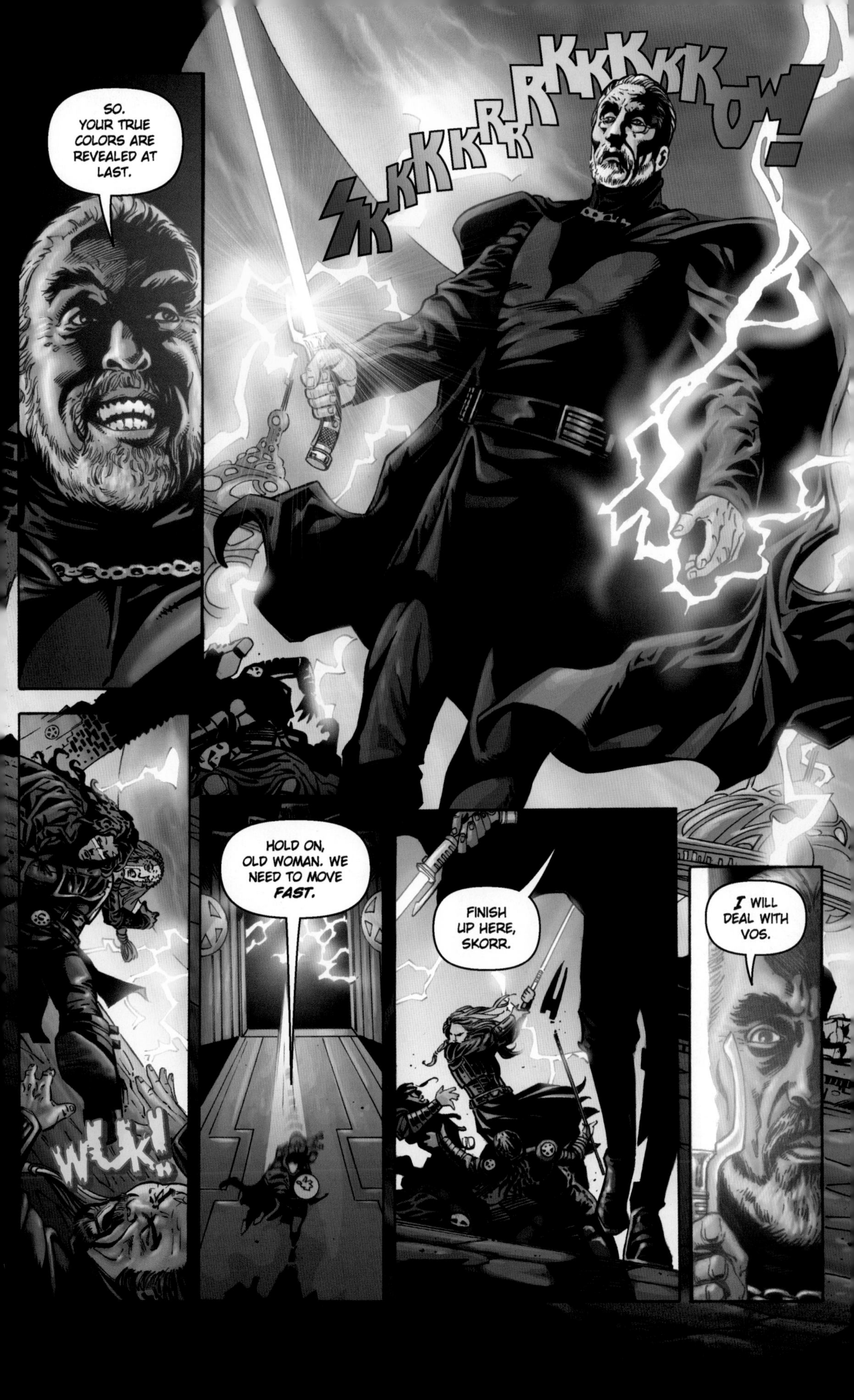
SO. YOUR TRUE COLORS ARE REVEALED AT LAST.
SKKKKRRRRKKKKKKOW!
WUK!
HOLD ON, OLD WOMAN. WE NEED TO MOVE FAST.
FINISH UP HERE, SKORR.
I WILL DEAL WITH VOS.

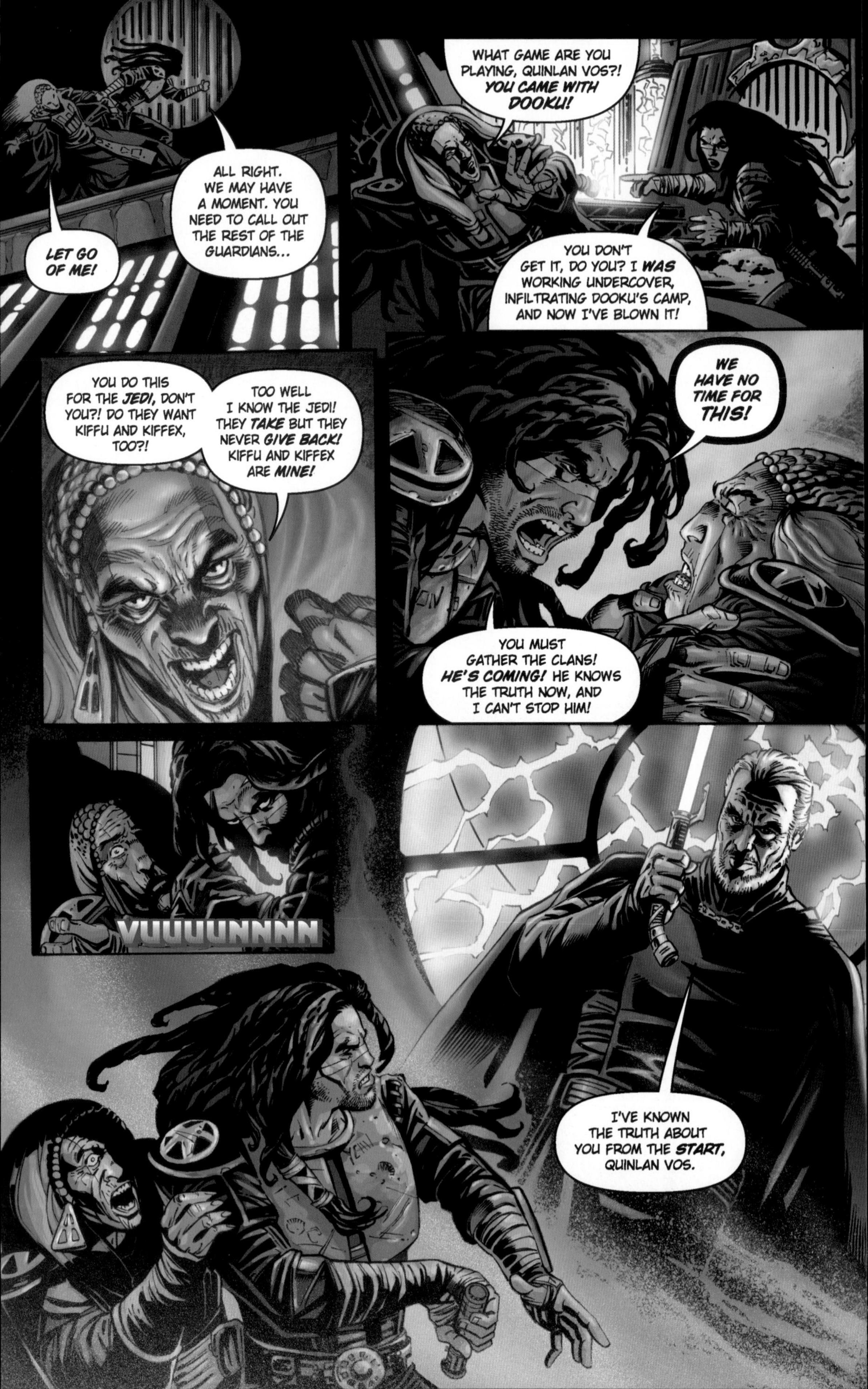
LET GO OF ME!
ALL RIGHT. WE MAY HAVE A MOMENT. YOU NEED TO CALL OUT THE REST OF THE GUARDIANS...
WHAT GAME ARE YOU PLAYING, QUINLAN VOS?! YOU CAME WITH DOOKU!
YOU DON'T GET IT, DO YOU? I WAS WORKING UNDERCOVER, INFILTRATING DOOKU'S CAMP, AND NOW I'VE BLOWN IT!
YOU DO THIS FOR THE JEDI, DON'T YOU?! DO THEY WANT KIFFU AND KIFFEX, TOO?!
TOO WELL I KNOW THE JEDI! THEY TAKE BUT THEY NEVER GIVE BACK! KIFFU AND KIFFEX ARE MINE!
WE HAVE NO TIME FOR THIS!
YOU MUST GATHER THE CLANS! HE'S COMING! HE KNOWS THE TRUTH NOW, AND I CAN'T STOP HIM!
VUUUUNNNN
I'VE KNOWN THE TRUTH ABOUT YOU FROM THE START, QUINLAN VOS.

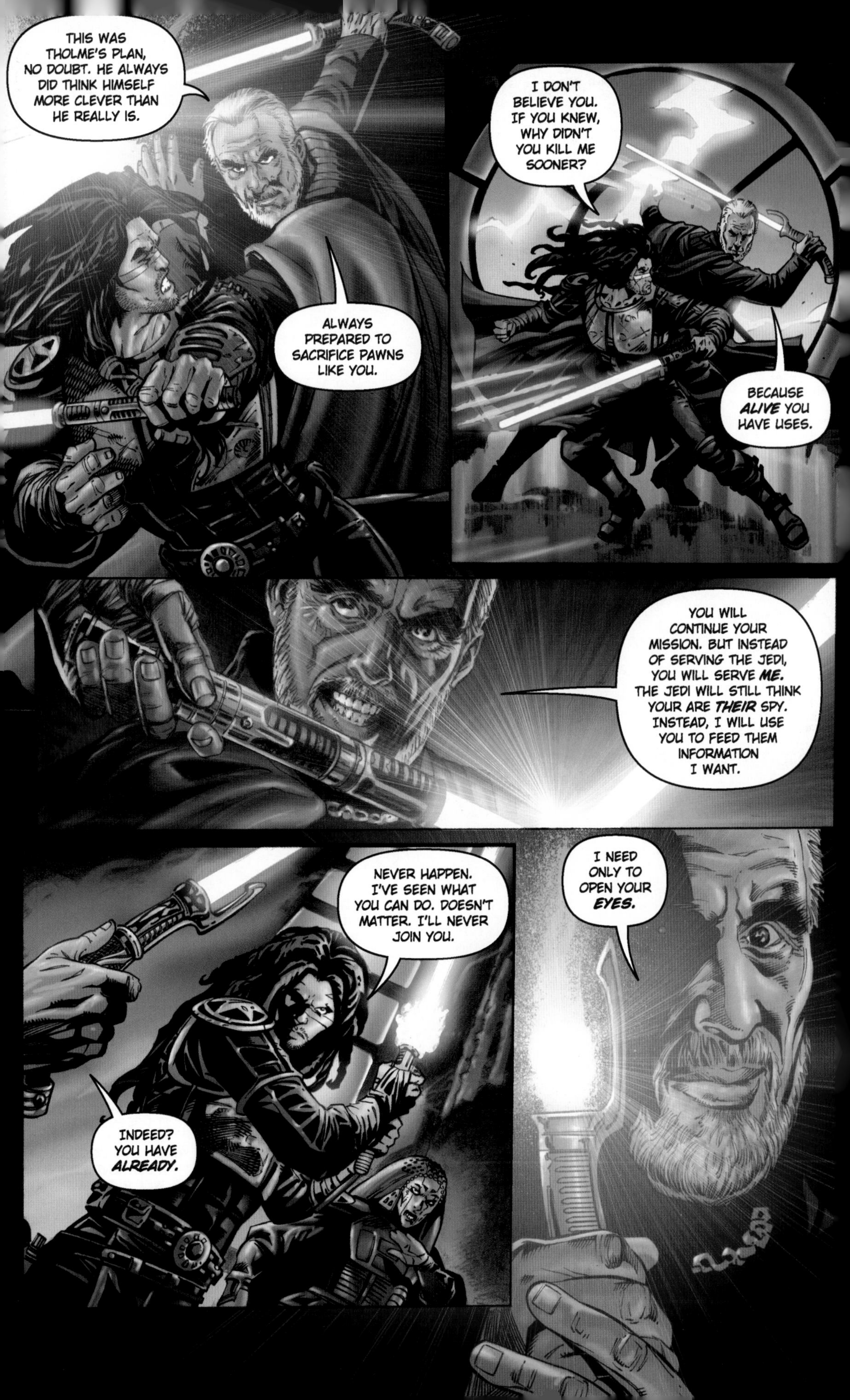
THIS WAS THOLME'S PLAN, NO DOUBT. HE ALWAYS DID THINK HIMSELF MORE CLEVER THAN HE REALLY IS.
ALWAYS PREPARED TO SACRIFICE PAWNS LIKE YOU.
I DON'T BELIEVE YOU. IF YOU KNEW, WHY DIDN'T YOU KILL ME SOONER?
BECAUSE ALIVE YOU HAVE USES.
YOU WILL CONTINUE YOUR MISSION. BUT INSTEAD OF SERVING THE JEDI, YOU WILL SERVE ME. THE JEDI WILL STILL THINK YOUR ARE THEIR SPY. INSTEAD, I WILL USE YOU TO FEED THEM INFORMATION I WANT.
NEVER HAPPEN. I'VE SEEN WHAT YOU CAN DO. DOESN'T MATTER. I'LL NEVER JOIN YOU.
INDEED? YOU HAVE ALREADY.
I NEED ONLY TO OPEN YOUR EYES.

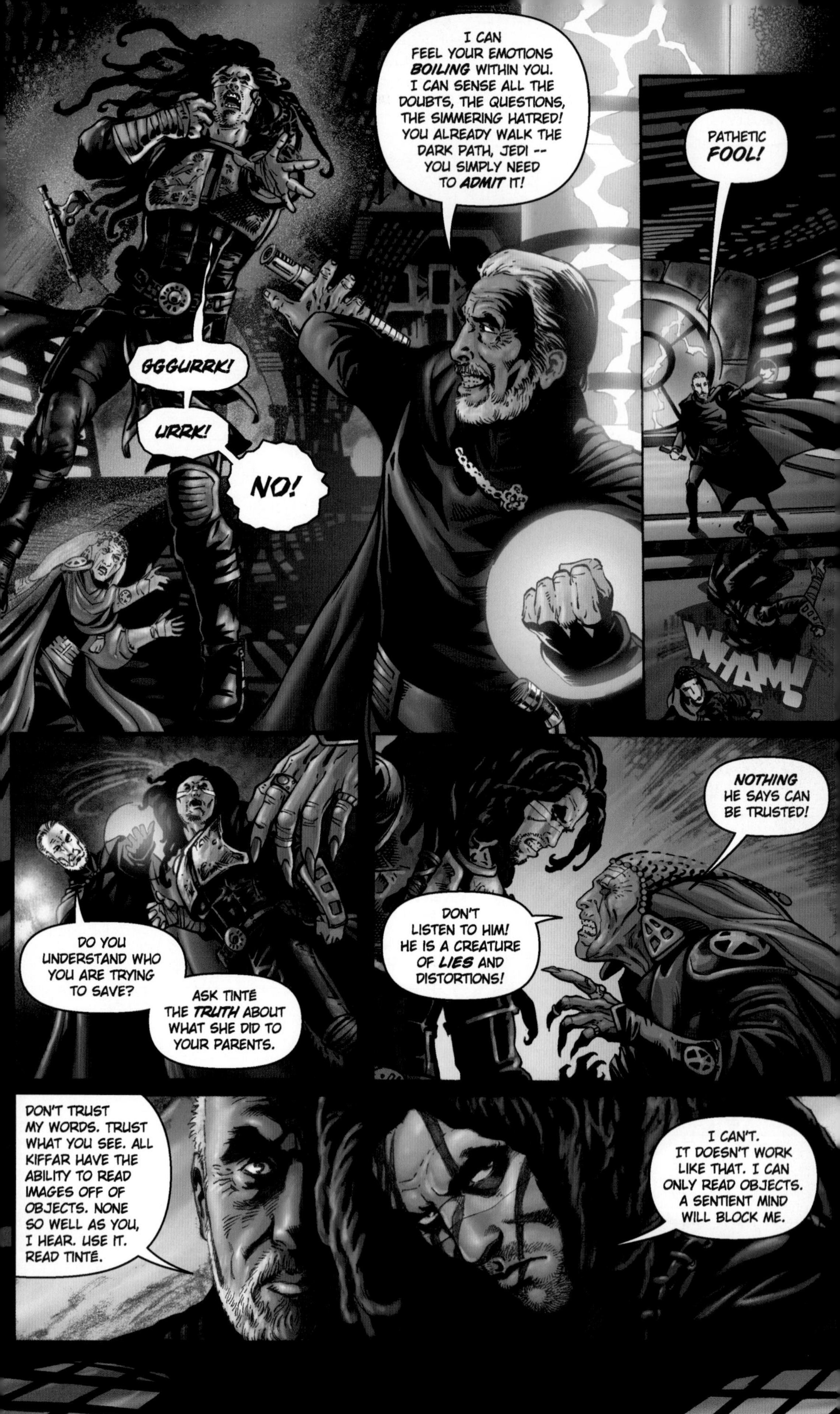
I CAN FEEL YOUR EMOTIONS BOILING WITHIN YOU. I CAN SENSE ALL THE DOUBTS, THE QUESTIONS, THE SIMMERING HATRED! YOU ALREADY WALK THE DARK PATH, JEDI -- YOU SIMPLY NEED TO ADMIT IT!
GGGURRK!
URRK!
NO!
PATHETIC FOOL!
WHAM!
DO YOU UNDERSTAND WHO YOU ARE TRYING TO SAVE?
ASK TINTÉ THE TRUTH ABOUT WHAT SHE DID TO YOUR PARENTS.
DON'T LISTEN TO HIM! HE IS A CREATURE OF LIES AND DISTORTIONS!
NOTHING HE SAYS CAN BE TRUSTED!
DON'T TRUST MY WORDS. TRUST WHAT YOU SEE. ALL KIFFAR HAVE THE ABILITY TO READ IMAGES OFF OF OBJECTS. NONE SO WELL AS YOU, I HEAR. USE IT. READ TINTÉ.
I CAN'T. IT DOESN'T WORK LIKE THAT. I CAN ONLY READ OBJECTS. A SENTIENT MIND WILL BLOCK ME.

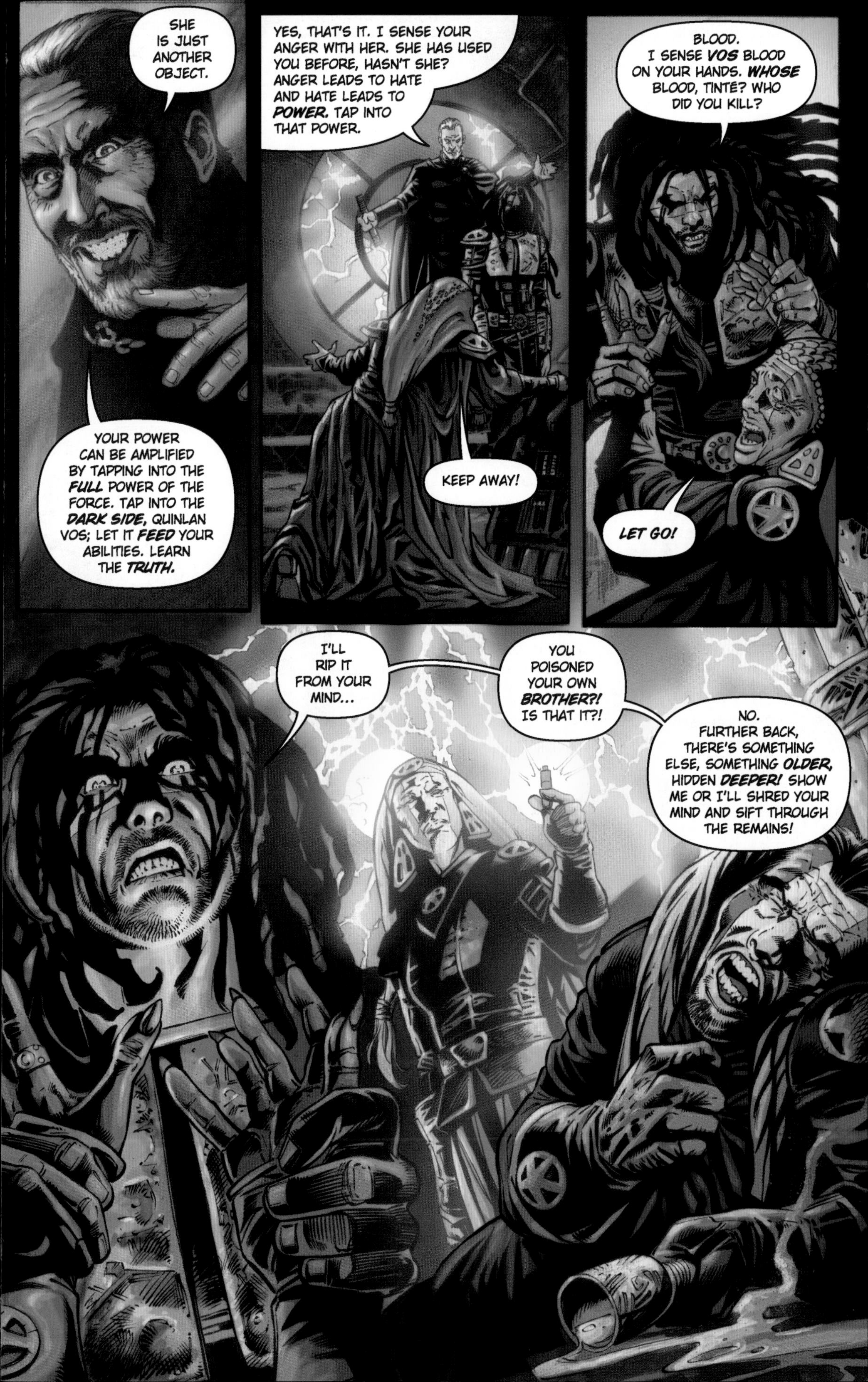
SHE IS JUST ANOTHER OBJECT.
YOUR POWER CAN BE AMPLIFIED BY TAPPING INTO THE FULL POWER OF THE FORCE. TAP INTO THE DARK SIDE, QUINLAN VOS; LET IT FEED YOUR ABILITIES. LEARN THE TRUTH.
YES, THAT'S IT. I SENSE YOUR ANGER WITH HER. SHE HAS USED YOU BEFORE, HASN'T SHE? ANGER LEADS TO HATE AND HATE LEADS TO POWER. TAP INTO THAT POWER.
KEEP AWAY!
BLOOD. I SENSE VOS BLOOD ON YOUR HANDS. WHOSE BLOOD, TINTÉ? WHO DID YOU KILL?
LET GO!
I'LL RIP IT FROM YOUR MIND...
YOU POISONED YOUR OWN BROTHER?! IS THAT IT?!
NO. FURTHER BACK, THERE'S SOMETHING ELSE, SOMETHING OLDER, HIDDEN DEEPER! SHOW ME OR I'LL SHRED YOUR MIND AND SIFT THROUGH THE REMAINS!

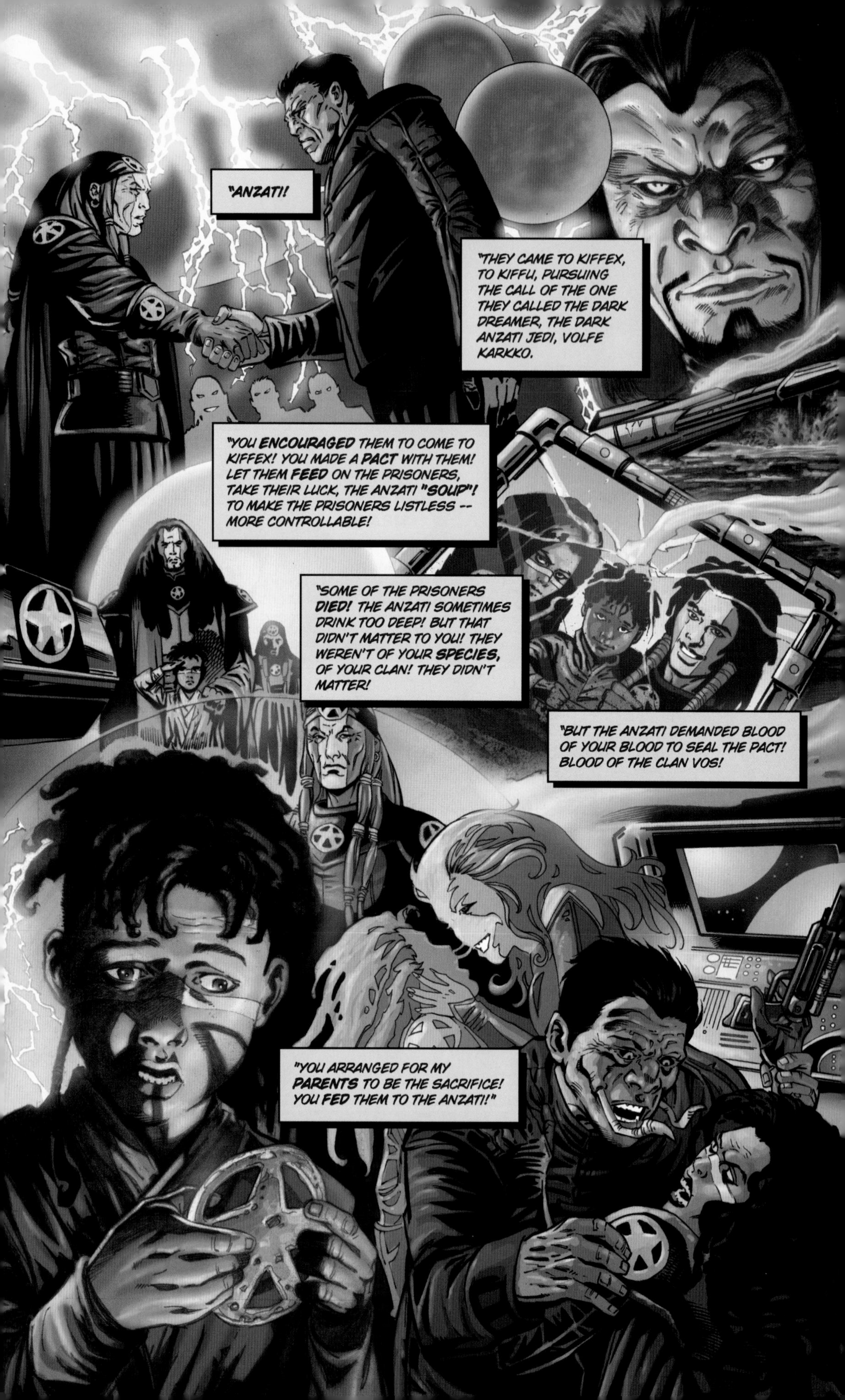
"ANZATI!
"THEY CAME TO KIFFEX, TO KIFFU, PURSUING THE CALL OF THE ONE THEY CALLED THE DARK DREAMER, THE DARK ANZATI JEDI, VOLFE KARKKO.
"YOU ENCOURAGED THEM TO COME TO KIFFEX! YOU MADE A PACT WITH THEM! LET THEM FEED ON THE PRISONERS, TAKE THEIR LUCK, THE ANZATI "SOUP"! TO MAKE THE PRISONERS LISTLESS -- MORE CONTROLLABLE!
"SOME OF THE PRISONERS DIED! THE ANZATI SOMETIMES DRINK TOO DEEP! BUT THAT DIDN'T MATTER TO YOU! THEY WEREN'T OF YOUR SPECIES, OF YOUR CLAN! THEY DIDN'T MATTER!
"BUT THE ANZATI DEMANDED BLOOD OF YOUR BLOOD TO SEAL THE PACT! BLOOD OF THE CLAN VOS!
"YOU ARRANGED FOR MY PARENTS TO BE THE SACRIFICE! YOU FED THEM TO THE ANZATI!"

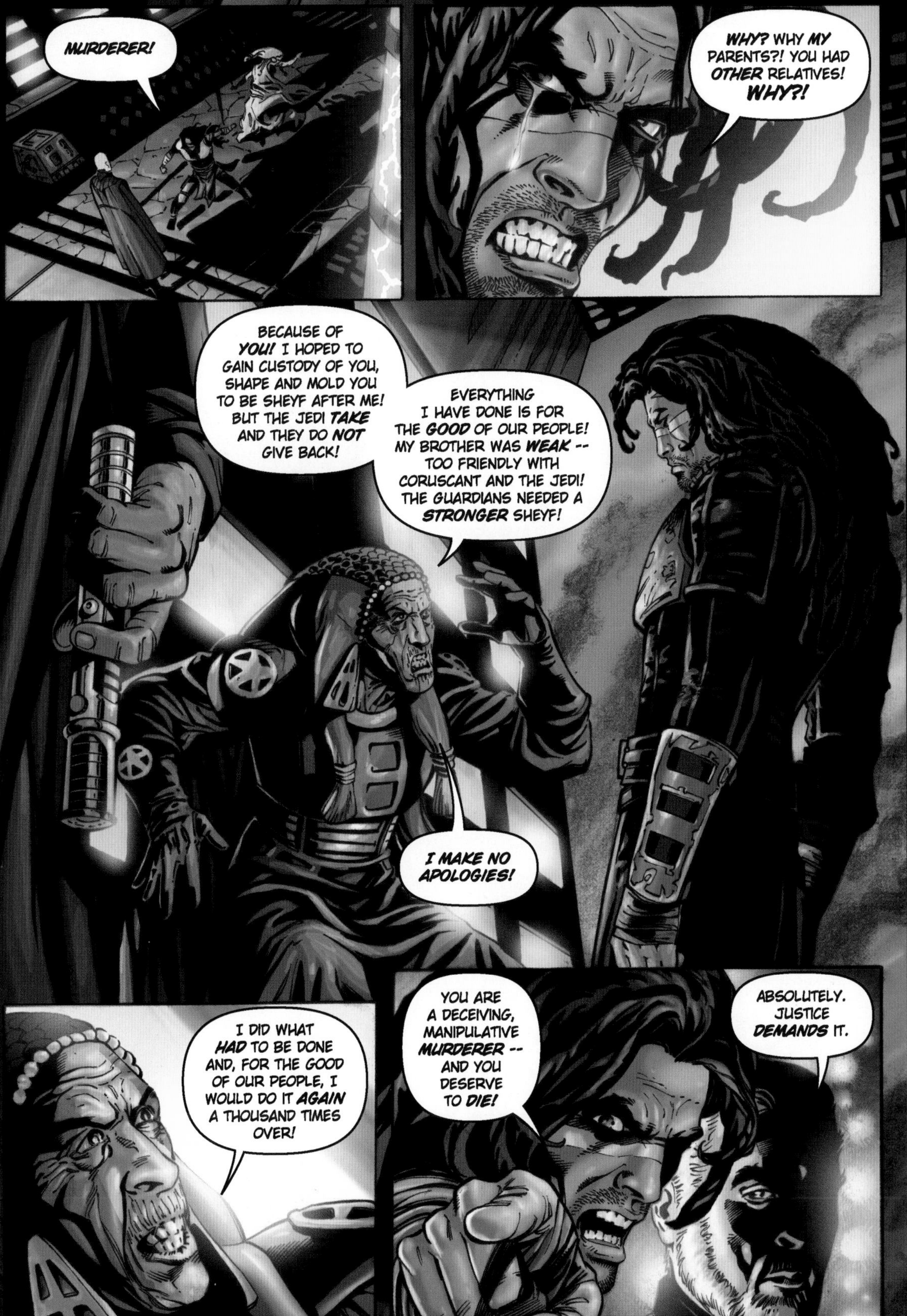
MURDERER!
WHY? WHY MY PARENTS?! YOU HAD OTHER RELATIVES! WHY?!
BECAUSE OF YOU! I HOPED TO GAIN CUSTODY OF YOU, SHAPE AND MOLD YOU TO BE SHEYF AFTER ME! BUT THE JEDI TAKE AND THEY DO NOT GIVE BACK!
EVERYTHING I HAVE DONE IS FOR THE GOOD OF OUR PEOPLE! MY BROTHER WAS WEAK -- TOO FRIENDLY WITH CORUSCANT AND THE JEDI! THE GUARDIANS NEEDED A STRONGER SHEYF!
I MAKE NO APOLOGIES!
I DID WHAT HAD TO BE DONE AND, FOR THE GOOD OF OUR PEOPLE, I WOULD DO IT AGAIN A THOUSAND TIMES OVER!
YOU ARE A DECEIVING, MANIPULATIVE MURDERER -- AND YOU DESERVE TO DIE!
ABSOLUTELY. JUSTICE DEMANDS IT.

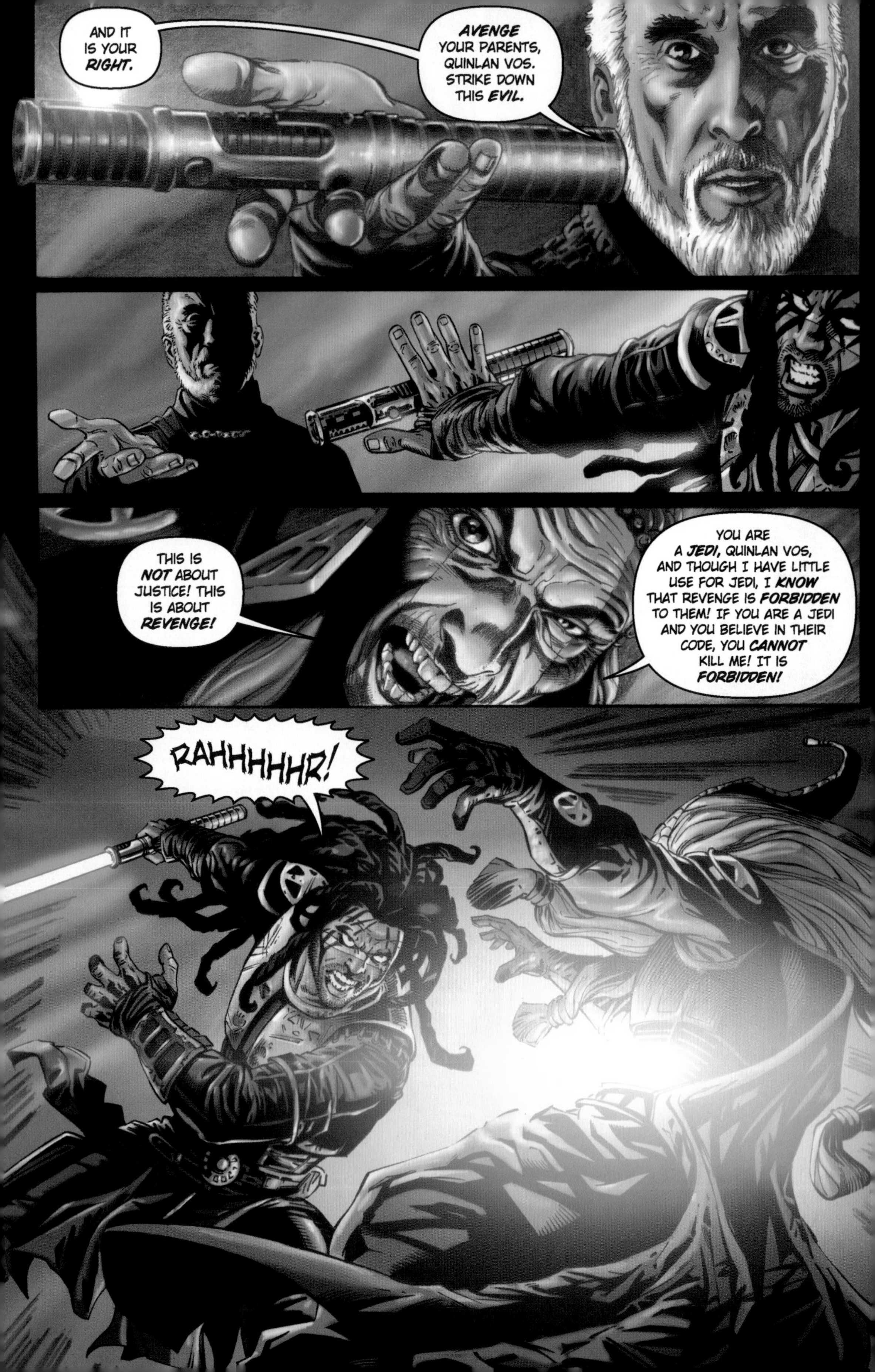
AND IT IS YOUR *RIGHT.*
AVENGE YOUR PARENTS, QUINLAN VOS. STRIKE DOWN THIS *EVIL.*
THIS IS *NOT* ABOUT JUSTICE! THIS IS ABOUT *REVENGE!*
YOU ARE A *JEDI,* QUINLAN VOS, AND THOUGH I HAVE LITTLE USE FOR JEDI, I *KNOW* THAT REVENGE IS *FORBIDDEN* TO THEM! IF YOU ARE A JEDI AND YOU BELIEVE IN THEIR CODE, YOU *CANNOT* KILL ME! IT IS *FORBIDDEN!*
RAHHHHHR!

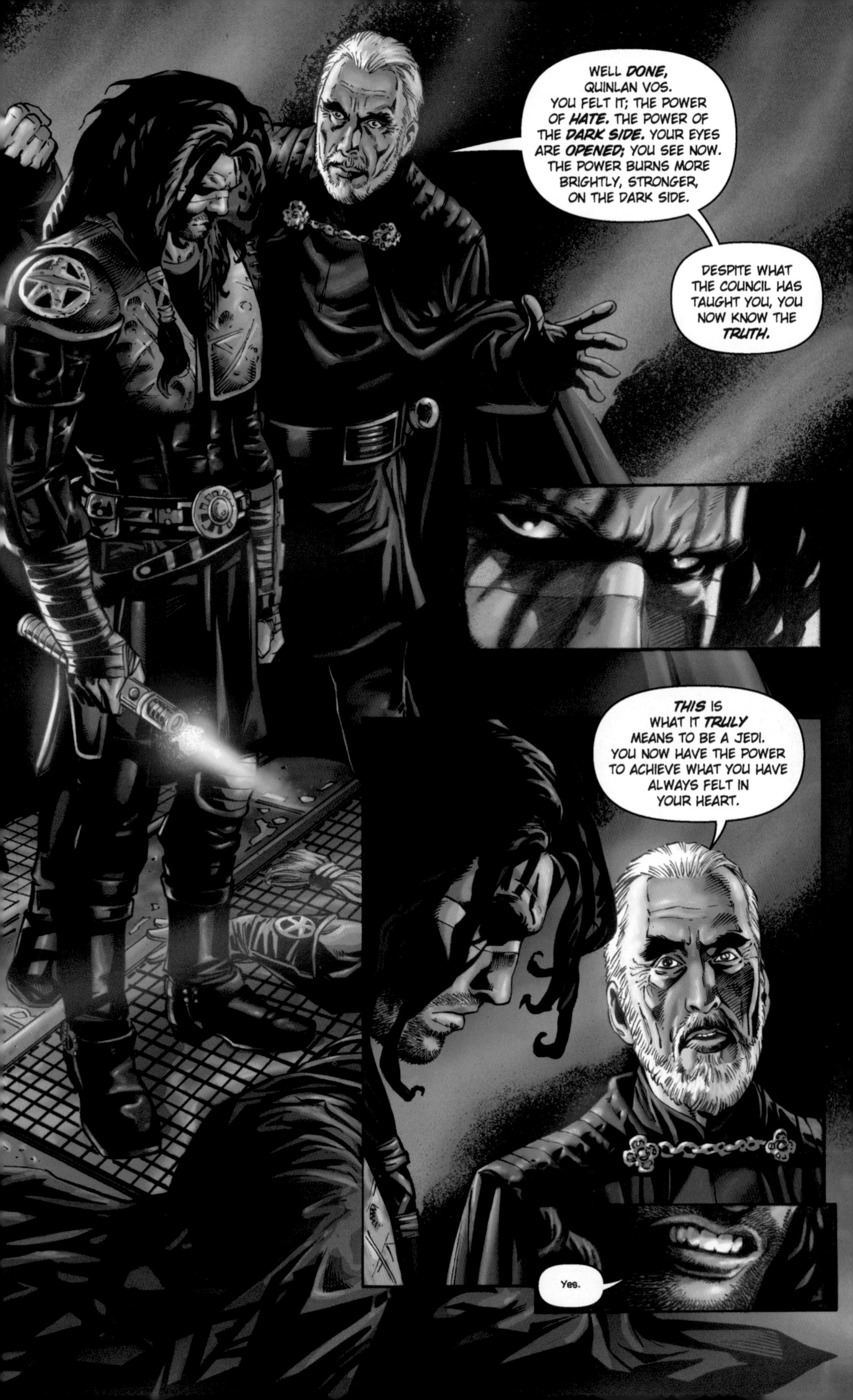
WELL **DONE,** QUINLAN VOS. YOU FELT IT; THE POWER OF **HATE.** THE POWER OF THE **DARK SIDE.** YOUR EYES ARE **OPENED;** YOU SEE NOW. THE POWER BURNS MORE BRIGHTLY, STRONGER, ON THE DARK SIDE.
DESPITE WHAT THE COUNCIL HAS TAUGHT YOU, YOU NOW KNOW THE **TRUTH.**
THIS IS WHAT IT **TRULY** MEANS TO BE A JEDI. YOU NOW HAVE THE POWER TO ACHIEVE WHAT YOU HAVE ALWAYS FELT IN YOUR HEART.
Yes.

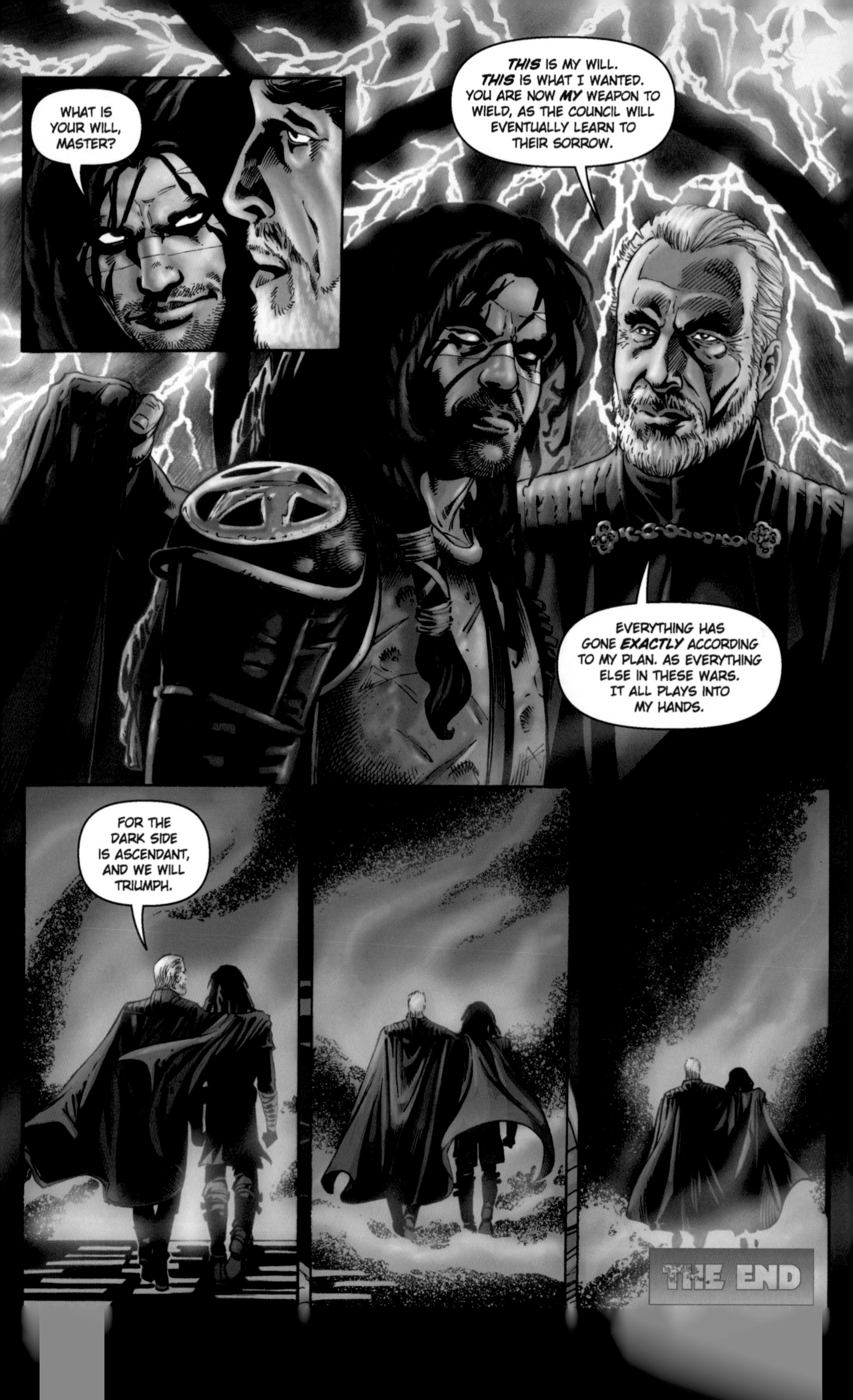
WHAT IS YOUR WILL, MASTER?
THIS IS MY WILL. THIS IS WHAT I WANTED. YOU ARE NOW MY WEAPON TO WIELD, AS THE COUNCIL WILL EVENTUALLY LEARN TO THEIR SORROW.
EVERYTHING HAS GONE EXACTLY ACCORDING TO MY PLAN. AS EVERYTHING ELSE IN THESE WARS. IT ALL PLAYS INTO MY HANDS.
FOR THE DARK SIDE IS ASCENDANT, AND WE WILL TRIUMPH.
THE END

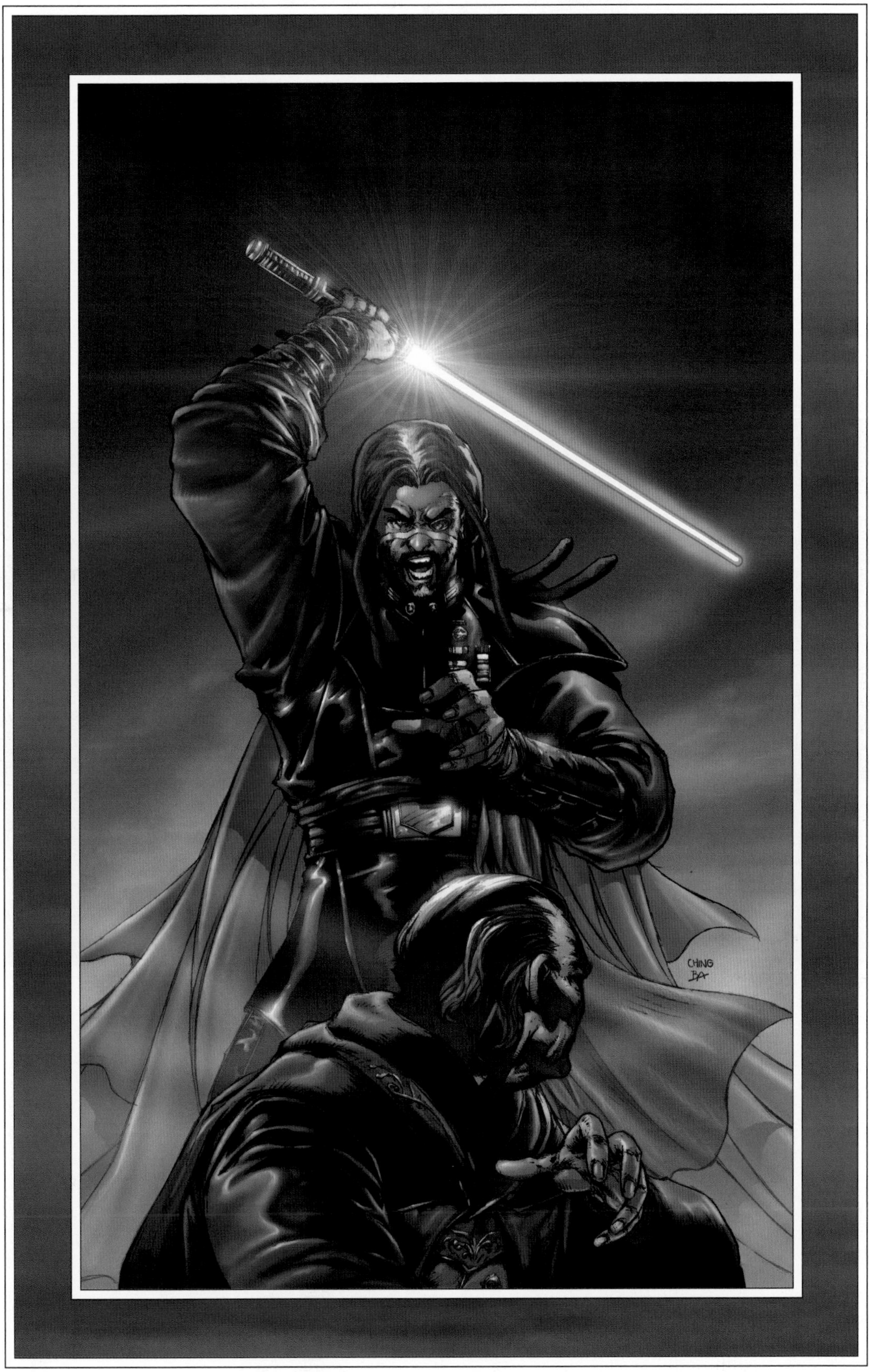
CHING
BA

SIXTEEN MONTHS AFTER
THE BATTLE OF GEONOSIS...

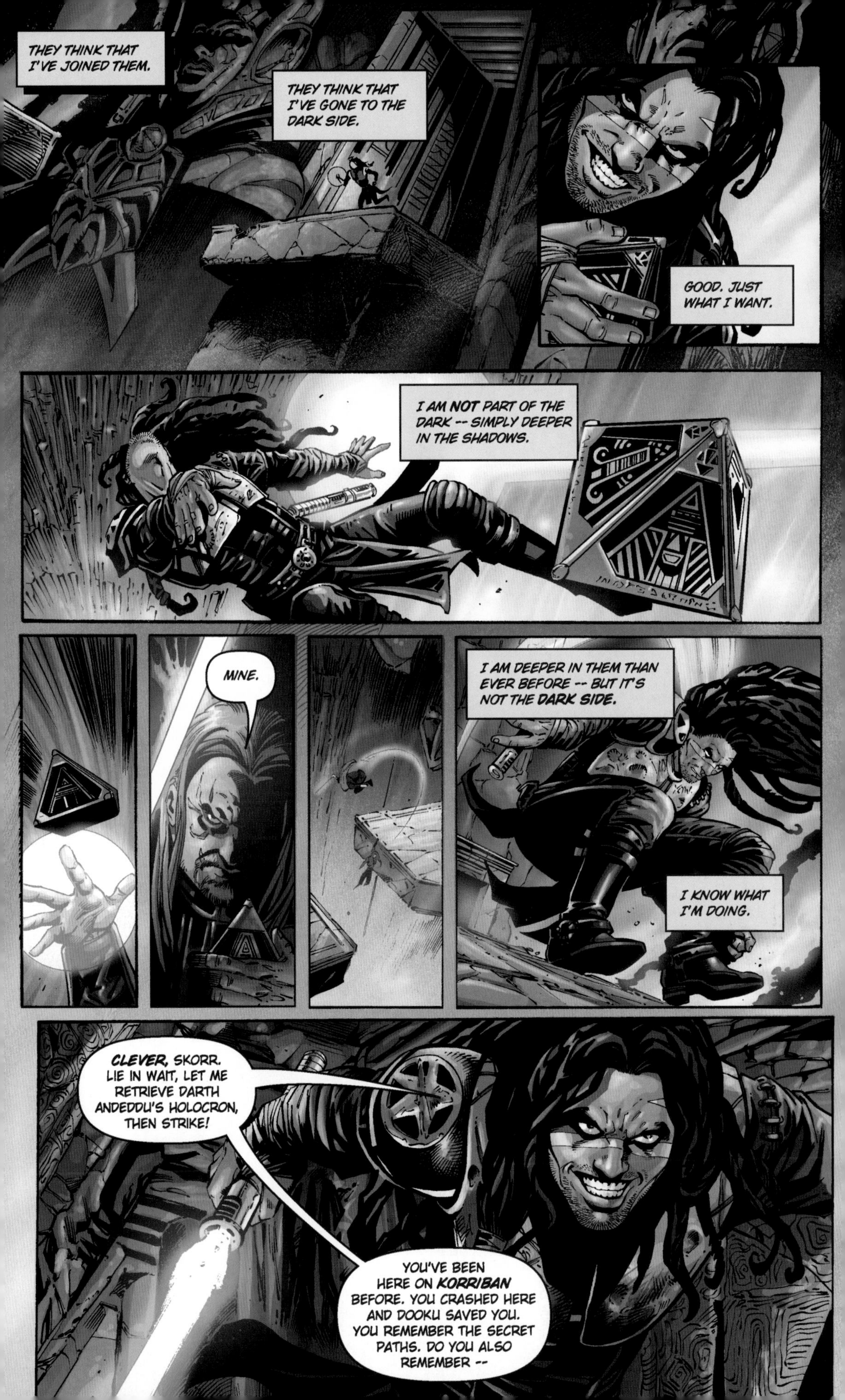
THEY THINK THAT I'VE JOINED THEM.
THEY THINK THAT I'VE GONE TO THE DARK SIDE.
GOOD. JUST WHAT I WANT.
I AM NOT PART OF THE DARK -- SIMPLY DEEPER IN THE SHADOWS.
MINE.
I AM DEEPER IN THEM THAN EVER BEFORE -- BUT IT'S NOT THE DARK SIDE.
I KNOW WHAT I'M DOING.
CLEVER, SKORR. LIE IN WAIT, LET ME RETRIEVE DARTH ANDEDDU'S HOLOCRON, THEN STRIKE!
YOU'VE BEEN HERE ON KORRIBAN BEFORE. YOU CRASHED HERE AND DOOKU SAVED YOU. YOU REMEMBER THE SECRET PATHS. DO YOU ALSO REMEMBER --

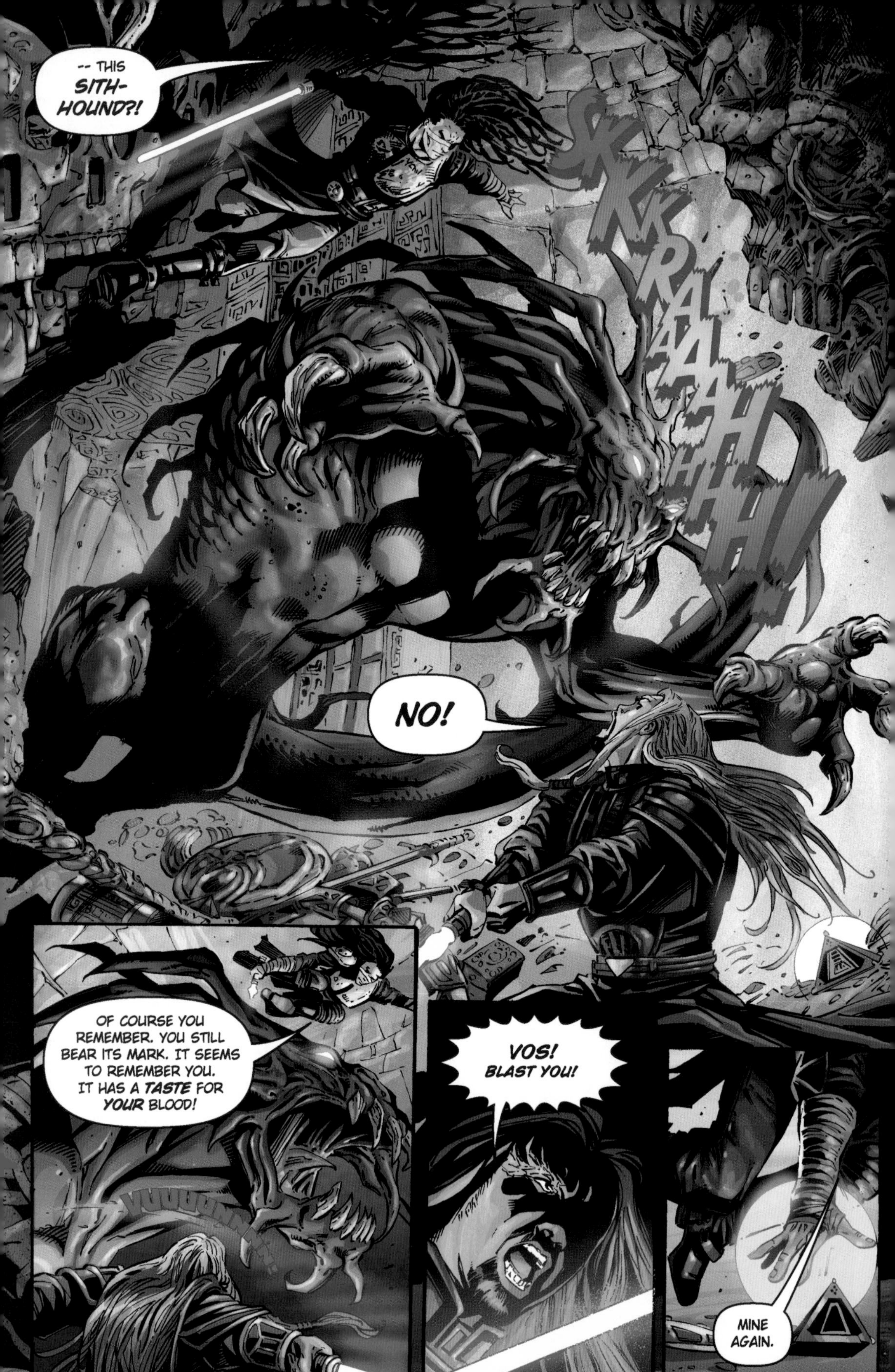
-- THIS SITH-HOUND?!
NO!
OF COURSE YOU REMEMBER. YOU STILL BEAR ITS MARK. IT SEEMS TO REMEMBER YOU. IT HAS A TASTE FOR YOUR BLOOD!
VOS! BLAST YOU!
MINE AGAIN.

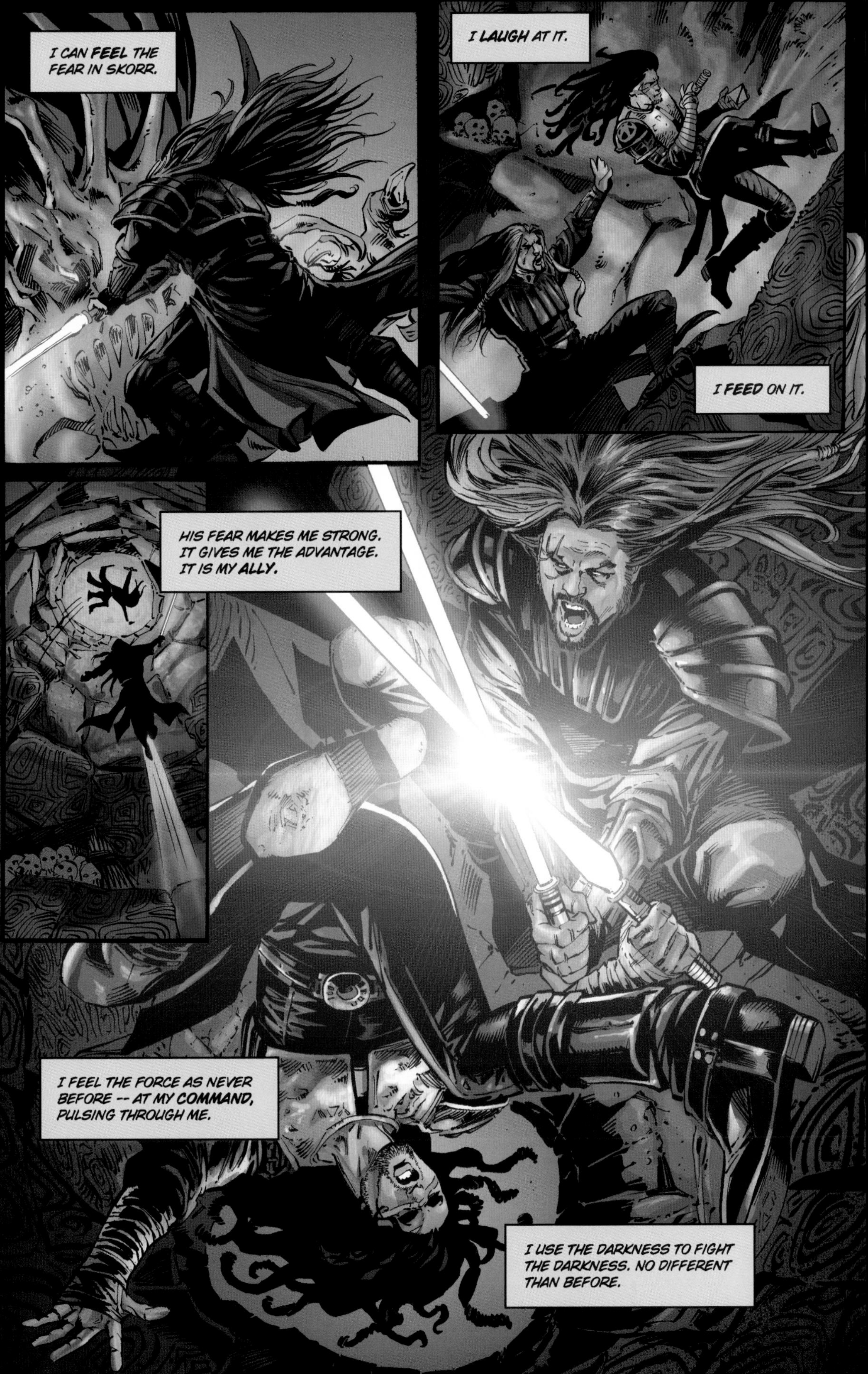
I CAN FEEL THE FEAR IN SKORR.
I LAUGH AT IT.
I FEED ON IT.
HIS FEAR MAKES ME STRONG. IT GIVES ME THE ADVANTAGE. IT IS MY ALLY.
I FEEL THE FORCE AS NEVER BEFORE -- AT MY COMMAND, PULSING THROUGH ME.
I USE THE DARKNESS TO FIGHT THE DARKNESS. NO DIFFERENT THAN BEFORE.

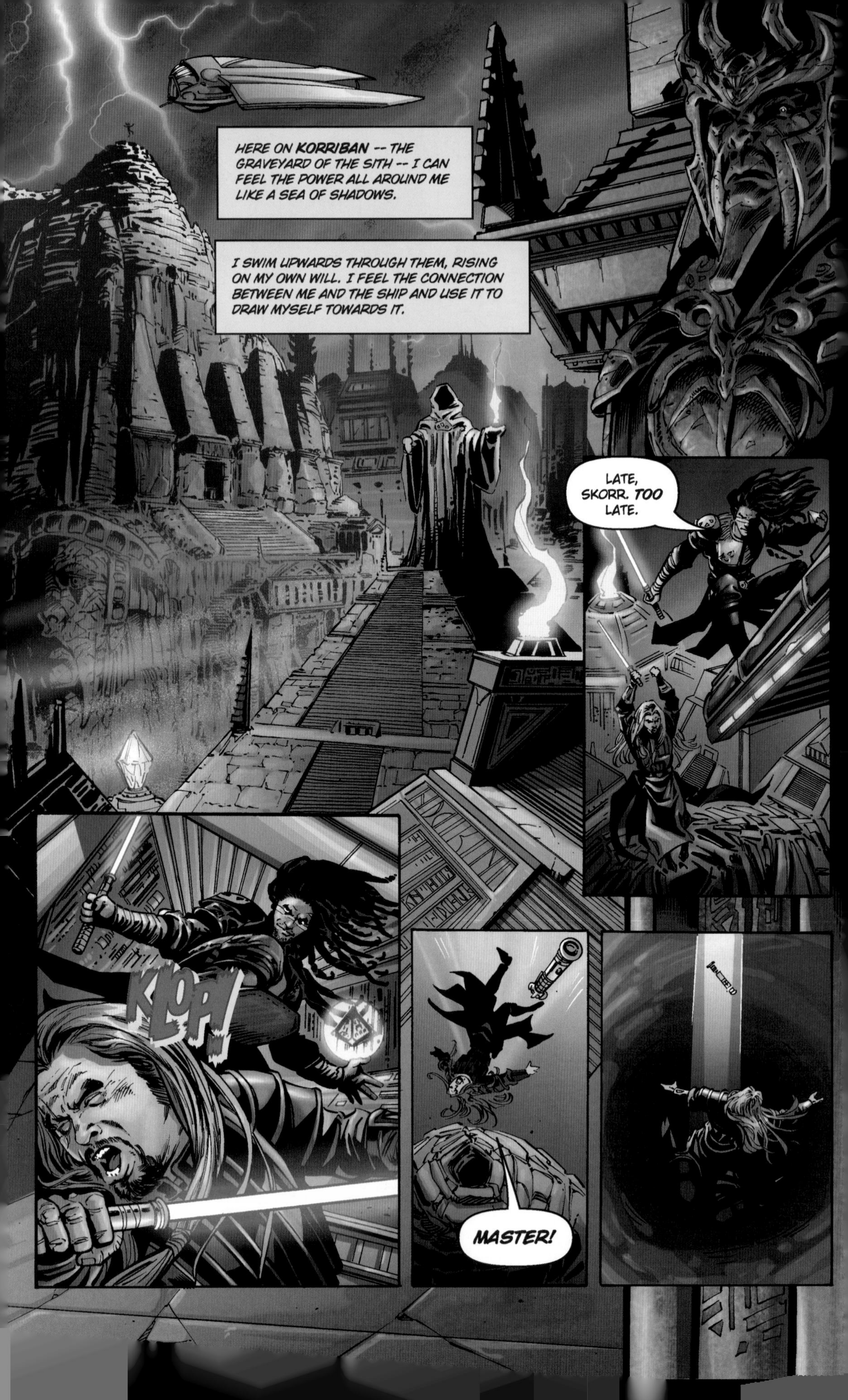
HERE ON KORRIBAN -- THE GRAVEYARD OF THE SITH -- I CAN FEEL THE POWER ALL AROUND ME LIKE A SEA OF SHADOWS.
I SWIM UPWARDS THROUGH THEM, RISING ON MY OWN WILL. I FEEL THE CONNECTION BETWEEN ME AND THE SHIP AND USE IT TO DRAW MYSELF TOWARDS IT.
LATE, SKORR. TOO LATE.
KLOP!
MASTER!

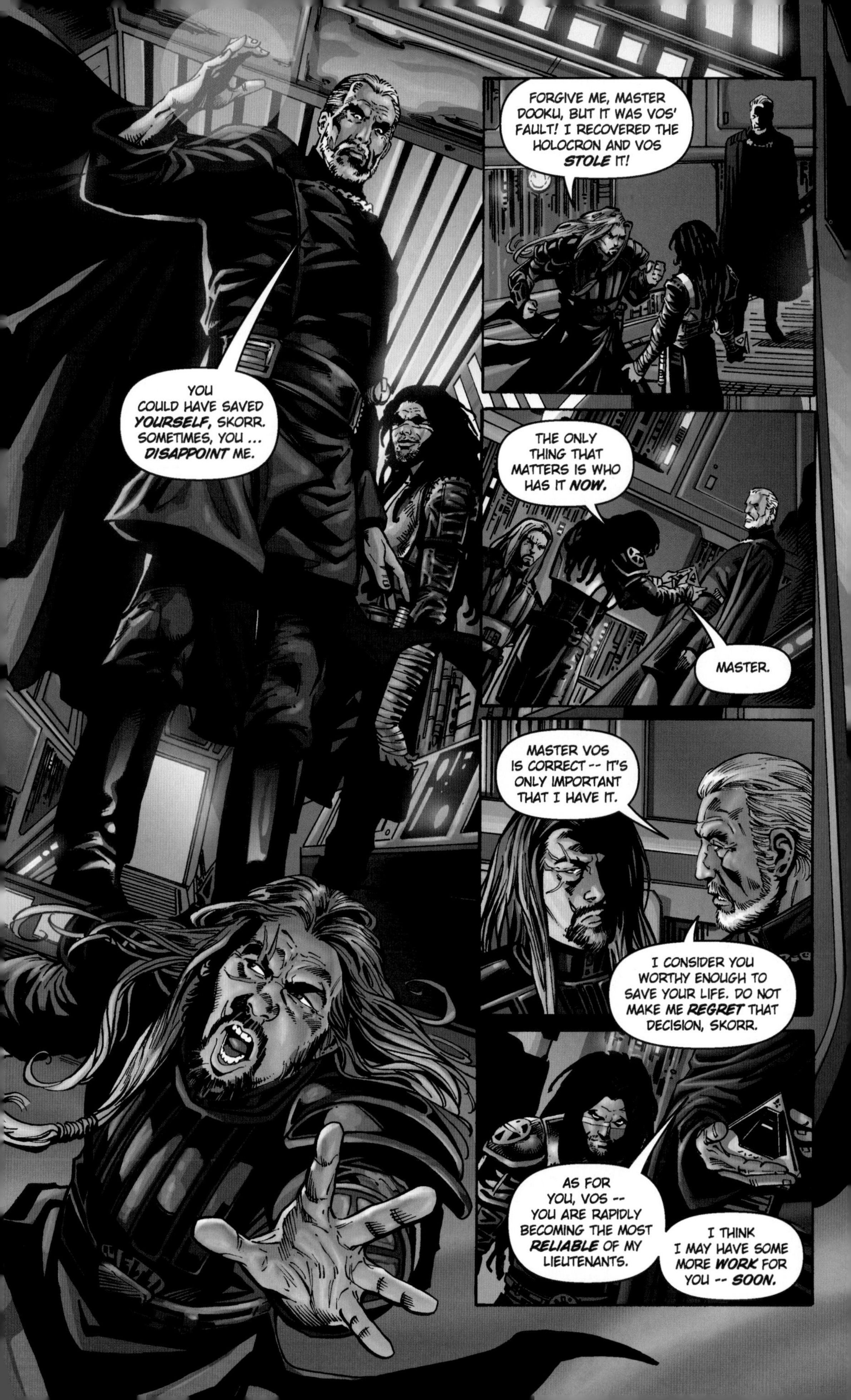

FORGIVE ME, MASTER DOOKU, BUT IT WAS VOS' FAULT! I RECOVERED THE HOLOCRON AND VOS STOLE IT!
YOU COULD HAVE SAVED YOURSELF, SKORR. SOMETIMES, YOU ... DISAPPOINT ME.
THE ONLY THING THAT MATTERS IS WHO HAS IT NOW.
MASTER.
MASTER VOS IS CORRECT -- IT'S ONLY IMPORTANT THAT I HAVE IT.
I CONSIDER YOU WORTHY ENOUGH TO SAVE YOUR LIFE. DO NOT MAKE ME REGRET THAT DECISION, SKORR.
AS FOR YOU, VOS -- YOU ARE RAPIDLY BECOMING THE MOST RELIABLE OF MY LIEUTENANTS.
I THINK I MAY HAVE SOME MORE WORK FOR YOU -- SOON.

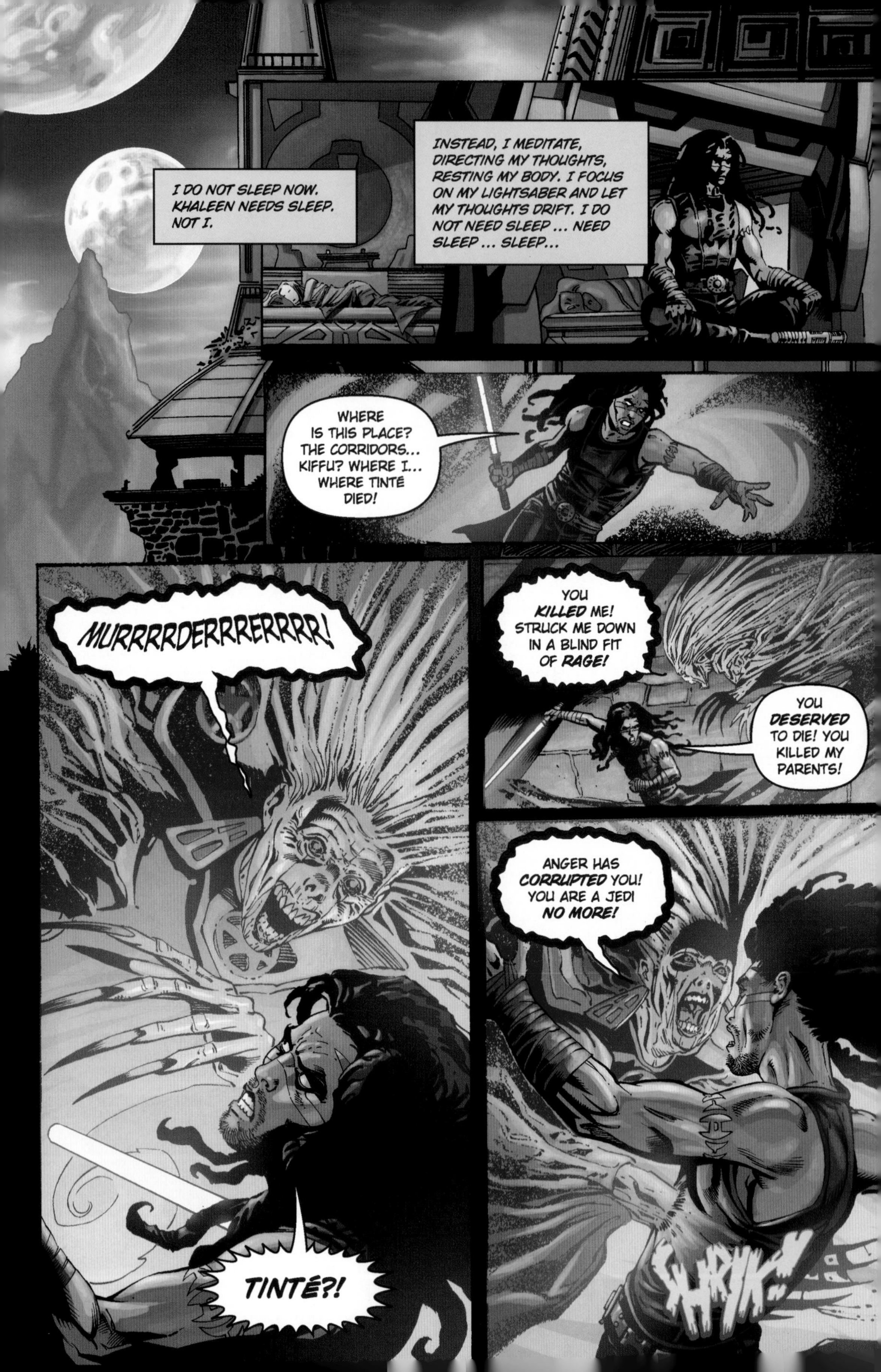
I DO NOT SLEEP NOW. KHALEEN NEEDS SLEEP. NOT I.
INSTEAD, I MEDITATE, DIRECTING MY THOUGHTS, RESTING MY BODY. I FOCUS ON MY LIGHTSABER AND LET MY THOUGHTS DRIFT. I DO NOT NEED SLEEP ... NEED SLEEP ... SLEEP...
WHERE IS THIS PLACE? THE CORRIDORS... KIFFU? WHERE I... WHERE TINTÉ DIED!
MURRRRDERRRERRRR!
TINTÉ?!
YOU KILLED ME! STRUCK ME DOWN IN A BLIND FIT OF RAGE!
YOU DESERVED TO DIE! YOU KILLED MY PARENTS!
ANGER HAS CORRUPTED YOU! YOU ARE A JEDI NO MORE!
SHRAK!

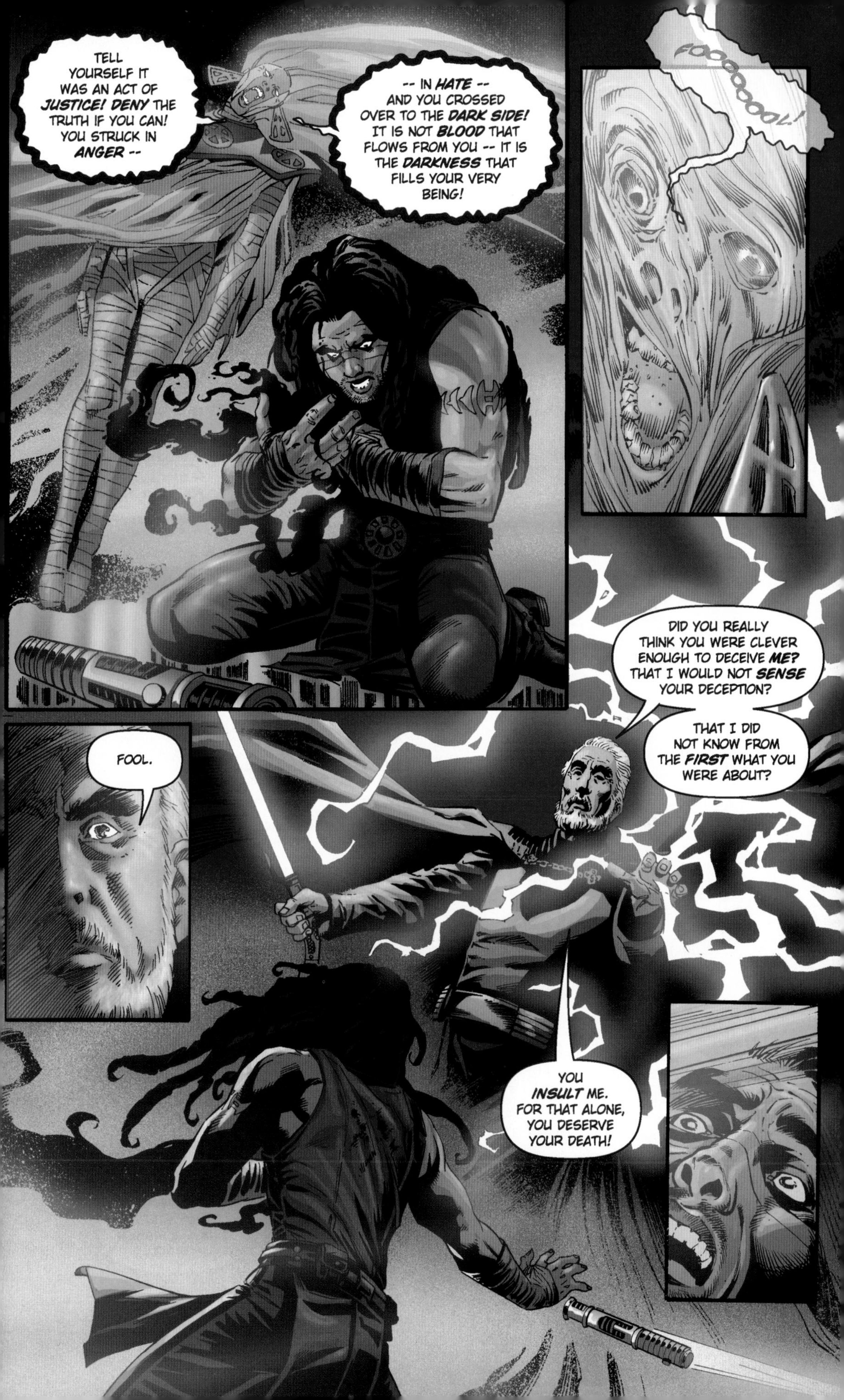
TELL YOURSELF IT WAS AN ACT OF JUSTICE! DENY THE TRUTH IF YOU CAN! YOU STRUCK IN ANGER --
-- IN HATE -- AND YOU CROSSED OVER TO THE DARK SIDE! IT IS NOT BLOOD THAT FLOWS FROM YOU -- IT IS THE DARKNESS THAT FILLS YOUR VERY BEING!
FOOOOOOOL!
FOOL.
DID YOU REALLY THINK YOU WERE CLEVER ENOUGH TO DECEIVE ME? THAT I WOULD NOT SENSE YOUR DECEPTION?
THAT I DID NOT KNOW FROM THE FIRST WHAT YOU WERE ABOUT?
YOU INSULT ME. FOR THAT ALONE, YOU DESERVE YOUR DEATH!

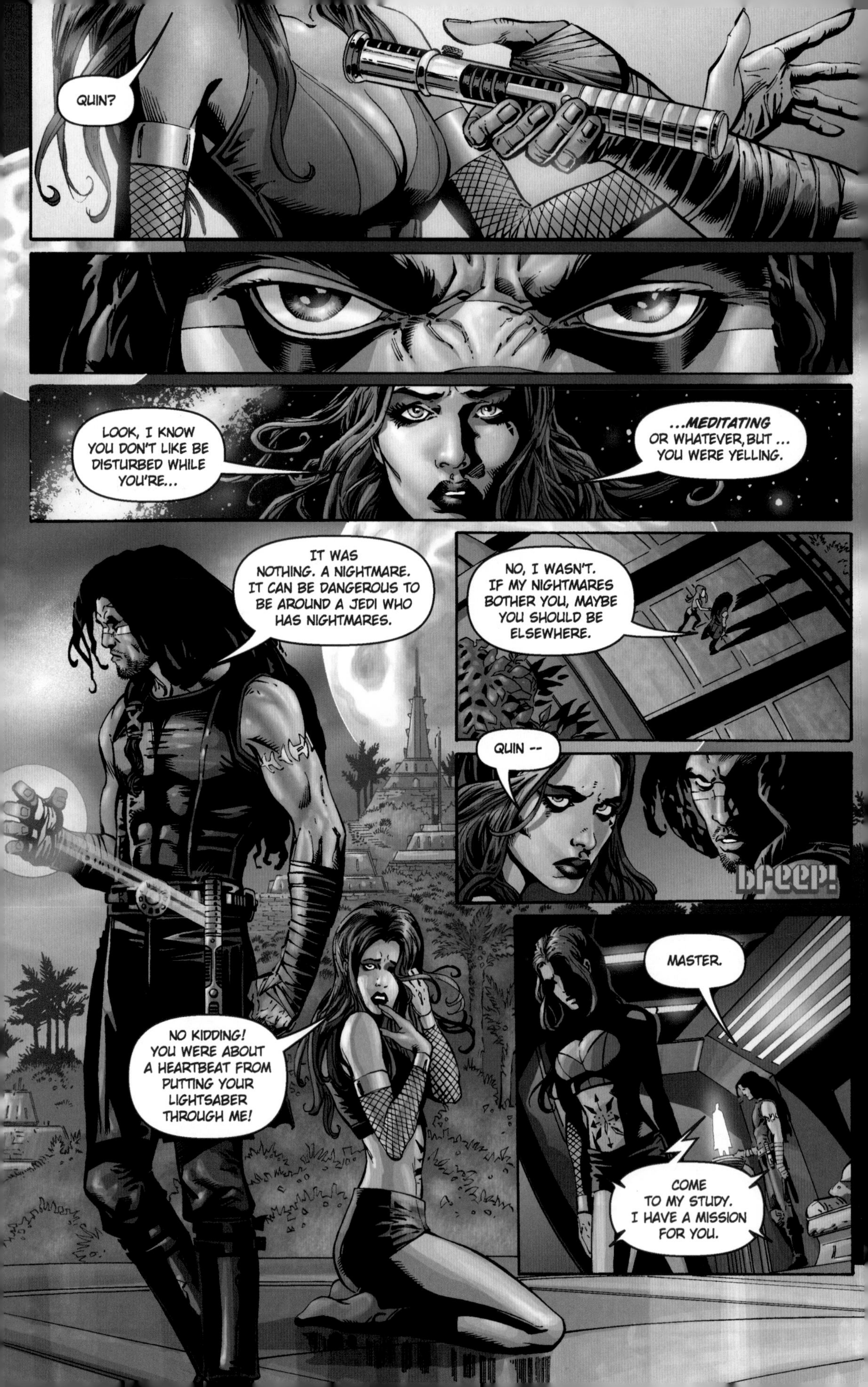
QUIN?
LOOK, I KNOW YOU DON'T LIKE BE DISTURBED WHILE YOU'RE...
...MEDITATING OR WHATEVER, BUT ... YOU WERE YELLING.
IT WAS NOTHING. A NIGHTMARE. IT CAN BE DANGEROUS TO BE AROUND A JEDI WHO HAS NIGHTMARES.
NO KIDDING! YOU WERE ABOUT A HEARTBEAT FROM PUTTING YOUR LIGHTSABER THROUGH ME!
NO, I WASN'T. IF MY NIGHTMARES BOTHER YOU, MAYBE YOU SHOULD BE ELSEWHERE.
QUIN --
breep!
MASTER.
COME TO MY STUDY. I HAVE A MISSION FOR YOU.

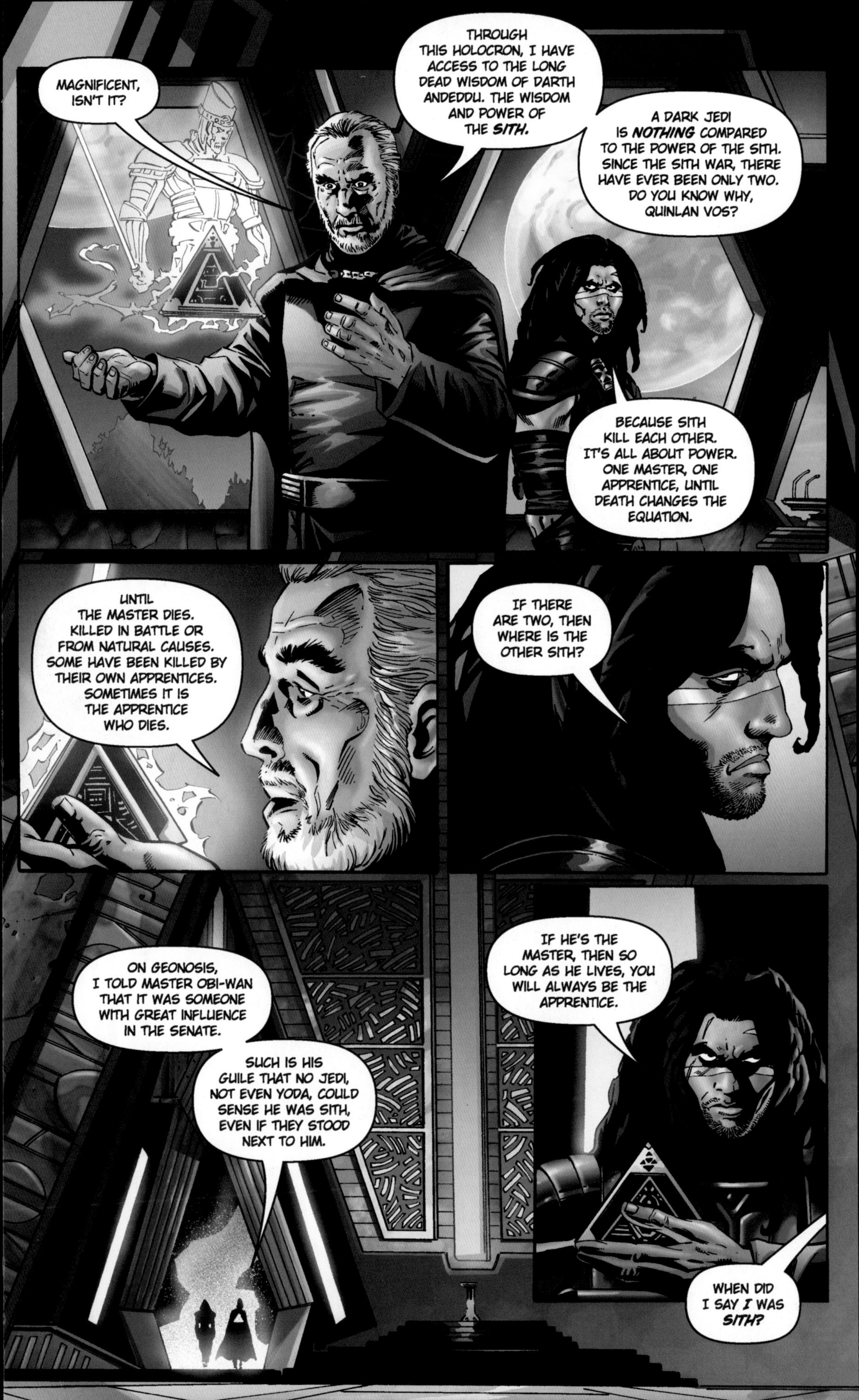
MAGNIFICENT, ISN'T IT?
THROUGH THIS HOLOCRON, I HAVE ACCESS TO THE LONG DEAD WISDOM OF DARTH ANDEDDU. THE WISDOM AND POWER OF THE *SITH.*
A DARK JEDI IS ***NOTHING*** COMPARED TO THE POWER OF THE SITH. SINCE THE SITH WAR, THERE HAVE EVER BEEN ONLY TWO. DO YOU KNOW WHY, QUINLAN VOS?
BECAUSE SITH KILL EACH OTHER. IT'S ALL ABOUT POWER. ONE MASTER, ONE APPRENTICE, UNTIL DEATH CHANGES THE EQUATION.
UNTIL THE MASTER DIES. KILLED IN BATTLE OR FROM NATURAL CAUSES. SOME HAVE BEEN KILLED BY THEIR OWN APPRENTICES. SOMETIMES IT IS THE APPRENTICE WHO DIES.
IF THERE ARE TWO, THEN WHERE IS THE OTHER SITH?
ON GEONOSIS, I TOLD MASTER OBI-WAN THAT IT WAS SOMEONE WITH GREAT INFLUENCE IN THE SENATE.
SUCH IS HIS GUILE THAT NO JEDI, NOT EVEN YODA, COULD SENSE HE WAS SITH, EVEN IF THEY STOOD NEXT TO HIM.
IF HE'S THE MASTER, THEN SO LONG AS HE LIVES, YOU WILL ALWAYS BE THE APPRENTICE.
WHEN DID I SAY *I* WAS *SITH?*

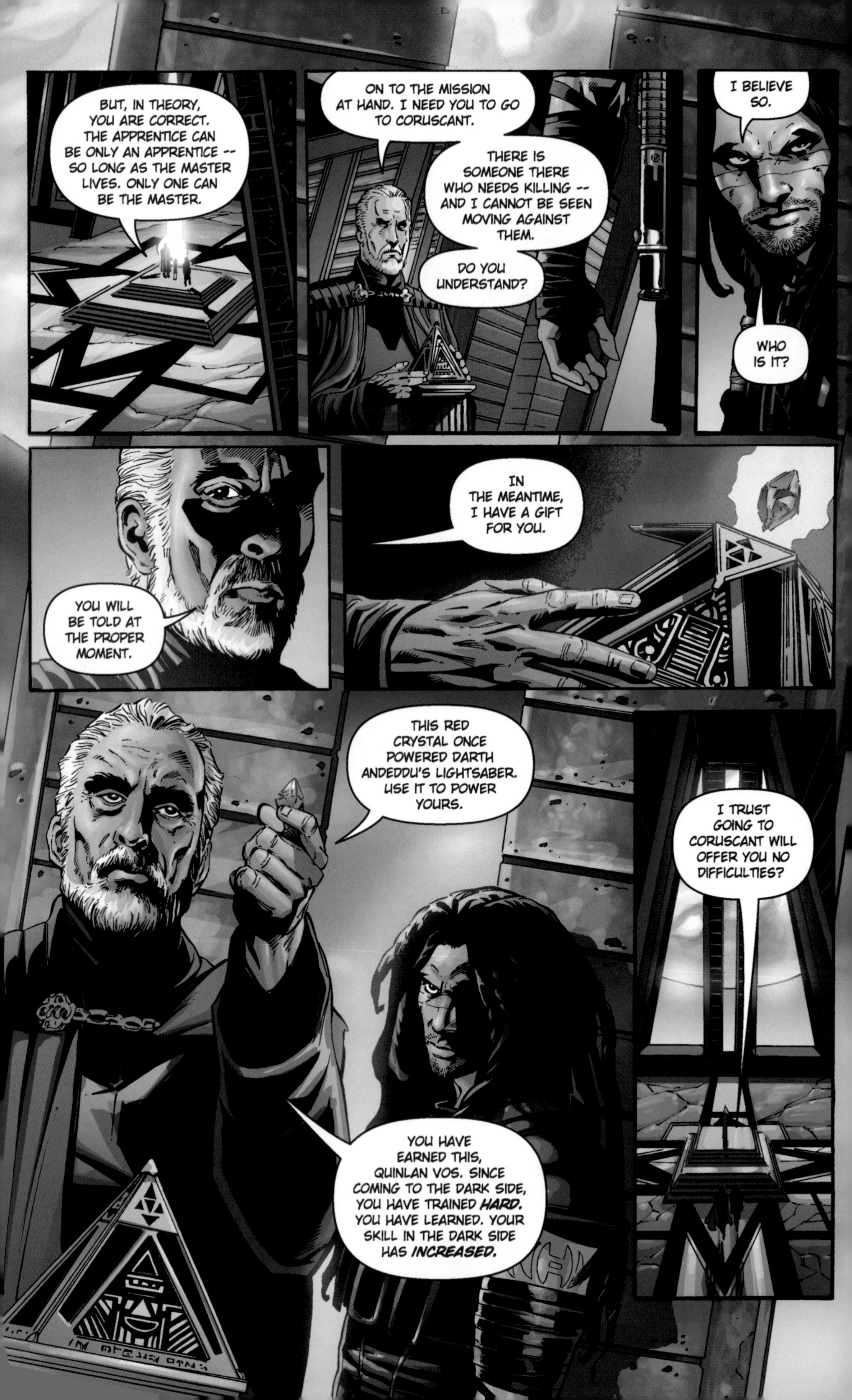
BUT, IN THEORY, YOU ARE CORRECT. THE APPRENTICE CAN BE ONLY AN APPRENTICE -- SO LONG AS THE MASTER LIVES. ONLY ONE CAN BE THE MASTER.
ON TO THE MISSION AT HAND. I NEED YOU TO GO TO CORUSCANT.
THERE IS SOMEONE THERE WHO NEEDS KILLING -- AND I CANNOT BE SEEN MOVING AGAINST THEM.
DO YOU UNDERSTAND?
I BELIEVE SO.
WHO IS IT?
YOU WILL BE TOLD AT THE PROPER MOMENT.
IN THE MEANTIME, I HAVE A GIFT FOR YOU.
THIS RED CRYSTAL ONCE POWERED DARTH ANDEDDU'S LIGHTSABER. USE IT TO POWER YOURS.
YOU HAVE EARNED THIS, QUINLAN VOS. SINCE COMING TO THE DARK SIDE, YOU HAVE TRAINED *HARD.* YOU HAVE LEARNED. YOUR SKILL IN THE DARK SIDE HAS *INCREASED.*
I TRUST GOING TO CORUSCANT WILL OFFER YOU NO DIFFICULTIES?

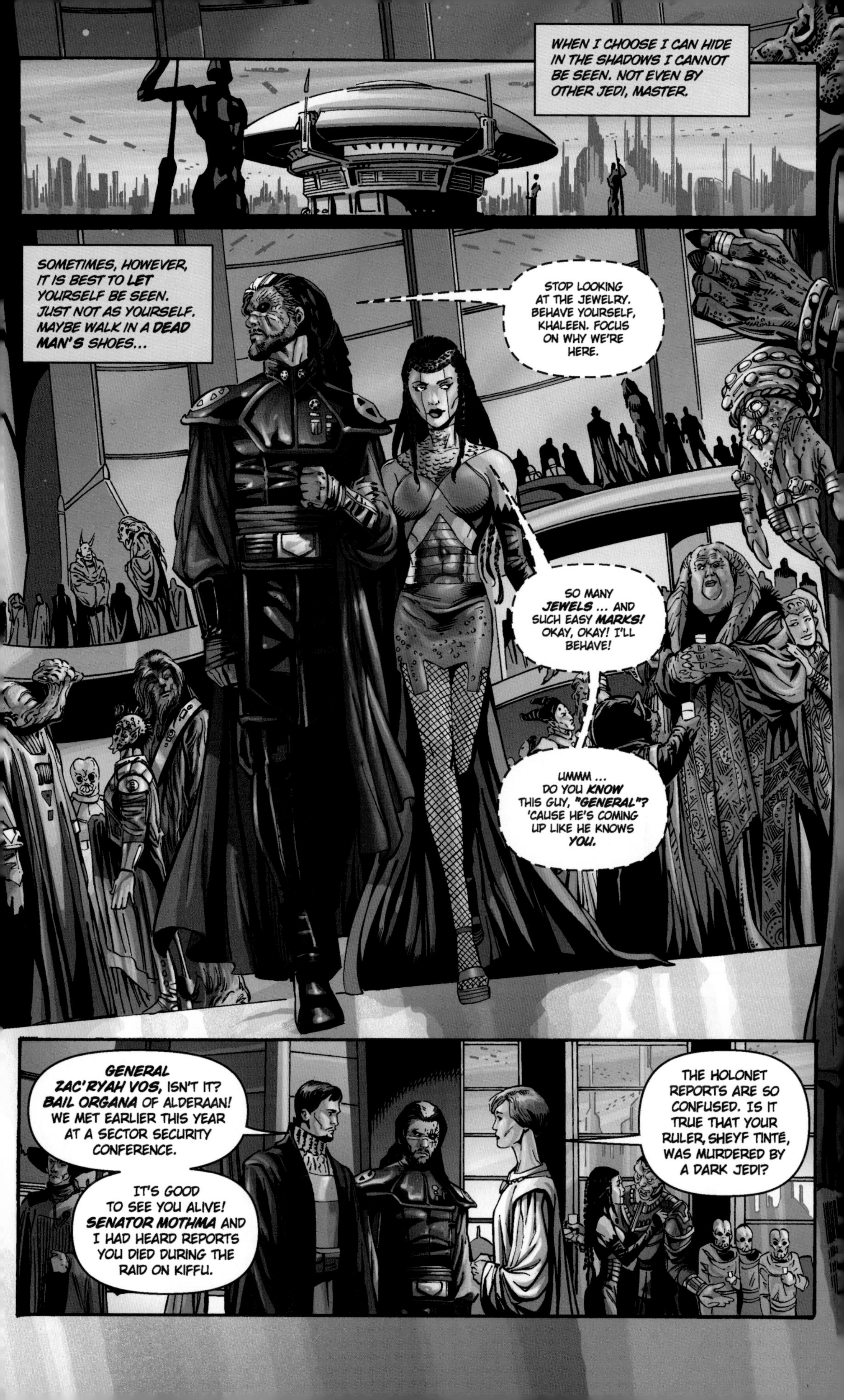
WHEN I CHOOSE I CAN HIDE IN THE SHADOWS I CANNOT BE SEEN. NOT EVEN BY OTHER JEDI, MASTER.
SOMETIMES, HOWEVER, IT IS BEST TO LET YOURSELF BE SEEN. JUST NOT AS YOURSELF. MAYBE WALK IN A DEAD MAN'S SHOES...
STOP LOOKING AT THE JEWELRY. BEHAVE YOURSELF, KHALEEN. FOCUS ON WHY WE'RE HERE.
SO MANY JEWELS ... AND SUCH EASY MARKS! OKAY, OKAY! I'LL BEHAVE!
UMMM ... DO YOU KNOW THIS GUY, "GENERAL"? 'CAUSE HE'S COMING UP LIKE HE KNOWS YOU.
GENERAL ZAC'RYAH VOS, ISN'T IT? BAIL ORGANA OF ALDERAAN! WE MET EARLIER THIS YEAR AT A SECTOR SECURITY CONFERENCE.
IT'S GOOD TO SEE YOU ALIVE! SENATOR MOTHMA AND I HAD HEARD REPORTS YOU DIED DURING THE RAID ON KIFFU.
THE HOLONET REPORTS ARE SO CONFUSED. IS IT TRUE THAT YOUR RULER, SHEYF TINTÉ, WAS MURDERED BY A DARK JEDI?

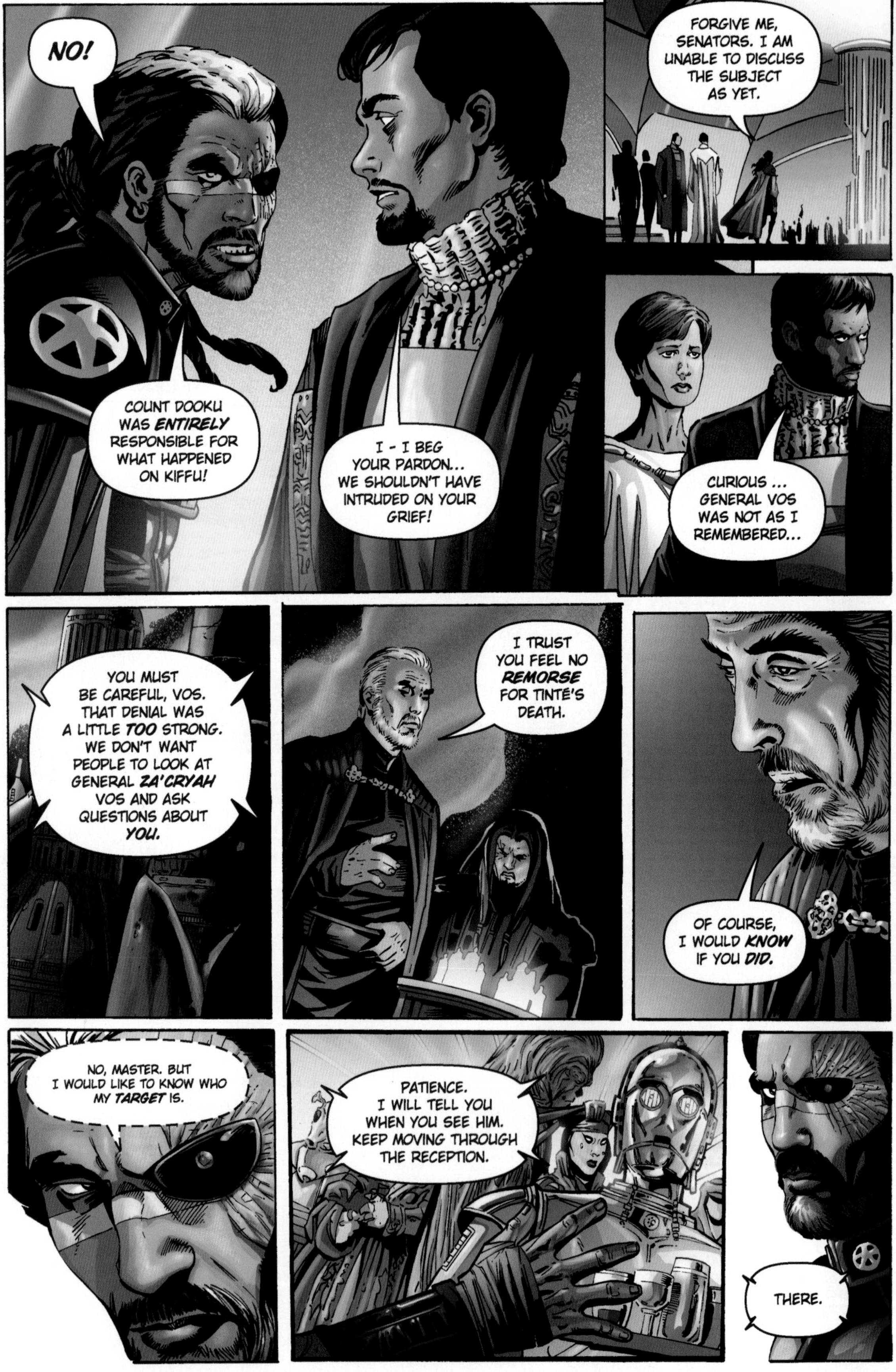
NO!
COUNT DOOKU WAS ENTIRELY RESPONSIBLE FOR WHAT HAPPENED ON KIFFU!
I - I BEG YOUR PARDON... WE SHOULDN'T HAVE INTRUDED ON YOUR GRIEF!
FORGIVE ME, SENATORS. I AM UNABLE TO DISCUSS THE SUBJECT AS YET.
CURIOUS ... GENERAL VOS WAS NOT AS I REMEMBERED...
YOU MUST BE CAREFUL, VOS. THAT DENIAL WAS A LITTLE TOO STRONG. WE DON'T WANT PEOPLE TO LOOK AT GENERAL ZA'CRYAH VOS AND ASK QUESTIONS ABOUT YOU.
I TRUST YOU FEEL NO REMORSE FOR TINTÉ'S DEATH.
OF COURSE, I WOULD KNOW IF YOU DID.
NO, MASTER. BUT I WOULD LIKE TO KNOW WHO MY TARGET IS.
PATIENCE. I WILL TELL YOU WHEN YOU SEE HIM. KEEP MOVING THROUGH THE RECEPTION.
THERE.

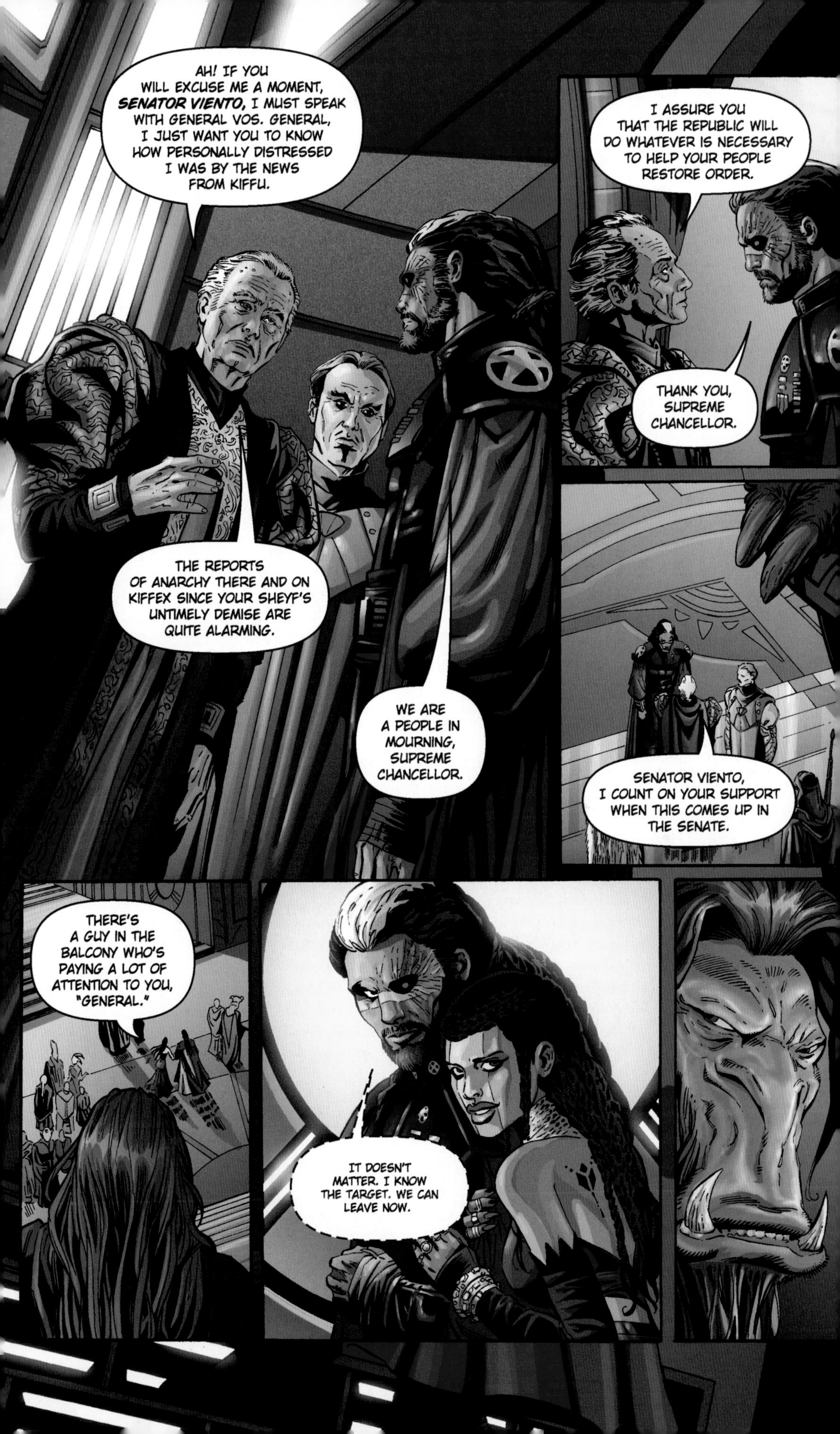
AH! IF YOU WILL EXCUSE ME A MOMENT, SENATOR VIENTO, I MUST SPEAK WITH GENERAL VOS. GENERAL, I JUST WANT YOU TO KNOW HOW PERSONALLY DISTRESSED I WAS BY THE NEWS FROM KIFFU.
THE REPORTS OF ANARCHY THERE AND ON KIFFEX SINCE YOUR SHEYF'S UNTIMELY DEMISE ARE QUITE ALARMING.
WE ARE A PEOPLE IN MOURNING, SUPREME CHANCELLOR.
I ASSURE YOU THAT THE REPUBLIC WILL DO WHATEVER IS NECESSARY TO HELP YOUR PEOPLE RESTORE ORDER.
THANK YOU, SUPREME CHANCELLOR.
SENATOR VIENTO, I COUNT ON YOUR SUPPORT WHEN THIS COMES UP IN THE SENATE.
THERE'S A GUY IN THE BALCONY WHO'S PAYING A LOT OF ATTENTION TO YOU, "GENERAL."
IT DOESN'T MATTER. I KNOW THE TARGET. WE CAN LEAVE NOW.

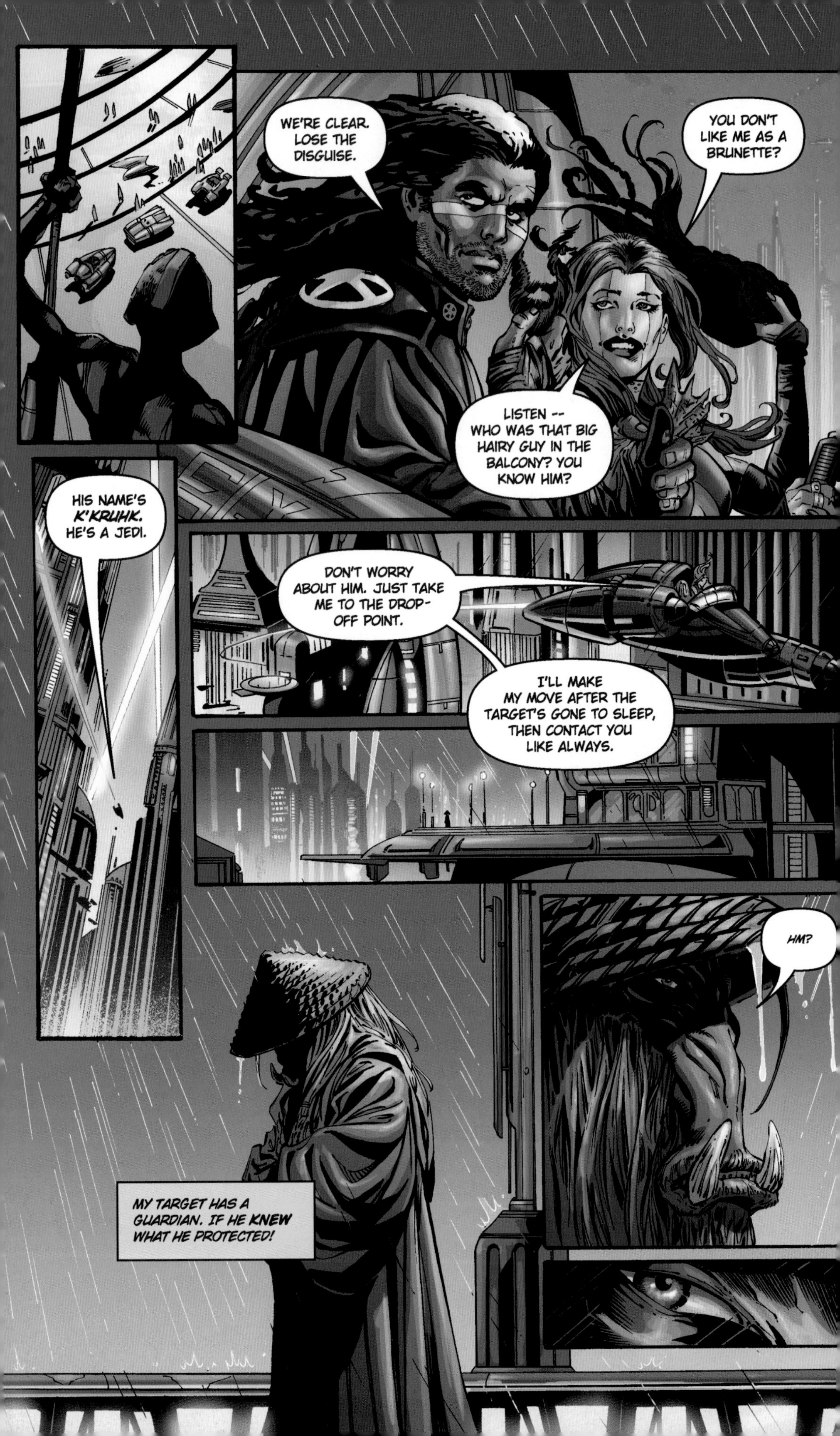

WE'RE CLEAR. LOSE THE DISGUISE.
YOU DON'T LIKE ME AS A BRUNETTE?
LISTEN -- WHO WAS THAT BIG HAIRY GUY IN THE BALCONY? YOU KNOW HIM?
HIS NAME'S ***K'KRUHK.*** HE'S A JEDI.
DON'T WORRY ABOUT HIM. JUST TAKE ME TO THE DROP-OFF POINT.
I'LL MAKE MY MOVE AFTER THE TARGET'S GONE TO SLEEP, THEN CONTACT YOU LIKE ALWAYS.
HM?
MY TARGET HAS A GUARDIAN. IF HE ***KNEW*** *WHAT HE PROTECTED!*

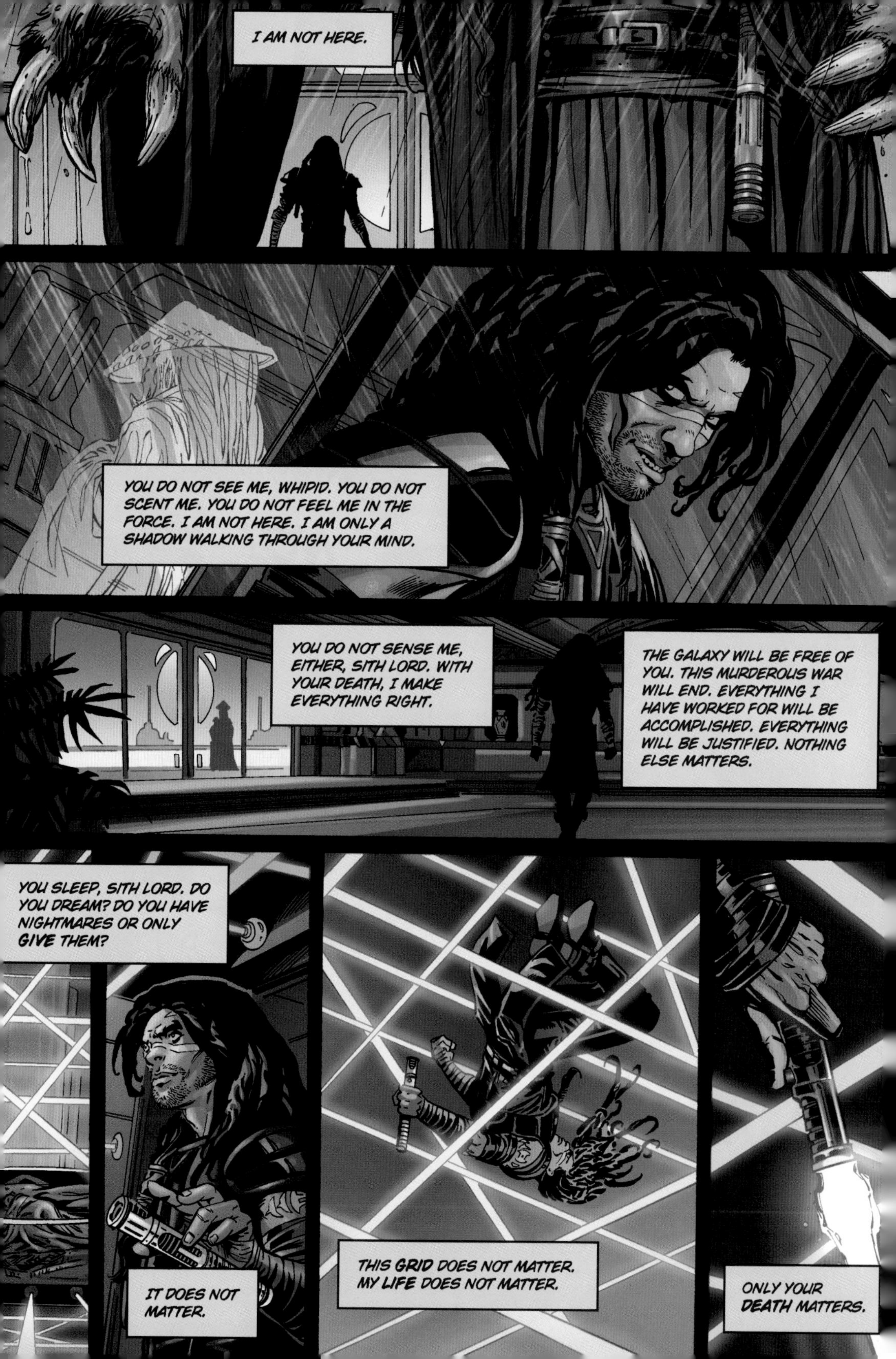
I AM NOT HERE.
YOU DO NOT SEE ME, WHIPID. YOU DO NOT SCENT ME. YOU DO NOT FEEL ME IN THE FORCE. I AM NOT HERE. I AM ONLY A SHADOW WALKING THROUGH YOUR MIND.
YOU DO NOT SENSE ME, EITHER, SITH LORD. WITH YOUR DEATH, I MAKE EVERYTHING RIGHT.
THE GALAXY WILL BE FREE OF YOU. THIS MURDEROUS WAR WILL END. EVERYTHING I HAVE WORKED FOR WILL BE ACCOMPLISHED. EVERYTHING WILL BE JUSTIFIED. NOTHING ELSE MATTERS.
YOU SLEEP, SITH LORD. DO YOU DREAM? DO YOU HAVE NIGHTMARES OR ONLY GIVE THEM?
IT DOES NOT MATTER.
THIS GRID DOES NOT MATTER. MY LIFE DOES NOT MATTER.
ONLY YOUR DEATH MATTERS.

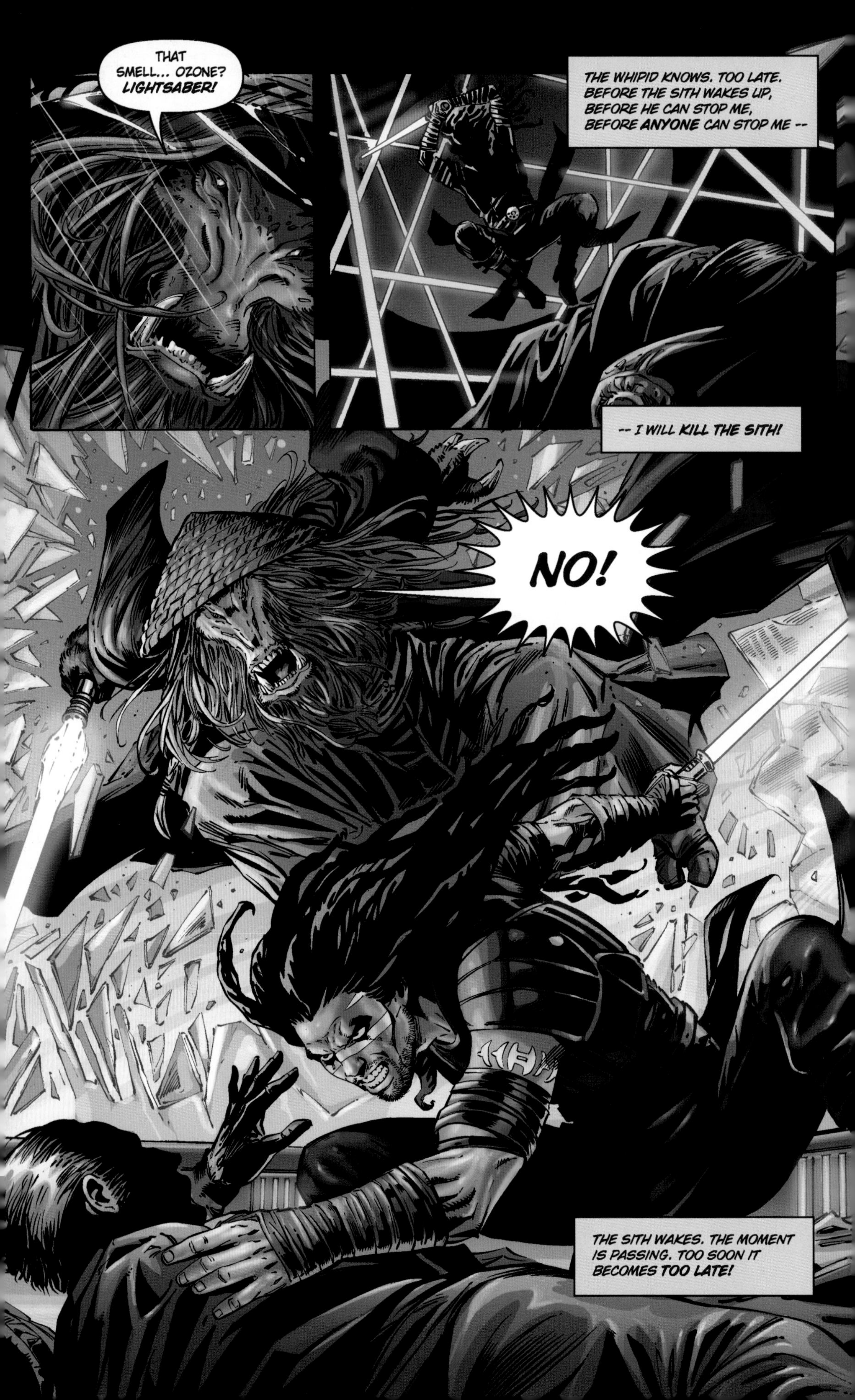
THAT SMELL... OZONE? LIGHTSABER!
THE WHIPID KNOWS. TOO LATE. BEFORE THE SITH WAKES UP, BEFORE HE CAN STOP ME, BEFORE ANYONE CAN STOP ME --
-- I WILL KILL THE SITH!
NO!
THE SITH WAKES. THE MOMENT IS PASSING. TOO SOON IT BECOMES TOO LATE!

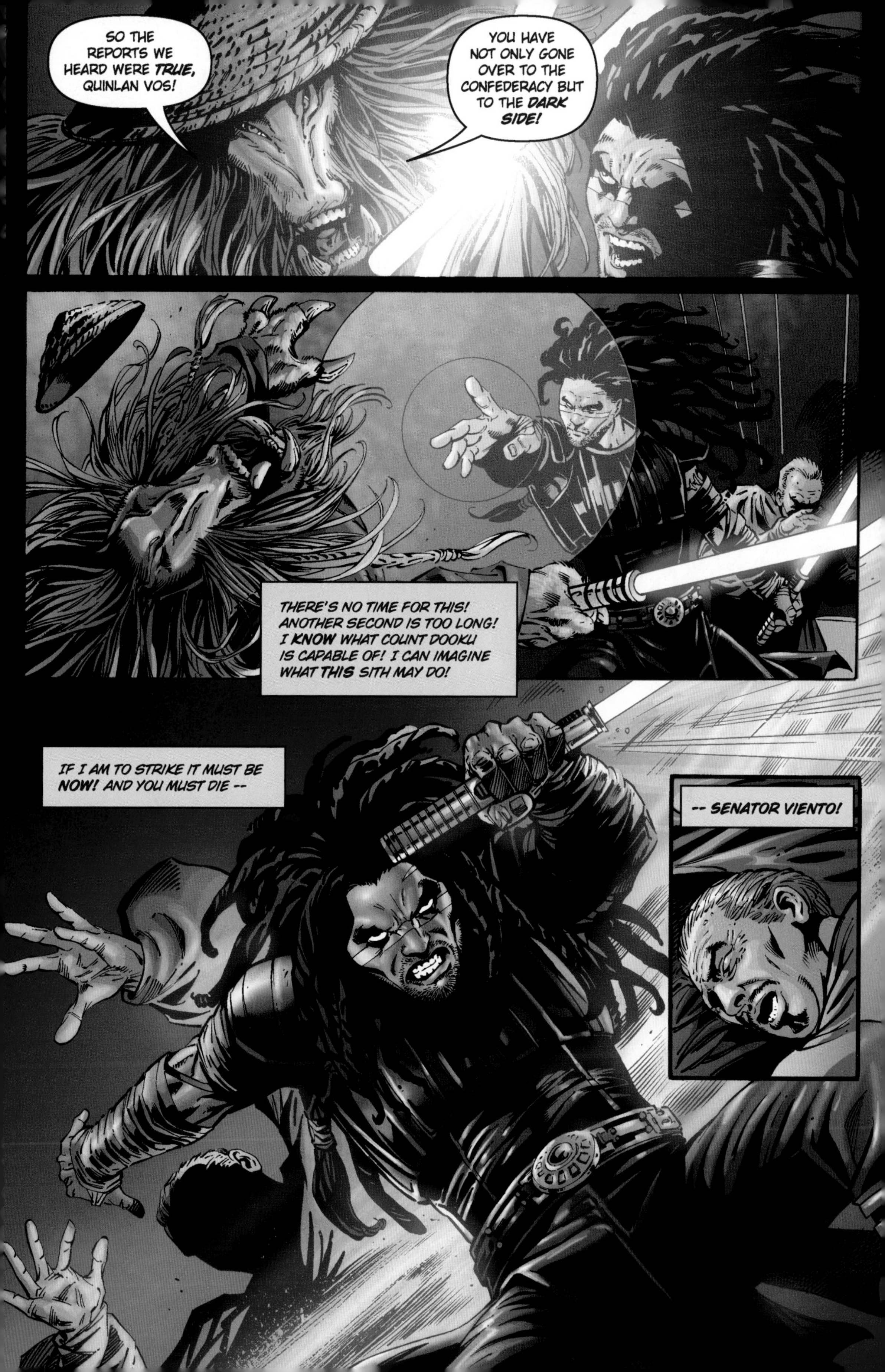
SO THE REPORTS WE HEARD WERE TRUE, QUINLAN VOS!
YOU HAVE NOT ONLY GONE OVER TO THE CONFEDERACY BUT TO THE DARK SIDE!
THERE'S NO TIME FOR THIS! ANOTHER SECOND IS TOO LONG! I KNOW WHAT COUNT DOOKU IS CAPABLE OF! I CAN IMAGINE WHAT THIS SITH MAY DO!
IF I AM TO STRIKE IT MUST BE NOW! AND YOU MUST DIE --
-- SENATOR VIENTO!

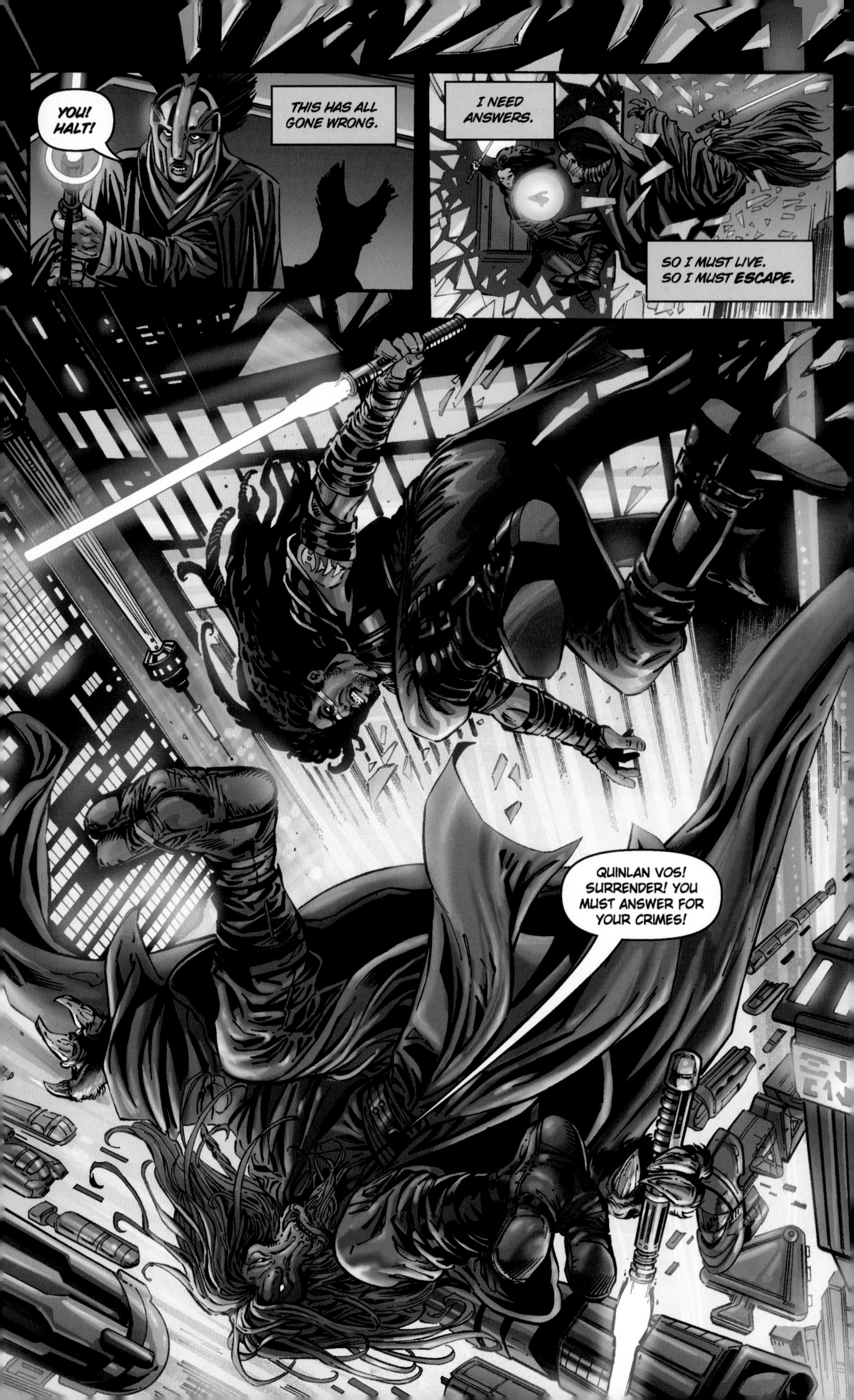
YOU! HALT!
THIS HAS ALL GONE WRONG.
I NEED ANSWERS.
SO I MUST LIVE. SO I MUST ESCAPE.
QUINLAN VOS! SURRENDER! YOU MUST ANSWER FOR YOUR CRIMES!

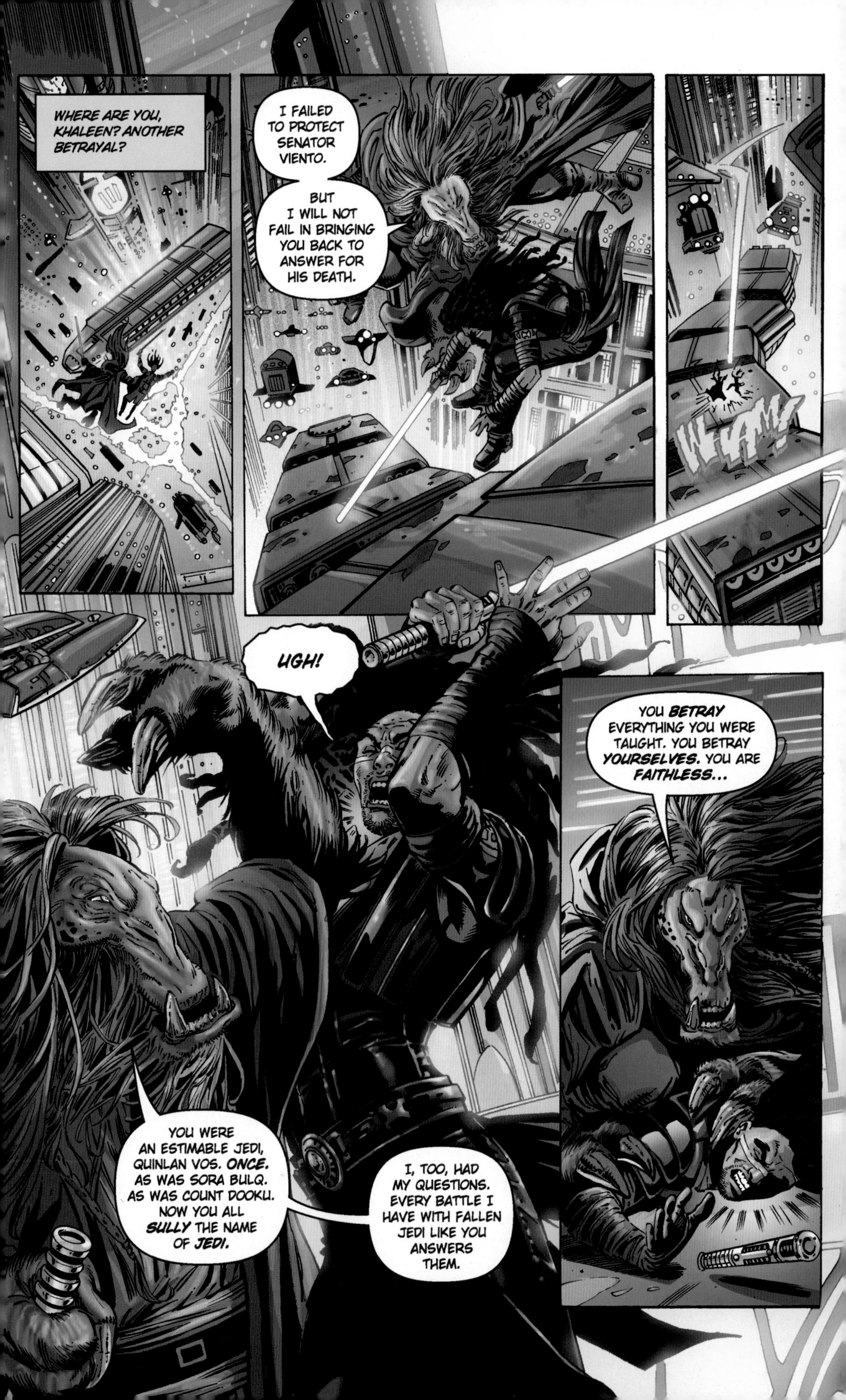

WHERE ARE YOU, KHALEEN? ANOTHER BETRAYAL?
I FAILED TO PROTECT SENATOR VIENTO.
BUT I WILL NOT FAIL IN BRINGING YOU BACK TO ANSWER FOR HIS DEATH.
WHAM!
UGH!
YOU BETRAY EVERYTHING YOU WERE TAUGHT. YOU BETRAY YOURSELVES. YOU ARE FAITHLESS...
YOU WERE AN ESTIMABLE JEDI, QUINLAN VOS. ONCE. AS WAS SORA BULQ. AS WAS COUNT DOOKU. NOW YOU ALL SULLY THE NAME OF JEDI.
I, TOO, HAD MY QUESTIONS. EVERY BATTLE I HAVE WITH FALLEN JEDI LIKE YOU ANSWERS THEM.

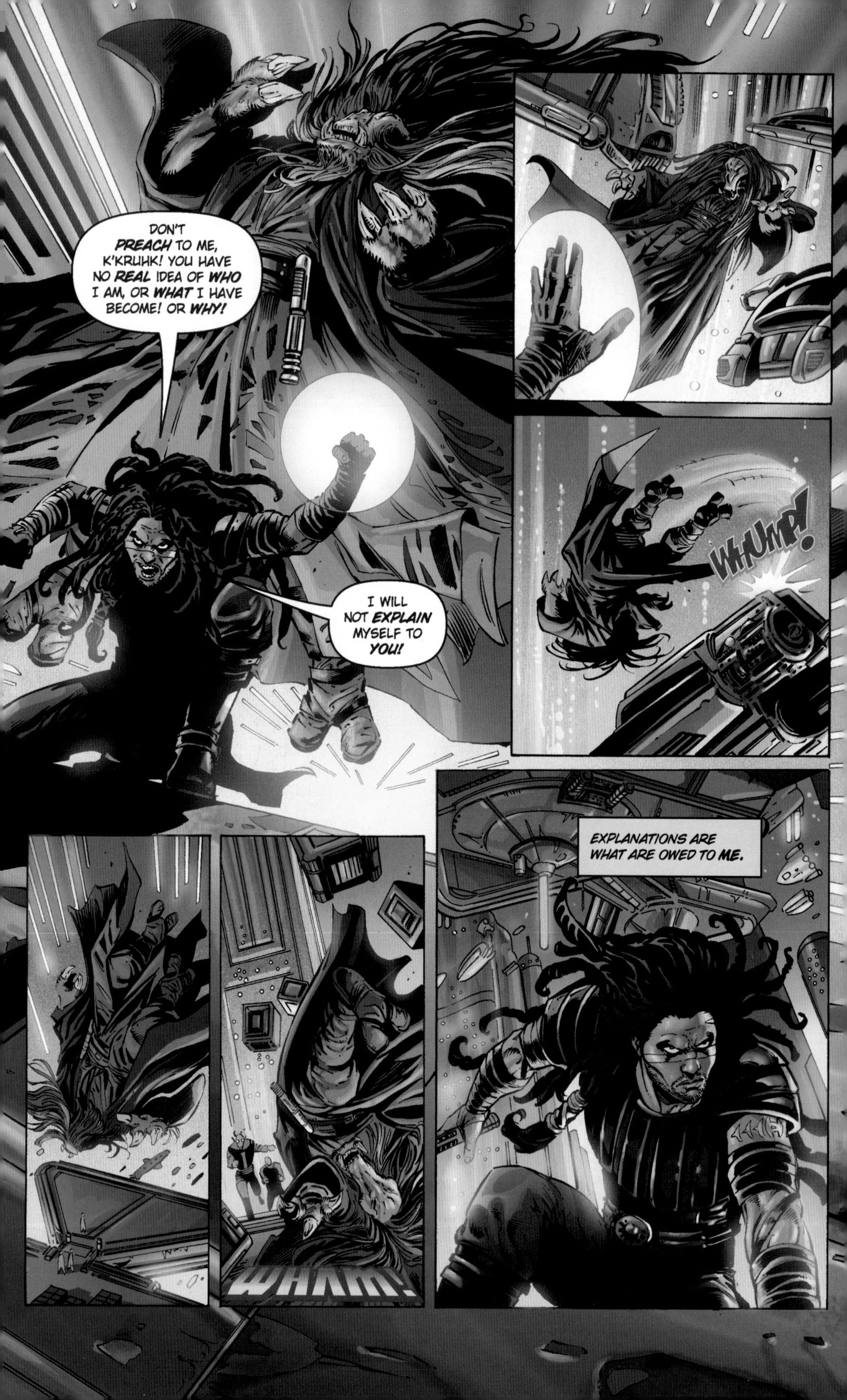
DON'T PREACH TO ME, K'KRUHK! YOU HAVE NO REAL IDEA OF WHO I AM, OR WHAT I HAVE BECOME! OR WHY!
I WILL NOT EXPLAIN MYSELF TO YOU!
WHUMP!
WHAM!
EXPLANATIONS ARE WHAT ARE OWED TO ME.

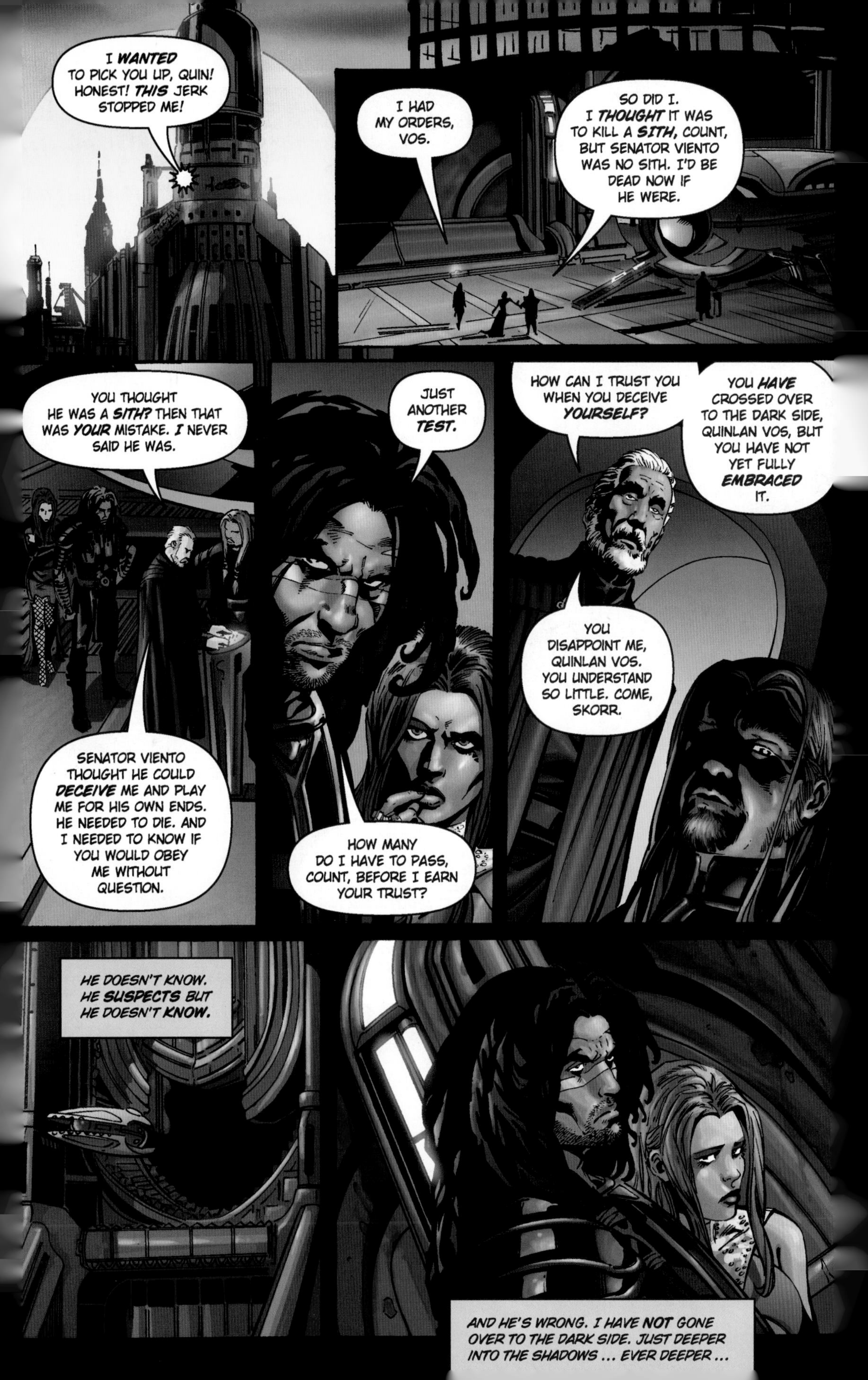
I WANTED TO PICK YOU UP, QUIN! HONEST! THIS JERK STOPPED ME!
I HAD MY ORDERS, VOS.
SO DID I. I THOUGHT IT WAS TO KILL A SITH, COUNT, BUT SENATOR VIENTO WAS NO SITH. I'D BE DEAD NOW IF HE WERE.
YOU THOUGHT HE WAS A SITH? THEN THAT WAS YOUR MISTAKE. I NEVER SAID HE WAS.
SENATOR VIENTO THOUGHT HE COULD DECEIVE ME AND PLAY ME FOR HIS OWN ENDS. HE NEEDED TO DIE. AND I NEEDED TO KNOW IF YOU WOULD OBEY ME WITHOUT QUESTION.
JUST ANOTHER TEST.
HOW MANY DO I HAVE TO PASS, COUNT, BEFORE I EARN YOUR TRUST?
HOW CAN I TRUST YOU WHEN YOU DECEIVE YOURSELF?
YOU HAVE CROSSED OVER TO THE DARK SIDE, QUINLAN VOS, BUT YOU HAVE NOT YET FULLY EMBRACED IT.
YOU DISAPPOINT ME, QUINLAN VOS. YOU UNDERSTAND SO LITTLE. COME, SKORR.
HE DOESN'T KNOW. HE SUSPECTS BUT HE DOESN'T KNOW.
AND HE'S WRONG. I HAVE NOT GONE OVER TO THE DARK SIDE. JUST DEEPER INTO THE SHADOWS ... EVER DEEPER ...

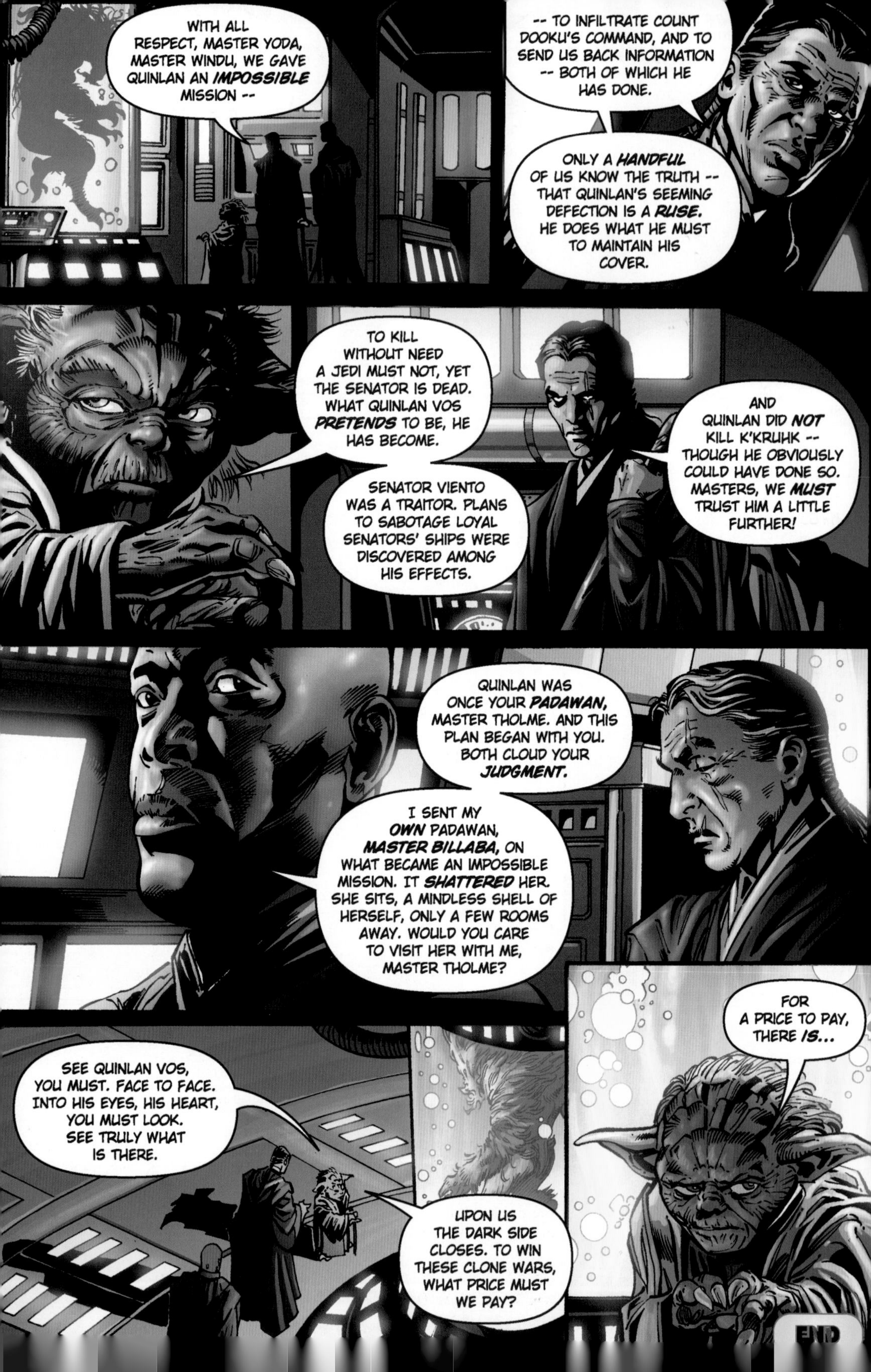
WITH ALL RESPECT, MASTER YODA, MASTER WINDU, WE GAVE QUINLAN AN *IMPOSSIBLE* MISSION --
-- TO INFILTRATE COUNT DOOKU'S COMMAND, AND TO SEND US BACK INFORMATION -- BOTH OF WHICH HE HAS DONE.
ONLY A *HANDFUL* OF US KNOW THE TRUTH -- THAT QUINLAN'S SEEMING DEFECTION IS A *RUSE.* HE DOES WHAT HE MUST TO MAINTAIN HIS COVER.
TO KILL WITHOUT NEED A JEDI MUST NOT, YET THE SENATOR IS DEAD. WHAT QUINLAN VOS *PRETENDS* TO BE, HE HAS BECOME.
SENATOR VIENTO WAS A TRAITOR. PLANS TO SABOTAGE LOYAL SENATORS' SHIPS WERE DISCOVERED AMONG HIS EFFECTS.
AND QUINLAN DID *NOT* KILL K'KRUHK -- THOUGH HE OBVIOUSLY COULD HAVE DONE SO. MASTERS, WE *MUST* TRUST HIM A LITTLE FURTHER!
QUINLAN WAS ONCE YOUR *PADAWAN,* MASTER THOLME. AND THIS PLAN BEGAN WITH YOU. BOTH CLOUD YOUR *JUDGMENT.*
I SENT MY *OWN* PADAWAN, *MASTER BILLABA,* ON WHAT BECAME AN IMPOSSIBLE MISSION. IT *SHATTERED* HER. SHE SITS, A MINDLESS SHELL OF HERSELF, ONLY A FEW ROOMS AWAY. WOULD YOU CARE TO VISIT HER WITH ME, MASTER THOLME?
SEE QUINLAN VOS, YOU MUST. FACE TO FACE. INTO HIS EYES, HIS HEART, YOU MUST LOOK. SEE TRULY WHAT IS THERE.
UPON US THE DARK SIDE CLOSES. TO WIN THESE CLONE WARS, WHAT PRICE MUST WE PAY?
FOR A PRICE TO PAY, THERE *IS...*
END